WHAT SHE SAID

THE ART OF INSPIRING ACTION THROUGH SPEECH

MONICA LUNIN

First published in 2022 by John Wiley & Sons Australia, Ltd
42 McDougall St, Milton Qld 4064
Office also in Melbourne

Typeset in Utopia Std 10.5/14pt

© John Wiley & Sons Australia, Ltd 2022

The moral rights of the author have been asserted

ISBN: 978-0-730-39983-4

A catalogue record for this
book is available from the
National Library of Australia

Cover design by Wiley

Cover Image: © Angelina Bambina/Shutterstock

Disclaimer

Contents

Introduction   *v*

1. Providing guidance, advice and wisdom   1

    Michelle Obama: *When they go low, we go high*   5

    Nora Ephron: *Be the heroine of your life*   15

    Florence Nightingale: *What makes a good nurse*   25

    Virginia Woolf: *Shakespeare's sister*   35

2. Sharing complex thoughts and ideas   47

    Brené Brown: *The power of vulnerability*   51

    Hannah Arendt: *What remains? The language remains*   61

    Marie Curie: *Radium and the new concepts in chemistry*   71

    Margaret Atwood: *Payback: Debt and the shadow side of wealth* 79

3. Opening hearts and minds   87

    Eleanor Roosevelt: *On the adoption of the Universal Declaration of Human Rights*   91

    Nancy Astor: *Maiden speech*   101

    Malala Yousafzai: *One girl among many*   109

    Naomi Klein: *This changes everything*   119

4. Beckoning the waves of feminism   127

    Mary Wollstonecraft: *I have a dream*   131

    Emmeline Pankhurst: *Why we are militant*   139

    Betty Friedan: *Call to women's strike for equality*   149

    Audre Lorde: *The Transformation of Silence*   157

5. Demanding respect   165

    Julia Gillard: *Misogyny speech*   169

    Sylvia Rivera: *Y'all better quiet down*   177

Margaret Thatcher: *The lady's not for turning* 183

Hillary Clinton: *Women's rights are human rights* 191

6. Arguing a position **199**

Ruth Bader Ginsburg: *Argument in Frontiero v. Richardson* 203

Barbara Jordan: *Articles of Impeachment during Watergate* 215

Margaret Sanger: *The morality of birth control* 225

Angela Merkel: *Speech to US Congress* 231

7. Inspiring action **239**

Queen Elizabeth I: *The heart and stomach of a king* 243

Sojourner Truth: *Ain't I a woman?* 251

Dolores Ibárruri: *They shall not pass!* 259

Greta Thunberg: *Our house is on fire* 265

8. Using humour to connect and persuade **273**

Nellie McClung: *Should men vote?* 277

Dorothy Parker: *Hollywood, the land I won't return to* 285

Roxane Gay: *Confessions of a bad feminist* 295

Ruby Wax: *What's so funny about mental illness?* 303

9. Encouraging inclusion **311**

Jacinda Ardern: *They were New Zealanders. They are us* 315

Faith Bandler: *Faith, hope and reconciliation* 323

Indira Gandhi: *Last speech of Indira Gandhi at Bhubaneswar* 333

Linda Burney: *Inaugural speech* 341

10. Harnessing the power of stories **351**

Eva Kor: *Surviving the Angel of Death* 355

Josephine Baker: *March on Washington* 365

Svetlana Alexievich: *On the battle lost* 375

Maya Angelou: *On the pulse of morning* 383

Sources *391*

Index *397*

Introduction

Words have the power to change the world. A speech that is masterfully delivered, well timed and beautifully constructed can change someone's mind, open their heart and inspire them to act. Women and men have been making speeches and making a difference in the world around them for as long as civilisation has existed. It is time to hold up the speeches made by women, so often overlooked, to examine their power, extract their wisdom and spread them as examples for other women and girls.

Why I wrote this book

I have chosen each of the forty speeches included in this book for the lessons it contains. All of the women featured here used their voice, and their will, to bring about change in some way. I believe we should celebrate their commitment and their decision to speak up, without needing to interrogate the significance of their historic contribution.

My purpose is not to criticise either the content or delivery, and nor is it to suggest how the speech might have been done better. I don't provide any analysis of the opinions, ideology or beliefs of any of those whose words I have selected.

If you were to pull down from the bookshelf any anthology of famous speeches you would likely find the content overwhelmingly skewed towards men. I have found such speeches to be sources of inspiration and instruction throughout my life, but I have come to wonder if the gender imbalance is justified. Of course, we know that women, historically, have not enjoyed equality when it comes to positions of power or platforms for speechmaking, so perhaps that is our default explanation. Do you accept, however, that because women did not have a platform, they did not have a voice?

I have come to the realisation that, in my mind, I lived in a post-feminist world. I believed my teachers and my parents when they told me I could do whatever I wanted to do. The men in my life — my dad, husband business partner and close friends — have never dissuaded me of this belief. I have surrounded myself with empowered and intelligent women who have carved out their place in the world. But when you look at the facts — the number of women in leadership roles in business and politics, for example, or the pay gap and rates of violence against women — I recognised that I have been deluding myself.

So what can I do to close the gap? Well, speaking has always been my thing. I am particularly interested in the intersection of communication and leadership and in my professional practice I work with people to help them find their mojo. We can all learn from the great speakers who have gone before us, no matter their gender. It is my hope that this collection will help other women develop their communication confidence and skill through seeing examples they might be better able to relate to.

At first glance, you may think some of the speakers identified in the pages of this book are too different from you to provide any useful advice. What could Queen Elizabeth I, who reigned in the sixteenth century, possibly have to teach a young woman working hard to be noticed in her job? How could a business leader extract any meaningful insight from the stories shared by a Russian novelist? Could a lawyer or an engineer learn from the early suffragettes? When you dig a bit deeper, however, you realise we can all learn something from each of these speeches. And these lessons can be found when we examine each speech according to its persuasive intent.

How to use this book

This book is more than a celebration of the speeches given by women. It is also a practical toolkit that you can use to help you inspire, motivate or educate others. We never just speak for the sake of it. When making a speech to any number of people, large or small, you want them to feel something. Similarly, your presentations are delivered to achieve something. Whatever your purpose, you will find guidance from those who have gone before you.

The ten chapters in this book, each including four speeches, have been created to organise the collection into categories of purpose, rather than a simple chronological order. For example, in the following chapters you can find:

- speeches that bestow guidance, advice and wisdom

- expert speeches that show creative ways to share complex ideas, concepts and theories sparking interest from new audiences

- inspiring speeches that honour all the women who have lent their voice to the advancement of other women in the waves of feminism

- fiery speeches that are delivered when you need to draw the line or demand respect, and those that instead use humour to pave the way to understanding.

The lessons provided from each of the speeches can be applied to your own practice of communication. Sometimes you will need to present in a way that encourages people to do something, to act in some way, or to change their behaviour. Plenty of trailblazers are included here for you to follow. At other times, of course, a softer touch is what you need, to open a closed mind — just a crack — so that you might sow the seeds of change, and examples of these speeches are also included here.

Among the women featured in this book, you will find a wide variation in style. Some are confident, some are shy. Some are fighters and some are thinkers. Some have built up their public-speaking skills over a lifetime and some are uncomfortable in the limelight. All are worthy of listening to and learning from.

We tend to think rational arguments are formed purely based on fact. However, eloquence — and guidance — can also be found in unexpected places. Many speeches through this book can help you learn how to animate your technical or logical presentations to make other people see things your way.

And along with the beauty in the speeches that serves to bring people closer together, lessons can be found here too. If you have ever faced the challenge of fostering inclusion, you will no doubt be moved by the speeches in this book that enhance existing bonds and create new connections among seemingly disparate groups. And finally you have the treat of looking to the words of some master storytellers to encourage you in the ongoing journey of developing your own voice.

But this book is more than a collection of inspiring and powerful speeches. I also provide some context as an introduction for each speech. And after the inclusion of each speech (either the whole speech or a substantial extract from it), I then break down three observations that make the speech so powerful. So you not only have 'what she said' but also 'how she did that'.

This book is intended as a celebration of diversity. Once you start to look you will find gems of oratory in every pocket of humanity. No limits based on ethnicity, background, education, race, age or even gender exist when it comes to the power of the spoken word. Once I set my intention these speeches were not hard to find. We have only to look a little further than the prevailing popular orations, no matter how good these might be. It is time to cast the net wider.

In the words of Margaret Atwood, 'a word, after a word, after a word has power'. So let's learn how to harness and leverage the power we all have.

1

Providing guidance, advice and wisdom

Appreciating the nature of the relationship between speaker and audience is important in crafting and delivering a speech that bestows guidance, advice and wisdom.

This relationship is usually somewhat unequal. This is not to say that the speaker is in any way better but, in the context of the advice, they have the upper hand. Their expertise, achievement, seniority (or some other distinguishing factor) creates in the minds of the audience a desire to listen and to extract meaning.

Think about all the scenarios in which this might happen — a classroom where the teacher is naturally in charge, for example, a church where parishioners settle in for the insight of a sermon, or a graduation ceremony where a keynote speaker is scheduled to punctuate the formalities.

The same relationship might arise in a professional context. You might have a manager inducting a group of new recruits, for example, an outgoing executive sharing the lessons learned during their tenure, or an experienced professional speaking at an industry conference.

If you find yourself in any of these scenarios, you can assume a certain amount of receptivity in the crowd before you begin. Unlike a political speech, you probably won't need to worry about hecklers or even anyone directly challenging your opinion. For the most part, your audience will be ready and willing to listen to you. This is a warm room.

Of course, that doesn't mean this type of speech is easy. Mastering a few fundamentals will make sure you build on the credibility that has already been bestowed upon you.

You will need to rise to the occasion. A hierarchy exists here, no matter how slight, and you are the senior. You need to assume the role. Be yourself, but the confident, assured, professional and accomplished version of yourself. Avoid apologising, demurring or otherwise giving away your power. Stand your ground, feel secure in yourself, open strongly and the rest will follow.

When providing guidance, giving advice or sharing wisdom, you have a fair amount of latitude when it comes to content — so get creative. You might want to choose a structure like 'my top ten tips' to give shape to your thoughts, share a personal story or even set the whole talk in the future. Organising your content into some sort of structure will help your audience stay with you as you work through your speech.

These types of speeches also allow for 'big picture' thinking. Concepts that might sound esoteric or idealistic can find a perfect home in this talk. A great example is Michelle Obama's claiming of the moral high ground in her speech at the Democratic National Convention supporting Hillary Clinton's presidential campaign.

You can also draw from your own experiences in formulating content in these types of speeches, sharing stories and lessons learned. Put yourself in the message as much as possible. You are there to speak because of your personal experience or track record. People want to connect with you. So sharing a little bit of yourself can be helpful — as you can see with Nora Ephron's speech at Wellesley College. Avoid disembodied advice in favour of wisdom that you earned from your own wins and losses.

This might even be an opportunity for you to set the bar a little higher. Consider Florence Nightingale, reaching out to us from a very different time. She was clear about the principles she considered vital for a nurse to adopt and nurture for a successful career, and she created an aspirational target for young women. In your world, this approach could have the added benefit of serving as a yardstick for future conversations.

The wisdom you share might be closely linked to your own area of expertise. You might begin by considering why you have been asked to speak, and what it is about your unique set of experiences that means others will want to listen. In the case of Virginia Woolf speaking about 'women in fiction' at Cambridge University in 1928, the skills of the novelist are leveraged to create a beautifully enigmatic piece, 'Shakespeare's sister'.

Your success in delivering an impactful and inspirational speech of guidance, advice or wisdom will depend on your own self-belief and your commitment to connect with and truly help each person in your audience. Be generous of spirit, remember they want to hear what you have to say, and you will make a difference.

... I wake up every morning in a house that was built by slaves. And I watch my daughters, two beautiful, intelligent, Black young women, playing with their dogs on the White House lawn. And because of Hillary Clinton, my daughters, and all our sons and daughters, now take for granted that a woman can be president of the United States.

Michelle Obama

Michelle Obama

Former First Lady of the United States, author and speaker

B: *17 January 1964, Chicago, IL, United States*

When they go low, we go high

When: *26 July 2016*

Where: *Democratic National Convention (DNC) in Philadelphia*

Audience: *50 000 people*

On 26 July 2016, the First Lady of the United States, Michelle Obama, spoke in support of Hillary Clinton in front of approximately 50 000 people at the Democratic National Convention (DNC) in Philadelphia. This convention confirmed Hillary Clinton as the Democratic nominee for president in the upcoming election, opposing Donald Trump as the Republican nominee.

Leading up to this speech, the world had witnessed the maturation of Obama's public-speaking ability and presence as she was thrust into the spotlight in correlation with the political career of her husband, Barack Obama. At times, we had seen her unsure of herself and rather guarded; at other times, she had been forthright and direct. Over time, she developed a style that was all her own.

Obama's speech at the DNC preceding the 2016 election was one of her finest moments at the microphone. A beautiful combination of emotion, conviction and technique, this speech provoked an overwhelming response from the assembled audience — including a standing ovation that appeared to be a genuine spontaneous response.

Obama's degree of influence in the United States and across the globe grew throughout and beyond her husband's presidency. With the publication of her book *Becoming* and the associated lecture tour, she has emerged as a role model in her own right.

Her signature speaking style is down to earth, and her language typically includes notes of colloquialism and candour. We often hear references to family, Black history and patriotism. On this occasion, Obama's speech was well crafted and expertly delivered, as the extracts included here show. She doesn't mention Trump at any point. Instead, her speech is imbued with values, triumph and optimism.

<u>WHAT</u> SHE SAID

"

Thank you all. Thank you so much. You know, it's hard to believe that it has been eight years since I first came to this convention to talk with you about why I thought my husband should be president.

Remember how I told you about his character and convictions, his decency and his grace, the traits that we've seen every day that he's served our country in the White House?

I also told you about our daughters, how they are the heart of our hearts, the centre of our world. And during our time in the White House, we've had the joy of watching them grow from bubbly little girls into poised young women, a journey that started soon after we arrived in Washington.

When they set off for their first day at their new school, I will never forget that winter morning as I watched our girls, just seven and ten years old, pile into those black SUVs with all those big men with guns.

And I saw their little faces pressed up against the window, and the only thing I could think was, what have we done?

See, because at that moment I realised that our time in the White House would form the foundation for who they would become. And how well we managed this experience could truly make or break them. That is what Barack and I think about every day as we try to guide and protect our girls through the challenges of this unusual life in the spotlight, how we urge them to ignore those who question their father's citizenship or faith.

How we insist that the hateful language they hear from public figures on TV does not represent the true spirit of this country.

How we explain that when someone is cruel or acts like a bully, you don't stoop to their level. No, our motto is when they go low, we go high.

With every word we utter, with every action we take, we know our kids are watching us. We as parents are their most important role models. And let me tell you, Barack and I take that same approach to our jobs as President and First Lady because we know that our words and actions matter, not just to our girls, but the children across this country, kids who tell us 'I saw you on TV', 'I wrote a report on you for school'.

Kids like the little Black boy who looked up at my husband, his eyes wide with hope and he wondered, *Is my hair like yours?*

… And I am here tonight because I know that that is the kind of president that Hillary Clinton will be. And that's why in this election I'm with her.

You see, Hillary understands that the president is about one thing and one thing only: it's about leaving something better for our kids. That's how we've always moved this country forward, by all of us coming together on behalf of our children, folks who volunteer to coach that team, to teach that Sunday school class, because they know it takes a village.

… Leaders like Hillary Clinton, who has the guts and the grace to keep coming back and putting those cracks in that highest and hardest glass ceiling until she finally breaks through, lifting all of us along with her.

That is the story of this country, the story that has brought me to this stage tonight, the story of generations of people who felt the lash of bondage, the shame of servitude, the sting of segregation, but who kept on striving and hoping and doing what needed to be done so that today I wake up every morning in a house that was built by slaves.

And I watch my daughters, two beautiful, intelligent, Black young women, playing with their dogs on the White House lawn.

And because of Hillary Clinton, my daughters, and all our sons and daughters, now take for granted that a woman can be president of the United States.

So, look, so don't let anyone ever tell you that this country isn't great, that somehow we need to make it great again. Because this right now is the greatest country on Earth!

And as my daughters prepare to set out into the world, I want a leader who is worthy of that truth, a leader who is worthy of my girls' promise and all our kids' promise, a leader who will be guided every day by the love and hope and impossibly big dreams that we all have for our children.

So in this election, we cannot sit back and hope that everything works out for the best. We cannot afford to be tired or frustrated or cynical. No, hear me. Between now and November, we need to do what we did eight years ago and four years ago.

We need to knock on every door, we need to get out every vote, we need to pour every last ounce of our passion and our strength and our love for this country into electing Hillary Clinton as president of the United States of America!

So let's get to work.

Thank you all and God bless.

99

<u>HOW</u> SHE DID THAT

Connect the personal to the universal

Long after we have forgotten the context of this speech or the fact that it was delivered at the Democratic National Convention in 2016, we will remember the claim of the moral imperative — 'when they go low, we go high'. This is the lesson Michelle Obama imparts through her words. By examining how she gets there, we can extract some meaningful lessons for aspiring speakers. Obama begins, as she often does, with reference to her family. We are invited to view her as a mother first. We are there with her when her two young girls, then only seven and ten, first took up residence in the White House.

Just like all parents, the Obamas were concerned with how to instil ethical practice and some sort of moral compass in the minds of their children. What were these two girls to do when faced with the inevitable attacks on both their parents from the opposition and from the media? Just like every other parent, Obama mused, 'How we explain that when someone is cruel or acts like a bully, you don't stoop to their level.' For Obama, the answer was clear: 'No, our motto is when they go low, we go high.' Unlike every other parent, Obama ushered her two girls through adolescence under the constant gaze of the public and the scrutiny of the media. Her approach for dealing with this, however, is universally accessible.

What might otherwise have sounded preachy, suddenly becomes the admirable and approachable insight from a 'mom'.

Apply rhetorical flourishes

It is well known that Michelle Obama worked closely with a professional speechwriter for this and many of her other addresses. Perhaps that is why we see several classical rhetorical devices at work in this particular speech. They are all cleverly applied, and fade into the background as they should, but it can be useful for those looking to polish their craft to identify a few examples.

Repetition of a word or phrase — in this case, 'kids'— is used several times. In the full speech (available online — see the Sources section at the end of this book), she also uses the lead-in statement 'I want' four times, followed by 'someone', 'a president' (twice) and 'a leader'. (You can see her final use of this lead-in statement in the extract provided.) This establishes a rhythm and builds towards a crescendo. Using these three variants of what Obama wants is one of several examples of *tricolon* — that satisfying rule of three first identified by Aristotle. (See Emmeline Pankhurst's speech in chapter 4 for more on this concept.)

Embody the delivery

Rhetoric and metaphor are useful in producing a speech as powerful as this one, but there is much more is going on here. The carefully crafted words must be artfully delivered. A great script is nothing without an equally powerful performance. What Michelle Obama achieved on this occasion was nothing short of masterful.

Her pace was perfect — a little bit fast with the slightest touch of breathlessness. This served to amplify the importance of the occasion and the gravity of the message. She achieved the often-elusive emotional resonance. We could see and hear how she felt about her content. When she picks up the personal story and returns to her daughters playing on the White House lawn, she is visibly choked up. This is the moment the audience rises to their feet and the cheering intensifies. This is oratorical alchemy.

One person in the audience, and their reaction, stands out — former President Bill Clinton. At this crucial moment, he mouths the word 'wow' and stands to applaud. He is clearly affected by the statement and the emotion with which Mrs Obama says, 'And because of Hillary Clinton, my daughters, and all our sons and daughters, now take for granted that a woman can be president of the United States.' Now, Bill Clinton is one of the most adept practitioners of pathos I have ever observed — he has that power to inspire deep emotion. His response makes the moment significant.

If you are making a point — indeed, if you are overtly claiming the high ground — your audience needs to believe you are fully committed. Otherwise, you may be met with the scepticism of a naughty teenager getting a lecture. Michelle Obama's speech at the DNC in 2016 is a fine example of a great speech expertly delivered.

What I'm saying is don't delude yourself that the powerful cultural values that wrecked the lives of so many of my classmates have vanished from the Earth.

Nora Ephron

Nora Ephron

Writer and filmmaker

B: *19 May 1941, New York City, NY, United States*

D: *26 June 2012, New York City, NY, United States*

Be the heroine of your life

When: *03 June 1996*

Where: *Wellesley College*

Audience: *Class of 1996*

Nora Ephron is the American writer and filmmaker that brought us such classics as *Silkwood, When Harry Met Sally, Sleepless in Seattle* and *Julie and Julia*. So, you would no doubt expect sharp wit combined with humour from her — and this speech delivers both. It is imbued with her trademark insight and personality. Ephron goes further than this, however, delivering a compelling feminist message and a warning to the graduating class of Wellesley College in 1996.

Throughout her career, Ephron took risks. At times, her films sailed close to the wind. She often surprised her audiences and made us laugh. She also took a stand when she knew it was the right thing to do. Early in her career she applied for a journalist position at *Newsweek* magazine, but had to accept a role as a mail girl because at that time women were not permitted to write for the publication. Later she quit, brought a sexual discrimination case against *Newsweek* and wrote the book *Good Girls Revolt* based on her experiences, which was later made into a movie.

Years after her experiences at *Newsweek*, she was invited to address the graduating class of her alma mater, the prestigious Wellesley College in Massachusetts, United States, delivering what's known as the 'commencement' speech. Here she addressed the 'class of 1996' — the women graduating from Wellesley College — and their friends, family and various college dignitaries. She warned these young graduating women against complacency. Reminding them to use their talents to become the heroines of their life, she argued they should avoid being trapped in a mere supporting role.

Commencement speeches are usually well crafted and delivered to receptive audiences that are pre-disposed to respond favourably. This one is no exception. The gravity of Ephron's advice is further amplified because she herself is a Wellesley graduate. The assembled crowd would be well aware of Ephron's work, her professional accomplishments and her ability to capture and celebrate human interactions.

Ephron has left behind an impressive legacy in the realm of popular culture. In the extracts of this speech included here, she offers the wisdom of her experience tempered by her trademark insights. To paraphrase the famous line from *When Harry Met Sally*, 'We'll have what she's having …'

<u>WHAT</u> SHE SAID

66

President Walsh, trustees, faculty, friends, noble parents ... and dear class of 1996, I am so proud of you. Thank you for asking me to speak to you today. I had a wonderful time trying to imagine who had been ahead of me on the list and had said no; I was positive you'd have to have gone to Martha Stewart first. And I meant to call her to see what she would have said, but I forgot. She would probably be up here telling you how to turn your lovely black robes into tents. I will try to be at least as helpful, if not quite as specific as that.

I'm very conscious of how easy it is to let people down on a day like this, because I remember my own graduation from Wellesley very, very well, I am sorry to say. The speaker was Santha Rama Rau, who was a woman writer, and I was going to be a woman writer. And, in fact, I had spent four years at Wellesley going to lectures by women writers hoping that I would be the beneficiary of some terrific secret — which I never was. And now here I was at graduation, under these very trees, absolutely terrified. Something was over. Something safe and protected. And something else was about to begin. I was heading off to New York and I was sure that I would live there forever and never meet anyone and end up dying one of those New York deaths where no one even notices you're missing until the smell drifts into the hallway weeks later. And I sat here thinking, *OK, Santha, this is my last chance for a really terrific secret, lay it on me*, and she spoke about the need to place friendship over love of country, which I must tell you had never crossed my mind one way or the other.

... My class went to college in the era when you got a master's degrees in teaching because it was 'something to fall back on' in the worst-case scenario, the worst-case scenario being that no-one married you and you actually had to go to work. As this same classmate said at our reunion, 'Our education was a dress rehearsal for a life we never led.' Isn't that the saddest line? We weren't meant to have futures, we were meant to marry them. We weren't meant to have politics, or careers that mattered, or opinions, or lives; we were meant to marry them. If you wanted to be an architect, you married an architect. *Non Ministrare sed Ministrari* — you know the old joke, not to be ministers but to be ministers' wives.

… What I'm saying is don't delude yourself that the powerful cultural values that wrecked the lives of so many of my classmates have vanished from the Earth. Don't let the *New York Times* article about the brilliant success of Wellesley graduates in the business world fool you — there's still a glass ceiling. Don't let the number of women in the work force trick you — there are still lots of magazines devoted almost exclusively to making perfect casseroles and turning various things into tents.

Don't underestimate how much antagonism there is toward women and how many people wish we could turn the clock back. One of the things people always say to you if you get upset is don't take it personally, but listen hard to what's going on and, please, I beg you, take it personally. Understand: every attack on Hillary Clinton for not knowing her place is an attack on you. Underneath almost all those attacks are the words: get back, get back to where you once belonged. When Elizabeth Dole pretends that she isn't serious about her career, that is an attack on you. The acquittal of OJ Simpson is an attack on you. Any move to limit abortion rights is an attack on you — whether or not you believe in abortion. The fact that Clarence Thomas is sitting on the Supreme Court today is an attack on you.

Above all, be the heroine of your life, not the victim. Because you don't have the alibi my class had — this is one of the great achievements and mixed blessings you inherit: unlike us, you can't say nobody told you there were other options. Your education is a dress rehearsal for a life that is yours to lead. Twenty-five years from now, you won't have as easy a time making excuses as my class did. You won't be able to blame the deans, or the culture, or anyone else: you will have no one to blame but yourselves. Whoa.

So what are you going to do? This is the season when a clutch of successful women — who have it all — give speeches to women like you and say, to be perfectly honest, you can't have it all. Maybe young women don't wonder whether they can have it all any longer, but in case any of you are wondering, of course you can have it all. What are you going to do? Everything, is my guess. It will be a little messy, but embrace the mess. It will be complicated, but rejoice in the complications. It will not be anything like what you think it will be like, but surprises are good for you. And don't be frightened: you can always change your mind. I know: I've had four careers and three husbands. And this is something else I want to tell you, one of the hundreds of things I didn't know when I was sitting here so many years ago: you are not going to be you, fixed and immutable you, forever. We have a game we play when we're waiting for tables in restaurants, where you have to write the five things that describe yourself on a piece of paper. When I was your age, I would have put: ambitious, Wellesley graduate, daughter, Democrat, single. Ten years later not one of those five things turned up on my list. I was: journalist, feminist, New Yorker, divorced, funny. Today not one of those five things turns up in my list: writer, director, mother, sister, happy. Whatever those five things are for you today, they won't make the list in ten years — not that you still won't be some of those things, but they won't be the five most important things about you. Which is one of the most delicious things available to women, and more particularly to women than to men. I think. It's slightly easier for us to shift, to change our minds, to take another path. Yogi Berra, the former New York Yankee who made a specialty of saying things that were famously maladroit, quoted himself at a recent commencement speech he gave.

'When you see a fork in the road,' he said, 'take it.' Yes, it's supposed to be a joke, but as someone said in a movie I made, don't laugh this is my life, this is the life many women lead: two paths diverge in a wood, and we get to take them both. It's another of the nicest things about being women; we can do that. Did I say it was hard? Yes, but let me say it again so that none of you can ever say the words, nobody said it was so hard. But it's also incredibly interesting. You are so lucky to have that life as an option.

… Whatever you choose, however many roads you travel, I hope that you choose not to be a lady. I hope you will find some way to break the rules and make a little trouble out there. And I also hope that you will choose to make some of that trouble on behalf of women. Thank you. Good luck. The first act of your life is over. Welcome to the best years of your lives.

<u>HOW</u> SHE DID THAT

Let the stories do the work

In the first two-thirds of this speech, Nora Ephron builds connection and credibility with her audience — not by telling them why they should listen, but by showing them. Stringing together a series of anecdotes about her time at Wellesley shows us that she knows of what she speaks. These are well-crafted windows into her experience using the poignant, evocative language of a writer and movie-maker.

In the full speech (see Sources for details), Ephron recounts the story of the limiting life advice she received from her class dean, saying the dean told her, 'You've worked so hard at Wellesley, when you marry, take a year off. Devote yourself to your husband and your marriage.' On hearing details such as these, we share in her incredulity. The women graduating in 1996 would have known, of course, that girls could choose what they wanted to be when they grow up — just as much as a boy. In fact, they would have been certain in this knowledge. In typical Ephron style, she reads the room and provides just the right contrast in the form of this anecdote and the advice to devote her life to the proper care of her husband.

Personal stories do much of the work here. They serve to make the message more fun, more powerful and more memorable than a speech filled with warnings and wisdom — no matter how appropriate. Try using the contrast effect, cleverly demonstrated by Ephron, to bring your point into sharp relief. If you are looking to warn people off a particular choice, you might consider painting the picture of an undesirable outcome, in the form of a story.

Select a theme and create a structure

Often a speech is aided by the use of structure. This can help keep the speaker and the audience on track. In this case, Nora Ephron uses a comedic hook, referring to her own time at the college back in the early sixties. Again in the full version, Ephron repeatedly poses the rhetorical question, 'How long ago was it?', using this to set up a series of vignettes, sharing her memories of how life was in the college for her generation (touching on subjects as diverse as lesbianism, curfews and tuition fees). She returns to this device repeatedly throughout the first part of the speech, and her chosen organising structure is part of what makes this address so easy to listen to.

Ephron lulls us along with the familiar arrangement of, 'How long ago was it?' and then, 'It was so long ago ...', setting up a few funny tidbits to follow. She then rather jarringly but purposefully changes the antecedent — and we are jolted into not so funny reminiscences about illegal abortions.

The lesson is to use familiar language techniques to invite your audiences in. Get them laughing with you and merrily following along before you shift to more serious matters. You can judge where to start and the right notes to hit at the outset by reflecting on the context and expectations in the room. Try channelling Nora Ephron's use of structure and variation of expected speech patterns to make an impact.

Change gears to land a serious message

Nora Ephron springboards from her series of amusing anecdotes and interesting insights to arrive at her central point. This is a serious message, and though slightly preachy, it works well in this context. The contrast with the humorous, endearing part of the speech is strong. When she changes gears in this way, her language and pace also shift. This change of pace makes the audience lean forward and listen up. Note the subtle uplift in speed and intensity when she delivers this part:

> Understand: every attack on Hillary Clinton for not knowing her place is an attack on you. Underneath almost all those attacks are the words: get back, get back to where you once belonged.

She goes on, riding the momentum she created, to name a series of insidious and damaging 'attacks' in the contemporary social and political landscape that may (or may not) have escaped the attention of these ambitious young women.

Heading towards the conclusion of the speech, Nora Ephron manages to lift the mood. Changing tone again, she shifts to her main piece of advice, one that is empowering and appropriate for the audience and the occasion: 'Above all, be the heroine of your own life'.

Then a good woman should be thorough. Thoroughness in a nurse is a matter of life and death to the patient.

Florence Nightingale

Florence Nightingale

Statistician, social reformer and founder of modern nursing

B: *12 May 1820, Florence, Italy*

D: *13 August 1910, London, England, United Kingdom*

___

What makes a good nurse

When: *May 1881*

Where: *A letter*

Audience: *Trainee nurses at St Thomas' Hospital*

The 'Lady with the Lamp' — Florence Nightingale — is a symbol of care and compassion, making the rounds of wounded soldiers during the Crimean War.

In 1860 she established a secular school for nursing at St Thomas' Hospital in London and set about professionalising the role of the nurse for women. Her legacy continues in the profession with the Nightingale Pledge and the Florence Nightingale Medal.

In 1881, in a letter to trainee nurses at St Thomas' Hospital — women typically as young as sixteen — Nightingale set down her advice. Only snippets of her recorded voice remain, so you will have to use your imagination to bring her words to life. Access your best *Downtown Abbey*-inspired English aristocratic accent, pitch your voice quite high, clip your vowels a little and you've got it. Now imagine yourself in a room full of fresh-faced new recruits — all young women. Florence is at the front, the master-trainer, sharing her wisdom.

Extracts from her advice are included here. Reading this advice today is at once challenging, amusing and infuriating. Parts of this address are likely off-putting — especially all the talk about obedience and what makes a good woman. But if you can contextualise that, and look beyond the anachronistic nature of the language, there is much to recommend Florence Nightingale's advice to young nurses.

WHAT SHE SAID

To our beginners, good courage

… To be a good nurse one must be a good woman, here we shall all agree. It is the old, old story. But some of us are new to the start.

What is it to be 'like a woman'? 'Like a woman' — 'a very woman' is sometimes laid as a word of contempt; sometimes as a word of tender admiration.

What makes a good woman is the better or higher of their nature:

Quietness

Gentleness

Patience

Endurance

Forbearance

With:

Her patients

Her fellow workers

Her supervisors

Her equals.

We need above all to remember that we come to learn, to be taught. Hence we come to obey.

No one ever was able to govern who was not able to obey.

No one ever was able to teach who was not able to learn.

The best scholars make the best teachers — those who obey best, the best rulers.

... You are here to be trained for nurses — attending on the wants of the sick — helpers in carrying out doctor's orders (not medical students, though theory is very helpful when carried out by practice). Theory without practice is ruinous to nurses.

Then a good woman should be thorough. Thoroughness in a nurse is a matter of life and death to the patient.

Or, rather, without it she is no nurse. Especially thoroughness in the unseen work. Do that well and the other will be done well too. Be as careful in the cleaning of the used poultice basin as in your attendance at an antiseptic dressing. Don't care more about what meets the eye and gains attention.

'How do you know you have grace?' said a minister to a housemaid.

'Because I clean under the mats' was the excellent reply.

If a housemaid said that, how much more should a nurse, all whose vessels mean patients.

***

Now what does 'like a woman' mean when it is said in contempt?

Does it not mean what is petty, little selfishnesses, small meannesses; envy; jealousy; foolish talking; unkind gossip; love of praise.

Now while we try to be 'like women' in the noble sense of the word, let us fight as bravely against all such womanly weaknesses.

Let us be anxious to do well, not for selfish praise, but to honour and advance the cause, the work we have taken up.

Let us value our training, not as it makes us cleverer or superior to others, but inasmuch as it enables us to be more useful and helpful to our fellow creatures, the sick, who most want our help.

Let it be our ambition, good nurses, and never let us be ashamed of the name of 'nurse'.

* * *

This to our beginners, I had almost said. But those who have finished their year's training be the first to tell us they are only beginners — they have just learnt how to learn and how to teach.

When they are put into the responsibility of nurse or sister, then they know how to learn and how to teach something every day a year, which, without their thorough training, they would not know.

This is what they tell me.

Then their battle cry is 'be not weary in well-doing'. We will not forget that once we were ignorant, tiresome probationers.

We will not laugh at the mistakes of beginners, but it shall be our pride to help all who come under our influence to be better women, more thorough nurses.

What is influence? The most mighty, the most unseen engine we know.

The importance of one year or two in the work, over one month in the work is more mighty, altho' narrow than the influence of statesmen or sovereigns. The influences of a good woman and thorough nurse with all the new probationers who come under her care is untold.

This it is — the using such influences, for good or for bad, which either raises or lowers the tone of a hospital.

We all see how much easier it is to sink to the level of the low, than to rise to the level of the high — but dear friends all, we know how soldiers were taught to fight in the old times against desperate odds, standing shoulder to shoulder and back to back.

Let us each and all, realising the importance of our influences on others — stand shoulder to shoulder and not alone in the good cause.

But let us be quiet.

What is it that is said about the learner? Women's influence ever has been and ever should be quiet and gentle in the working like the learner. Never noisy or self-asserting.

Let us seek all of us rather to be good rather than clever nurses.

Now I am sure we will all give a grateful cheer to our matron and to our home sister and our medical instructors.

God bless you all, my dear, dear friends and I hope to see you all, one by one, this year.

<u>HOW</u> SHE DID THAT

Use contrast for clarity

Communication always involves some sort of transfer of meaning, and this transfer can be risky. The opportunity for things to get lost or misinterpreted is great. So many elements get in the way — the differing perspectives of the speaker and the audience, the use of language (including vague terminology or jargon), and varying expectations of what is required in any given situation.

In this address, we see several instances of Nightingale seeking to clarify her own meaning. She obviously wants to make sure that she limits the opportunity for misunderstanding as much as possible. This trait has likely developed over her many years spent teaching.

Even though the subject matter of this address is general — she is not teaching us how to change a bedpan or clean a wound — it is still important to be understood. For this, Nightingale effectively and repeatedly employs the technique of contrast. She provides her definition of what it means to be a nurse, explaining what it is and then what it is not.

She takes back the power of the previously pejorative phrase 'like a woman' and redefines it in the positive — much like the modern reinterpretation of what it means to 'run like a girl'. Nightingale prescribes three successive aspirations for the trainee nurse: to do your best, to value training, and to be a good nurse. For every piece of advice, she contrasts the opposite driver of the ambition so as to illuminate her true meaning. 'Let us be anxious to do well, not for selfish praise, but to honour and advance the cause ...' Try this technique of providing counterexamples to make sure your audience does not misinterpret your meaning.

Emphasise the nature of learning and leadership

Despite the anachronistic and in so many ways 'unfeminist' tone of this address, we can tell that Florence Nightingale holds her audience and their chosen profession in high regard. She bestows upon them some inspirational ideas about the nature of lifelong learning and the role of a leader.

We can take from her message that it is our duty to always be the student. Long after basic training is finished, we must be open to learning. That is the only way to become a teacher. She then connects her thinking to the role of the leader. If you are to lead — to command — you must learn to be a good follower. This is a lesson, buried in an antiquated document, that would benefit many aspiring leaders today.

There is a lesson here for those times you need to step into the role of trainer, teacher or facilitator, as most of us will from time to time. Learning to learn will help you better appreciate how to teach. Practising the art of 'follower-ship' will make you a better leader.

Encourage high virtue

If Florence Nightingale's new recruits, perhaps in their late teens, were raised in today's world, they might extract from this address the advice that they should be 'living their best life' — not in a post-worthy way, but in a way that allows what's best in you to shine. Your 'best life' should be intrinsically motivated.

This is the right context to impart the wisdom of experience and that is indeed what the audience will be expecting. Nightingale lists the virtues she believes are required: quietness, gentleness, patience, endurance, forbearance. Then she highlights the one she considers to be the ultimate virtue — thoroughness — and spends some time expounding on the nature of this, possibly overlooked, attribute of the 'good nurse'.

Nightingale is presumably aiming to set the tone and create a standard for assessment and self-reflection. Though many practical lessons will follow, this is a great place to emphasise the virtues that must underpin all the skills and knowledge these young women will now acquire.

Interestingly, Nightingale links her talk on virtue to her take on the concept of influence. 'What is influence? The most mighty, the most unseen engine we know.' Young women as influencers? Living their best life? Perhaps Florence Nightingale was ahead of her time after all.

The dead poet who was Shakespeare's sister will put on the body which she has so often laid down. Drawing her life from the lives of the unknown who were her forerunners, she will be born.

Virginia Woolf

Virginia Woolf

Author

B: *25 January 1882, London, England, United Kingdom*

D: *28 March 1941, East Sussex, England, United Kingdom*

Shakespeare's sister

When: *1928*

Where: *University of Cambridge*

Audience: *Female students from Newnham College and Girton College*

Bloomsbury novelist Virginia Woolf was known for her innovative approach to writing and her non-linear storylines. She was complicated and complex in both her character and the way she made sense of the world. The writer made a significant impact on modern fiction and continues to fascinate readers 80 years after she died. In addition to writing fiction, Woolf was prolific in her exploration of ideas and opinions through letters, essays and talks.

In 1928, Woolf was invited to speak to the female students from Newnham College and Girton College at the University of Cambridge on the subject of 'Women in fiction'. Her thoughts culminated in a piece called 'Shakespeare's sister', which was later included in her famous extended essay *A Room of One's Own*.

The piece is remarkable for its insight and creativity. The audience is delivered a slice of wisdom from the renowned author that is entertaining and thought-provoking. Nearly 100 years later, 'Shakespeare's sister' continues to inspire women, especially those looking to pursue a creative career. From Shakespeare's time, through that of the Bloomsbury Group in the early twentieth century, to our modern experience, Woolf shines a light on the inequity of the female experience. Her speech still sparks consideration and discussion on this matter, which is far from resolved.

Woolf's creation of 'Shakespeare's sister' is emblematic of all women who have faced the inequalities of opportunity. In continuing these ideas, *A Room of One's Own* sets out a case for the independent means a woman must fiercely acquire and protect in order to summon the creative forces she has. In Woolf's view, this independence is the minimum requirement for even a hope of equal participation.

Woolf's lecture continues to deliver guidance nearly a century after it was delivered. This speech (reproduced in full here) is also an exemplar of Virginia Woolf's meandering thoughts, so beautifully and hauntingly rendered.

<u>WHAT</u> SHE SAID

When you asked me to speak about women and fiction I sat down on the banks of a river and began to wonder what the words meant. They might mean simply a few remarks about Fanny Burney, a few more about Jane Austen, a tribute to the Brontës and a sketch of Haworth Parsonage under snow, and one would have done. But at second sight, the words seemed not so simple.

The title 'Women and fiction' might mean women and what they are like, or it might mean women and the fiction that they write, or it might mean women and the fiction that is written about them, or it might mean that somehow all three are inextricably mixed together and you want me to consider them in that light. But when I began to consider the subject in this last way, which seemed the most interesting, I soon saw that it had one fatal drawback: I should never be able to come to a conclusion.

All I could do was to offer you an opinion upon one minor point: a woman must have money and a room of her own if she is to write fiction; and that, as you will see, leaves the great problem of the true nature of woman and the true nature of fiction unsolved.

But in order to make some amends, I am going to do what I can to show you how I arrived at this opinion about the room and the money. I need not say that what I am about to describe has no existence; Oxbridge is an invention; 'I' is only a convenient term for somebody who has no real being. Lies will flow from my lips, but there may perhaps be some truth mixed up with them.

Here then was I (call me Mary Beton, Mary Seton, Mary Carmichael or by any name you please — it is not a matter of any importance) sitting on the banks of a river a week or two ago in fine October weather, lost in thought.

Thought — to call it by a prouder name than it deserved — had let its line down into the stream. It swayed, minute after minute, hither and thither among the reflections and the weeds, letting the water lift it and sink it until — you know the little tug — the sudden conglomeration of an idea at the end of one's line: and then the cautious hauling of it in, and the careful laying of it out? Alas, laid on the grass, how small, how insignificant this thought of mine looked; the sort of fish that a good fisherman puts back into the water so that it may grow fatter and be one day worth cooking and eating.

But however small it was, it had, nevertheless, the mysterious property of its kind — put back into the mind, it became at once very exciting, and important; and as it darted and sank, and flashed hither and thither, set up such a wash and tumult of ideas that it was impossible to sit still. It was thus that I found myself walking with extreme rapidity across a grass plot. Instantly a man's figure rose to intercept me. His face expressed horror and indignation. Instinct rather than reason came to my help; he was a beadle*, I was a woman. This was the turf; there was the path. Only the fellows and scholars are allowed here; the gravel is the place for me. Such thoughts were the work of a moment. As I regained the path, the arms of the beadle sank, his face assumed its usual repose, and though turf is better walking than gravel, no very great harm was done. The only charge I could bring against the fellows and scholars of whatever the college might happen to be was that, in protection of their turf, they had sent my little fish into hiding.

But curiosity remained.

For it is a perennial puzzle why no woman wrote a word of that extraordinary literature when every other man, it seemed, was capable of song or sonnet. What were the conditions in which women lived? I asked myself; for fiction, imaginative work that is, is not dropped like a pebble upon the ground, as science may

---

* A church leader.

be; fiction is like a spider's web, attached ever so lightly perhaps, but still attached to life at all four corners. Often the attachment is scarcely perceptible; Shakespeare's plays, for instance, seem to hang there complete by themselves. But when the web is pulled askew, hooked up at the edge, torn in the middle, one remembers that these webs are not spun in mid-air by incorporeal creatures, but are the work of suffering human beings, and are attached to grossly material things, like health and money and the houses we live in.

I went, therefore, to the shelf where the histories stand. I looked up 'Women', found 'position of' and turned to the pages indicated. 'Wife-beating,' I read, 'was a recognised right of man, and was practised without shame by high as well as low. Similarly,' the historian goes on, 'the daughter who refused to marry the gentleman of her parents' choice was liable to be locked up, beaten and flung about the room, without any shock being inflicted on public opinion.'

I could not help thinking, as I looked at the works of Shakespeare on the shelf, that it would have been impossible, completely and entirely, for any woman to have written the plays of Shakespeare in the age of Shakespeare. Let me imagine what would have happened had Shakespeare had a wonderfully gifted sister, called Judith, let us say. Shakespeare himself went, very probably — his mother was an heiress — to the grammar school, where he may have learnt Latin — Ovid, Virgil and Horace — and the elements of grammar and logic. He was, it is well known, a wild boy who poached rabbits, perhaps shot a deer, and had, rather sooner than he should have done, married a woman in the neighbourhood, who bore him a child rather quicker than was right.

That escapade sent him to seek his fortune in London. He had, it seemed, a taste for the theatre; he began by holding horses at the stage door. Very soon he got work in the theatre, became a successful actor, and lived at the hub of the universe, meeting everybody, knowing everybody, practising his art on the boards, exercising his wits in the streets, and even getting access to the palace of the queen. Meanwhile, his extraordinarily gifted sister, let us suppose, remained at home. She was as adventurous, as imaginative, as agog to see the world as he was. But she was not sent to school. She had no chance of learning grammar and logic, let alone of reading Horace and Virgil. She picked up a book now and then, one of her brother's perhaps, and read a few pages. But then her parents came in and told her to mend the stockings or mind the stew and not moon about with books and papers.

Perhaps she scribbled some pages up in an apple loft on the sly, but was careful to hide them or set fire to them. Soon, however, before she was out of her teens, she was to be betrothed to the son of a neighbouring wool stapler. She cried out that marriage was hateful to her, and for that she was severely beaten by her father. Then he ceased to scold her. He begged her instead not to hurt him, not to shame him in this matter of her marriage. He would give her a chain of beads or a fine petticoat, he said; and there were tears in his eyes. How could she disobey him? How could she break his heart?

The force of her own gift alone drove her to it. She made up a small parcel of her belongings, let herself down by a rope one summer's night and took the road to London. She was not 17. She had the quickest fancy, a gift like her brother's, for the tune of words. Like him, she had a taste for the theatre. She stood at the stage door; she wanted to act, she said. Men laughed in her face. The manager — a fat, loose lipped man — guffawed. He bellowed something about poodles dancing and women acting — no woman, he said, could possibly be an actress. He hinted — you can imagine what. She could get no training in her craft.

Yet her genius was for fiction and lusted to feed abundantly upon the lives of men and women and the study of their ways. At last — for she was very young, oddly like Shakespeare the poet in her face, with the same grey eyes — at last the manager took pity on her; she found herself with child by that gentleman and so — who shall measure the heat and violence of the poet's heart when caught and tangled in a woman's body? — killed herself one winter's night and lies buried at some crossroads where the omnibuses now stop outside the Elephant and Castle.

Here I would stop, but the pressure of convention decrees that every speech must end with a peroration. When I rummage in my own mind I find no noble sentiments about being companions and equals and influencing the world to higher ends. I find myself saying briefly and prosaically that it is much more important to be oneself than anything else. Do not dream of influencing other people, I would say, if I knew how to make it sound exalted. Think of things in themselves.

How can I further encourage you to go about the business of life? Young women, I would say — and please attend, for the peroration is beginning — my suggestion is a little fantastic; I prefer, therefore, to put it in the form of fiction. I told you that Shakespeare had a sister. Now my belief is that this poet who never wrote a word and was buried at the crossroads still lives. She lives in you and in me, and in many other women who are not here tonight, for they are washing up the dishes and putting the children to bed. But she lives, for great poets do not die; they are continuing presences; they need only the opportunity to walk among us in the flesh.

This opportunity is now coming within your power to give her. For my belief is that if we live another century or so — I am talking of the common life which is the real life and not of the little separate lives which we live as individuals — and have each of us rooms of our own; if we have the habit of freedom and the courage to write exactly what we think; if we escape a little from the common sitting-room and see human beings not always in their relation to each other but in relation to reality; if we face that there is no arm to cling to, but that we go alone and that our relation is to the world of reality and not only to the world of men and women, then the opportunity will come and the dead poet who was Shakespeare's sister will put on the body which she has so often laid down. Drawing her life from the lives of the unknown who were her forerunners, she will be born.

As for her coming without that preparation, without that effort on our part, without that determination that when she is born again she shall find it possible to live and write her poetry, that we cannot expect, for that would be impossible. But I maintain that she would come if we worked for her, and that so to work, even in poverty and obscurity, is worthwhile.

99

<u>HOW</u> SHE DID THAT

Invite the audience to do the work

At the time of this speech, Virginia Woolf was an author practised in the art of fiction, so she was adept at conjuring the imaginary world to make her point. In 'Shakespeare's sister' she creates a character, derived from a period in history, in the form of William Shakespeare's sister (whom she calls Judith), and she weaves for us a tale of what her life might have been like if we assume she possessed the same talents and drive as her brothers. Rather than telling us all the ways in which women were unfairly treated, she shows us through a tale of her own creation.

Woolf spells out her technique, telling us explicitly, 'I prefer, therefore, to put it in the form of fiction'. She steps in and out of the storyteller's shoes. When indulging in the fiction, she allows herself all of the expressive language and imagery that she is known for, bringing the story — and the injustice — to life. It is pleasing to follow her off on one tangent and then another, because somehow we know we are to extract the meaning from the tale.

In this story fragment, we are given a character, a setting and a struggle. With a few expert literary flourishes, Woolf provides us with all we need to come to our own realisation. Although technically her words were delivered as a lecture, they were not 'lecturing' in their delivery. Instead, a certain amount of faith is placed in the women from Cambridge to draw their own inferences and form personal impressions from the imagined life of Shakespeare's sister.

You don't need to play to the lowest (and least imaginative) common denominator in your audience. If you can find a way to present your ideas as a narrative — or even an image, example or allegory — and you can do it with panache, you might be able to make an even stronger impact. Could it be that your audience will be more convinced if they, themselves, decipher the moral of the story, as it were?

Use contrast to highlight your point

By using the very creative device of the imagined story of William Shakespeare's sister, Virginia Woolf is able to play with various rhetorical techniques, most notably the principle of contrast. Simply put, we are more able to notice the attributes of a particular thing when it is presented alongside something that is different.

Woolf creates her character and asks a simple question (of herself and her audience): what if the sister held similar aspirations to the brother? By creating this imagined parallel universe that runs alongside what we all already know of Shakespeare's success, Woolf amplifies her thesis. She doesn't have to lecture us of the inequalities and injustices the sister would have had to endure; we see it for ourselves, in sharp relief.

We can imagine the frustration of a woman pursuing a literary career when continually confronted with ridicule and the banal reality of bearing children and washing the dishes. The audience can conjure its own images of William Shakespeare kicking up his heels in a tavern or the court of Queen Elizabeth I, while his sister is doomed to a fate of domestic drudgery, beatings, forced marriage and terminal marginalisation.

Contrast sits at the very heart of Virginia Woolf's device — the imagined, disempowered life of Judith Shakespeare and the actual life of William Shakespeare. The brother's opportunity is contrasted with the sister's repression, the brother's education with the sister's benightedness, the brother's liberty with the sister's subjugation.

The overall impression Woolf seeks to create is one of oppression, which readies the audience for her eventual, somewhat enigmatic words of advice:

> ... if we have the habit of freedom and the courage to write exactly what we think; if we escape a little from the common sitting-room and see human beings not always in their relation to each other but in relation to reality; if we face that there is no arm to cling to, but that we go alone and that our relation is to the world of reality and not only to the world of men and

women, then the opportunity will come and the dead poet who was Shakespeare's sister will put on the body which she has so often laid down.

Expose the mechanics of your persuasion

From the very beginning of her lecture, Virginia Woolf shares her own creative meanderings. When considering the subject of women in fiction and working through what to say she tells her audience she 'sat down on the banks of a river and began to wonder what the words meant'. Throughout the speech, Woolf steps in and out of the roles of the advice giver, the storyteller and the speechmaker.

She goes on to tell us the central component of her idea, at once also sharing its limitations. Then she tells us she will take us through how she arrived at this opinion. Later, she indicates when she will be moving on to the peroration, or conclusion, of the lecture. It is as though she is exposing the formwork of her talk — in the same way as Brecht's plays in the 1920s aimed to expose the mechanisms of theatre — and I like to think this was, like Brecht, purposely done because it most definitely enhances the piece.

This is a useful and quite straightforward technique to use in your own presentations. When you have been invited to share your thoughts or personal experience and you are not sure how to structure your talk, perhaps, like Woolf, you could start with the topic you were given. Make it personal and begin with a first-person exposé of how you relate to the topic. 'Shakespeare's sister' is an enchanting example of how a speaker can think out loud, drawing their audience in and making them part of the wonder of discovery.

Sharing complex thoughts and ideas

Your expertise has no value to the world if it cannot be understood.

For your ideas to take hold, inspire others and create change, they must be transmitted. There is so much opportunity for confusion. Your audience will get confused if they don't understand the terms you're using or don't have the background knowledge required to appreciate the concepts. Even experts can become confused when delivering information because they have so much detail in their heads and a particularly deep understanding of their own field that they don't know where to start. Sometimes they jump around in their delivery, trying to fill in gaps, and then become overwhelmed or discouraged because their audience is just not getting it.

When planning a speech or presentation where you need to share complex ideas, first consider why the audience needs to know what you have to share. Decide on the most important benefit for them and then clarify their current level of understanding. In a broad sense, your job is to break down your concepts into their component parts and communicate each part in a manner that can be understood. You will need to make things as simple as possible, but no simpler. Before you craft your speech or presentation think about the audience, and then work out how to bridge the gap from the known to the unknown.

The speeches in this chapter are examples of women who have bridged this gap. Many of us have enjoyed learning about new concepts from the TED stage. Beginning in 1984 as a conference where Technology, Entertainment and Design converged, this lecture series now covers almost all topics — with the ambitious goal of lifting awareness in an age of reduced attention spans. Brené Brown's TED Talk on 'The power of vulnerability' is a master example of deep expertise made accessible to the mass market. Part of the secret here is to put yourself in the story. Brown takes the audience with her on her own journey of exploration and discovery. Who knew social science research could be so life-changing?

Sometimes your ideas will disrupt the status quo. Like philosopher Hannah Arendt, you may have an insight that is complex, potentially confusing, but ultimately necessary in advancing our understanding of the human condition. In this case, you have all the more reason to speak up. The world of academia would have you believe that you, as an individual, have no place in the research and that you need to anonymise your findings. You can challenge that paradigm if you want to transmit more than your knowledge, if you want to help people see why it matters.

Perhaps communicating to a general audience is a challenge for you. Marie Curie was a practised teacher, but she preferred to lecture students in chemistry and physics — an audience already equipped with a foundation of knowledge upon which she could build. Delivering a Nobel Lecture to a general audience upon the acceptance of her second Nobel Prize was a challenge. Her example reminds us to define any terms that may be ambiguous and to signpost the information to make sure nothing is lost. The world now has the cherished gift of Dr Curie explaining the significance of the discovery of radium in her own words.

You might be driven by your own curiosity about a topic or a personal quest for understanding. Margaret Atwood first started looking at the topic that would become the focus of her Massey Lecture Series 'Payback' for her own edification — that is, she wanted to understand the concept of debt and the shadow side of wealth. Her research began with the goal of enhancing her own knowledge, and then grew into a five-part lecture series. There is no better way to learn a concept, inside and out, than to teach it. You will likely see, as Atwood did, that an overwhelming amount of information needs to be broken down into categories, and then further reduced into bite-sized chunks. Atwood brings her superior literary capability to the lectern by sharing anecdotes and retelling ancient stories to help the audience understand complex ideas.

You cannot selectively numb. When we numb [hard feelings], we numb joy, we numb gratitude, we numb happiness. And then we are miserable, and we are looking for purpose and meaning, and then we feel vulnerable.

Brené Brown

Brené Brown

Leadership expert and author

B: *18 November 1965, San Antonio, Texas, United States*

The power of vulnerability

When: *2010*

Where: *Houston*

Audience: *TEDx*

Brené Brown launched herself into the public consciousness with a TED Talk. Her talk, delivered in June 2010 as part of TEDxHouston, is one of the most-viewed TED Talks of all available options, with close to 55 million views at the time of writing. The talk that captured the imagination of so many is about her social science research into vulnerability and shame.

This speech does many things at once. It is educational, entertaining and clear. But, most importantly, this TED Talk carries a nugget of wisdom that just might change somebody's life. It is a unique perspective — a fresh idea — and it is delivered from the heart.

Brené Brown breaks down her years of research to communicate a rare insight that sheds a little bit of light on what it means to be human. She is at once humbled and unafraid. Her manner is warm and her message is powerful. More than just a great example of an idea well communicated, this talk (extracts included here) encapsulates a remarkable life lesson.

A second or even third reading might be needed for you to see beyond the remarkable subject matter and observe the mechanics of communication. You can learn from Brown on two levels-of course, there is her remarkable insight, but there is also a wealth of technique in the way she shares her ideas.

<u>WHAT</u> SHE SAID

So, I'll start with this: a couple years ago, an event planner called me because I was going to do a speaking event. And she called and she said, 'I'm really struggling with how to write about you on the little flyer.' And I thought, *Well, what's the struggle?* And she said, 'Well, I saw you speak and I'm going to call you a researcher, I think, but I'm afraid if I call you a researcher, no-one will come, because they'll think you're boring and irrelevant.'

And I was like, 'Okay.' And she said, 'But the thing I liked about your talk is you're a storyteller. So I think what I'll do is just call you a storyteller.' And, of course, the academic, insecure part of me was like, 'You're going to call me a what?' And she said, 'I'm going to call you a storyteller.' And I was like, 'Why not "magic pixie"?'

…And I thought, you know, I am a storyteller. I'm a qualitative researcher. I collect stories; that's what I do. And maybe stories are just data with a soul. And maybe I'm just a storyteller … So I'm a researcher-storyteller, and I'm going to talk to you today — we're talking about expanding perception — and so I want to talk to you and tell some stories about a piece of my research that fundamentally expanded my perception and really actually changed the way that I live and love and work and parent.

…So very quickly — really about six weeks into this research — I ran into this unnamed thing that absolutely unravelled connection in a way that I didn't understand or had never seen. And so I pulled back out of the research and thought, *I need to figure out what this is.* And it turned out to be shame. And shame is really easily understood as the fear of disconnection: Is there something about me that, if other people know it or see it, I won't be worthy of connection?

The things I can tell you about it: It's universal; we all have it. The only people who don't experience shame have no capacity for human empathy or connection. No-one wants to talk about it, and the less you talk about it, the more you have it. What underpinned this shame, this 'I'm not good enough,' — which, we all know that feeling: 'I'm not blank enough. I'm not thin enough, rich enough, beautiful enough, smart enough, promoted enough.' The thing that underpinned this was excruciating vulnerability. This idea of, in order for connection to happen, we have to allow ourselves to be seen, really seen.

And you know how I feel about vulnerability. I hate vulnerability. And so I thought, this is my chance to beat it back with my measuring stick. I'm going in, I'm going to figure this stuff out, I'm going to spend a year, I'm going to totally deconstruct shame, I'm going to understand how vulnerability works, and I'm going to outsmart it. So I was ready, and I was really excited. As you know, it's not going to turn out well.

... And so here's what I found. What they [whole-hearted people who believe they are worthy of belonging] had in common was a sense of courage. And I want to separate courage and bravery for you for a minute. Courage, the original definition of courage, when it first came into the English language — it's from the Latin word 'cor', meaning 'heart' — and the original definition was to tell the story of who you are with your whole heart. And so these folks had, very simply, the courage to be imperfect. They had the compassion to be kind to themselves first and then to others, because, as it turns out, we can't practise compassion with other people if we can't treat ourselves kindly. And the last was they had connection, and — this was the hard part — as a result of authenticity, they were willing to let go of who they thought they should be in order to be who they were, which you have to absolutely do that for connection.

The other thing that they had in common was this: they fully embraced vulnerability. They believed that what made them vulnerable made them beautiful. They didn't talk about vulnerability being comfortable, nor did they really talk about it being excruciating — as I had heard it earlier in the shame interviewing. They just talked about it being necessary. They talked about the willingness to say, 'I love you' first … the willingness to do something where there are no guarantees … the willingness to breathe through waiting for the doctor to call after your mammogram. They're willing to invest in a relationship that may or may not work out. They thought this was fundamental.

… You can't numb those hard feelings without numbing the other affects, our emotions. You cannot selectively numb. So when we numb those, we numb joy, we numb gratitude, we numb happiness. And then we are miserable, and we are looking for purpose and meaning, and then we feel vulnerable, so then we have a couple of beers and a banana nut muffin. And it becomes this dangerous cycle.

One of the things that I think we need to think about is why and how we numb. And it doesn't just have to be addiction. The other thing we do is we make everything that's uncertain certain. Religion has gone from a belief in faith and mystery to certainty. 'I'm right, you're wrong. Shut up.' That's it. Just certain. The more afraid we are, the more vulnerable we are, the more afraid we are. This is what politics looks like today. There's no discourse anymore. There's no conversation. There's just blame. You know how blame is described in the research? A way to discharge pain and discomfort. We perfect. If there's anyone who wants their life to look like this, it would be me, but it doesn't work. Because what we do is we take fat from our butts and put it in our cheeks. Which just, I hope in 100 years, people will look back and go, 'Wow.'

…But there's another way, and I'll leave you with this. This is what I have found: To let ourselves be seen, deeply seen, vulnerably seen…to love with our whole hearts, even though there's no guarantee — and that's really hard, and I can tell you as a parent, that's excruciatingly difficult — to practise gratitude and joy in those moments of terror, when we're wondering, 'Can I love you this much? Can I believe in this this passionately? Can I be this fierce about this?' Just to be able to stop and, instead of catastrophising what might happen, to say, 'I'm just so grateful, because to feel this vulnerable means I'm alive.' And the last, which I think is probably the most important, is to believe that we're enough. Because when we work from a place, I believe, that says, 'I'm enough'…then we stop screaming and start listening, we're kinder and gentler to the people around us, and we're kinder and gentler to ourselves.

That's all I have. Thank you.

99

<u>HOW</u> SHE DID THAT

Bring awe and wonder to the process of discovery

When talking about shame and vulnerability, Brené Brown steps into the shoes of her research subjects. Typically, academic writing and the lectures that follow are rather impersonal. In fact, researchers are careful to remove any traces of themselves from their content. Add in generous doses of technical jargon and we are left with these disembodied voices with which audiences struggle to connect.

But Brown breaks the mould. Rather than telling us about a hypothesis she had and how she went about designing and executing a research study, she makes it personal. 'You know how I feel about vulnerability ...'

Speakers often find it challenging to make technical content relatable. For this problem, Brown's first TED talk delivers a critical lesson. Put yourself in the story, and make the problem, hypothesis and discovery your own. Frame your method in the first person. Don't present a report-like exposition of facts; instead, show us how you were feeling at the various stages of doubt. Display the emotions of wonder as you yourself made new connections.

When Brown uses phrases such as, 'So I was ready, and I was really excited', it is as though we are doing the research alongside her. We're shown how throwing your whole self into a project like this is anything but dull. We traverse the challenges and doubt with her and we laugh with her about the (not so) mini-breakdown, when her findings did not jive with her assumptions. These challenges, hurdles and mini-triumphs help us relate to the process of discovery. (Brown details her breakdown/spiritual awakening in the full version of her TED Talk — see Sources for details.)

Can you find ways to animate your research or technical content by putting yourself back in the picture? Many of your listeners will be drawn to a familiarity with you and that could be the gateway to gaining their attention and interest.

Establish synergy with your central idea

One of the interesting aspects that make this talk so remarkable is that Brené Brown lives and breathes the very subject of her thesis. Vulnerability is a necessary human condition. Simply saying those words, however, is not enough to convey meaning to the audience. Add the demonstration of the concept, throughout the talk, and you will impact the feeling as well as the thinking side of your audience member's mind.

What Brown manages, quite masterfully in this talk, is to consistently exhibit vulnerability. She takes the concept down from the academic shelf, tries it on and shows us how it looks on her. This not only enhances our understanding of the content, but also draws us closer to the speaker.

In a very un-technical way, Brown openly shares her need for and visits to a therapist. She talks about vulnerability while showing unmistakable vulnerability herself. In the full version of the talk, she explains how she told her therapist:

> I know that vulnerability is the core of shame and fear and our struggle for worthiness. But it appears that it is also the birthplace of joy and creativity, of belonging and love.

Even the tiny, seemingly throwaway lines — such as the 'academic, insecure part' of her asking why she wasn't being dubbed a 'magic pixie' — are tiny, self-deprecating examples of vulnerability. In the full version, Brown peppers her talk with similar comments — 'I have a slight office supply addiction, but that's another talk', 'I always go into this Jackson Pollock crazy thing'. This layering of her own vulnerability makes her more endearing and her ideas more enduring.

Take the time to connect

Imagine you were presenting the findings from years of your own research. Would you be able to do it effectively in just 20 minutes? This is about the maximum length for a TED talk, and with very good reason. The time frame is roughly correlated to our attention span. Given a tight time frame and an overwhelming amount of data, what do you do?

Well, the mistake many of us make is to try to cram in the maximum amount of content. We create data-dense slides and we push the limits to ensure we don't miss any important facts. A better approach is to work out the central idea. Define what you want your audience to take away and then work within the boundaries of the time permitted, with awareness of your audience's engagement, and hit the right note. After all, rushing or over-stuffing a presentation will only confuse and overwhelm your audience. This would ultimately be a waste of time.

Pace is cleverly used here to allow the listener time to assimilate the information. Brown also uses her pauses to connect with people in the audience. She makes eye contact and uses facial expressions that imply she is having a conversation. It feels natural and complements the familiar tone used throughout.

The close to 55 million views this talk has generated can be justified by interesting content — but it is greatly enhanced by Brené Brown delivering it with such care and compassion.

There are people who take it amiss — and I can understand that in a sense — that, for instance, I can still laugh.

Hannah Arendt

Hannah Arendt

Philosopher and writer

B: 14 October 1906, Linden - Mitte, Hanover, Germany

D: 4 December 1975, Upper West Side, NY, United States

What remains? The language remains

When: 1964

Where: West Germany

Audience: Television interview

Hannah Arendt was a German-born Jewish political theorist with first-hand experience of anti-semitism and the Nazi regime, from before and during World War II. Fleeing Germany in 1933 (the year Adolf Hitler came to power), she settled first in Paris and then in New York. During her time in the United States, she continued to develop her philosophical theories, with an interest in totalitarianism, war and revolution. Her work helps sharpen the perspective of the concept of evil, bringing it down to the complicity that exists at an individual level. As an example of this, she once said in an interview with the *New Yorker*, 'It is well known that the most radical revolutionary will become a conservative the day after the revolution.'

In 1961 Hannah Arendt was commissioned by the *New Yorker* magazine to report on the trial in Jerusalem of Adolf Eichmann. Eichmann was a Nazi official who, among other things, was responsible for the isolation of Jews into ghettos in the major cities of Germany and elsewhere in Europe.

Arendt's articles later culminated in the book *Eichmann in Jerusalem: A Report on the Banality of Evil*. This publication sparked a wave of protest, particularly with regards to her portrayal of Eichmann as a dull, unimaginative automaton — a 'clown' — rather than the evil monster the world expected. Arendt also questioned the actions of some Jewish leaders associated with the Jewish Councils, arguing these leaders cooperated perhaps too readily with Eichmann and, without this cooperation, more Jewish lives would have been saved. These views attracted condemnation from many of her peers and even some of her friends. Arendt's views were sometimes misunderstood as providing a defence of the Nazi regime. Her theories illuminate the mechanics of evil regimes and the role of the individual in supporting the enabling infrastructure.

Amid the controversy, Arendt spoke out repeatedly in defence of her intellectual argument.

On 28 October 1964, she appeared in a televised conversation with German journalist Günter Gaus, which was broadcast in West Germany. This interview was conducted in Arendt's native tongue and broadcast very early in the days of television and before the talk show format really existed. The audience were accustomed to the portrait and Q&A style of interview used by Gaus from previous shows featuring political figures as well as artists and philosophers.

Not exactly a speech, the interview does cover a lot of ground and Arendt presents her arguments clearly. When Gaus turns to the question of the Eichmann matter, Arendt responds with force and reason. Evident in this interview is her characteristic commitment to uncovering the truth, her deference to logos over pathos — and her endless chain-smoking habit.

WHAT SHE SAID

Gaus: Miss Arendt, your book on the trial of Eichmann in Jerusalem was published this fall in the Federal Republic. Since its publication in America, your book has been very heatedly discussed. From the Jewish side, especially, objections have been raised which you say are partly based on misunderstandings and partly on an intentional political campaign. Above all, people were offended by the question you raised about the extent to which Jews are to blame for their passive acceptance of the German mass murders, or to what extent the collaboration of certain Jewish councils almost constitutes a kind of guilt of their own. In any case, for a portrait of Hannah Arendt, so to speak, a number of questions come out of this book. If I may begin with them: Is the criticism that your book is lacking in love for the Jewish people painful to you?

Arendt: First of all, I must, in all friendliness, state that you yourself have become a victim of this campaign. Nowhere in my book did I reproach the Jewish people with nonresistance. Someone else did that in the Eichmann trial, namely, Mr. Haussner of the Israeli public prosecutor's office. I called such questions directed to the witnesses in Jerusalem both foolish and cruel.

Gaus: I have read the book. I know that. But some of the criticisms made of you are based on the tone in which many passages are written.

Arendt: Well, that is another matter. What can I say? Besides, I don't want to say anything. If people think that one can only write about these things in a solemn tone of voice…Look, there are people who take it amiss — and I can understand that in a sense — that, for instance, I can still laugh. But I was really of the opinion that Eichmann was a buffoon. I'll tell you this: I read the transcript of his police investigation, thirty-six hundred pages, read it, and read it very carefully, and I do not know how many times I laughed — laughed out loud! People took this reaction in a bad way. I cannot do anything about that. But I know one thing: three minutes before certain death, I probably still would laugh. And that, they say, is the tone of voice. That the tone of voice is predominantly ironic is completely true. The tone of voice in this case is really the person. When people reproach me with accusing the Jewish people, that is a malignant lie and propaganda and nothing else. The tone of voice, however, is an objection against me personally. And I cannot do anything about that.

Gaus: You are prepared to bear that?

Arendt: Yes, willingly. What is one to do? I cannot say to people: You misunderstand me, and in truth this or that is going on in my heart. That's ridiculous.

...Gaus: Miss Arendt, do you feel that it is your duty to publish what you learn through political-philosophical speculation or sociological analysis? Or are there reasons to be silent about something you know?

Arendt: Yes, that is a very difficult problem. It is at bottom the sole question that interested me in the whole controversy over the Eichmann book. But it is a question that never arose unless I broached it. It is the only serious question — everything else is pure propaganda soup. So, fiat veritas, et pereat mundus [let truth be told though the world may perish]?d But the Eichmann book did not de facto touch upon such things. The book really does not jeopardize anybody's legitimate interests. It was only thought to do so.

Gaus: You must leave the question of what is legitimate open to discussion.

Arendt: Yes, that is true. You are right. The question of what is legitimate is still open to discussion. I probably mean by 'legitimate' something different from what the Jewish organizations mean. But let us assume that real interests, which even I recognize, were at stake.

Gaus: Might one then be silent about the truth?

Arendt: Might I have been? Yes! To be sure, I might have written it … But look here, someone asked me, if I had anticipated one thing or another, wouldn't I have written the Eichmann book differently? I answered: No. I would have confronted the alternative: to write or not to write. Because one can also hold one's tongue.

<u>HOW</u> SHE DID THAT

Be prepared to face the difficult questions

We all experience a strong temptation to sidestep the thorniest issues that are bound to create tension and ill will. The more difficult and challenging they are, the more likely we are to face criticism and rejection. But, as Hannah Arendt shows us, by tackling these issues and demonstrating tenacity and clear-headedness, the good outweighs the bad. The benefit of advancing human understanding is worth the risks of being misunderstood, in her view.

Building on the philosophical views of her contemporaries, and adding her unique perspective as a Jew and a woman, she illuminates a side of the situation not previously considered. This is a voice the world needed to hear and still does.

In today's world, Arendt would likely be accused of not 'managing the optics'. Perhaps her opponents would suggest she was tone-deaf. Long before the era of political correctness, Hannah Arendt demonstrated a willingness to stand by her convictions, to brave the storm of criticism in order to illuminate a deeper truth.

If your perspective is likely to be met with resistance or awkwardness, ask yourself why you need to speak out in the first place. If your reason is in service of a bigger purpose than your own gratification, perhaps you can summon some of Arendt's tenacity. By attaching yourself to a higher goal, you may just find the strength needed to take on questions and face down those who seek to downplay your contribution.

Once you have made the choice and you have taken a stand, you need to stick around for the fallout. Engage with your opponents. Demonstrate a willingness to debate. Be ready to entertain and discuss opposing viewpoints. Do not shrink away and wait for the dust to settle.

Accept complexity and nuance

So many ideas are swept away because they are difficult to articulate in a ten-second sound bite. Without catchphrases and mnemonics to assist us, we have to really pay attention. A reduced attention span has possibly become more commonplace with the changes in how we now consume media.

Arendt shows us that we needn't reduce our ideas any further than they should be. If meaning is at stake, the right thing to do is err on the side of complexity, but be deliberate in your language, and provide examples and explanations to ensure understanding. Doubting the intelligence of your audience is a mistake. In the long run, 'dumbing down' your ideas is futile.

When you know you will need to go into some detail in order to explain yourself properly, make sure you have chosen the right forum. Your audience should be prepped. You can indicate, as Arendt does in this interview, you are taking the matter seriously.

In defending your point of view while also communicating complex ideas, you may need to structure, segment and reiterate your points in different ways, for different audiences. Arendt is very clear, almost but not quite to the point of rudeness, in cleaving tone and content. She is aware that her tone may be problematic for some but she is forthright in explaining that her tone, lacking pathos as it does, has no bearing on her central idea — the banality of evil.

Deflect ad hominem attacks

After her article was published in the *New Yorker*, Arendt was criticised by some for being a Nazi sympathiser. Such an attack must have felt deeply personal and unjust. But, in this response, we see Arendt call out the fallacy for what it was, thus reclaiming the higher ground.

Not every criticism is worthy of a response. Often remarks made behind the mask of anonymity, such as social media trolling, are best left to die of natural causes or to be starved of oxygen.

If you find yourself face to face and need to argue your position, you are more likely to triumph if you expose faulty reasoning. Stay calm and don't overreact. Listen carefully for mistakes in the premise of the question or counterargument and respond on that level. Resist being drawn on irrational generalisations. Arendt did not, and should not have had to, defend her non–neo-Nazi status.

In this interview, Arendt cuts across the interviewer, she leans forward, she raises her voice slightly and she punctuates her words. She conveys immediate strength and makes her position known. At times she is willing to sit back and wax philosophical, while at other times she defends.

The world needs your ideas. Your ability to remain steadfast in the face of nastiness will make sure we really hear the crux of what you have to say.

We have here an entirely separate kind of chemistry for which the current tool we use is the electrometer, not the balance, and which we might well call the chemistry of the imponderable.

Marie Curie

Marie Curie

Chemist and physicist

B: *7 November 1867, Warsaw, Poland*

D: *4 July 1934, Passy, France*

Radium and the new concepts in chemistry

When: *11 December 1911*

Where: *Stockholm, Sweden*

Audience: *Nobel Committee, Swedish royalty, dignitaries and guests*

You might know Dr Marie Curie as 'Madame Curie', for that is often the moniker that accompanies the history lesson. Perhaps you also noticed the shift in title from 'Doctor' to 'Madame' or 'Mrs', and the subtle diminishment of female achievement in academia that still happens today.

Curie and her colleagues were among the first to conduct research into radioactivity, leading to the discovery of two new elements. These were remarkable and portentous achievements in science and came as the culmination of decades of focus and work by Curie.

She was one of the most impressive scientific contributors of the twentieth century. She was also a woman who refused to let her gender impede her professional pursuits, despite being constantly maligned. As a young woman, she was denied entry to university on the basis of gender, so she and her sister studied at the clandestine Flying University in Poland.

She was awarded not one but two Nobel Prizes in two separate categories: physics and then chemistry. She discovered not one but two new elements: radium and polonium. Her work was groundbreaking and she had to fight every step of the way — for resources, recognition and the right to pursue her scientific work. Merit, it seems, was not nearly enough.

Like many scientists, Curie eschewed the social and political realms. She was shy and sometimes wore a sling in social situations to avoid shaking hands. She did not travel to Stockholm with her husband to receive her first Nobel Prize, preferring to remain in Paris, working in her laboratory. She rarely wrote for the mainstream and avoided speaking in public.

We now cherish her Nobel Lecture, delivered upon acceptance of her second award, in Stockholm, Sweden, on 11 December 1911 to a formal assembly of the Nobel Committee, Swedish royalty, dignitaries and guests. Extracts of this talk are included here.

<u>WHAT</u> SHE SAID

66

Some 15 years ago the radiation of uranium was discovered by Henri Becquerel, and two years later the study of this phenomenon was extended to other substances, first by me, and then by Pierre Curie and myself. This study rapidly led us to the discovery of new elements, the radiation of which, while being analogous with that of uranium, was far more intense. All the elements emitting such radiation I have termed radioactive, and the new property of matter revealed in this emission has thus received the name radioactivity. Thanks to this discovery of new, very powerful radioactive substances, particularly radium, the study of radioactivity progressed with marvellous rapidity: Discoveries followed each other in rapid succession, and it was obvious that a new science was in course of development. The Swedish Academy of Sciences was kind enough to celebrate the birth of this science by awarding the Nobel Prize for Physics to the first workers in the field, Henri Becquerel, Pierre Curie and Marie Curie (1903).

From that time onward numerous scientists devoted themselves to the study of radioactivity. Allow me to recall to you one of them who, by the certainty of his judgement, and the boldness of his hypotheses and through the many investigations carried out by him and his pupils, has succeeded not only in increasing our knowledge but also in classifying it with great clarity; he has provided a backbone for the new science, in the form of a very precise theory admirably suited to the study of the phenomena. I am happy to recall that Rutherford came to Stockholm in 1908 to receive the Nobel Prize as a well-deserved reward for his work.

... It is therefore my task to present to you radium in particular as a new chemical element, and to leave aside the description of the many radioactive phenomena which have already been described in the Nobel Lectures of H. Becquerel, P. Curie and E. Rutherford.

Before broaching the subject of this lecture, I should like to recall that the discoveries of radium and of polonium were made by Pierre Curie in collaboration with me. We are also indebted to Pierre Curie for basic research in the field of radioactivity, which has been carried out either alone, or in collaboration with his pupils.

... We were thus led to create a new method of searching for new elements, a method based on radioactivity considered as an atomic property of matter. Each chemical separation is followed by a measurement of the activity of the products obtained, and in this way it is possible to determine how the active substance behaves from the chemical viewpoint. This method has come into general application, and is similar in some ways to spectral analysis. Because of the wide variety of radiation emitted, the method could be perfected and extended, so that it makes it possible, not only to discover radioactive materials, but also to distinguish them from each other with certainty.

... To conclude I should like to emphasise the nature of the new chemistry of radioactive bodies ... We are also accustomed to deal currently in the laboratory with substances the presence of which is only shown to us by their radioactive properties but which nevertheless we can determine, dissolve, reprecipitate from their solutions and deposit electrolytically. This means that we have here an entirely separate kind of chemistry for which the current tool we use is the electrometer, not the balance, and which we might well call the chemistry of the imponderable.

<u>HOW</u> SHE DID THAT

Give credit

Scientific discovery, as is the case in many other fields, is often the result of a group effort. Experimentation is iterative — each new experiment builds on the hypotheses and observations of previous attempts. Empiricists look to the work of others to first consider what has been proven — what is true. Success often relies on one's ability to put the ego aside.

In this case, Dr Marie Curie took care to attribute the importance of foundational discoveries and at the same time mark her gratitude for the first award. She notes, 'The Swedish Academy of Sciences was kind enough to celebrate the birth of this science by awarding the Nobel Prize for Physics to the first workers in the field, Henri Becquerel, Pierre Curie and Marie Curie (1903).'

In the full version of her speech (see Sources for details), Curie makes multiple references to other scientists, noting how their findings have informed her study and the advancement of the field in general. She goes further than just a bit of casual name-dropping. For example, she makes special mention of 'the most brilliant triumphs of the theory is the prediction that the gas helium, always present in radioactive minerals, can represent one of the end-products of the evolution of radium' noting the two researchers responsible — Ramsay and Soddy.

Sometimes we think that claiming all the credit for ourselves will elevate our status in the minds of our audience. Often the opposite is true. When you give credit, congratulations and recognition to others as it is due, you cast yourself in a more positive light. To make this technique work for you, remember to be specific — what are you giving credit for? How can you highlight the unique contributions of those you mention? If you are going to do it, be specific and genuine.

Claim credit

For Dr Marie Curie, the question of gender could not be separated from this lecture or the award itself. It was only on the insistence of her husband, Pierre Curie, that her name was included in the list of recipients of the 1903 Nobel Prize for discoveries in radiation. Curie chose not to attend the awards, electing to remain behind in Paris. At the time, the Swedish Academy of Sciences described her as a 'helpmeet' to her husband. Then, in 1911 she was awarded the Nobel Prize for Chemistry. This time she was the sole recipient and could not be relegated to the supporting role.

> Perhaps it was her awareness of the gender stigma that caused Curie to explicitly claim credit for her accomplishments in her speech, noting: Some 15 years ago the radiation of uranium was discovered by Henri Becquerel, and two years later the study of this phenomenon was extended to other substances, first by me, and then by Pierre Curie and myself.

If you find yourself in a situation where you need to establish credibility, this is a good way to do it. By stating objective facts you remove any taint of bragging. The coupling of credit-claiming with appropriate credit-giving works to elevate the trustworthiness of the speaker.

As it was, Curie was uncomfortable enough in delivering this lecture and it is clear she was not seeking attention for the purposes of vanity.

Signpost transitions

The full version of this lecture covers a lot of scientific ground. We know that Dr Marie Curie avoided public speaking and that she tended to write for technical publications, steering clear of the mainstream. So, we can assume that this is probably, for her, about as un-technical as it gets.

Even if you do not work in a particularly technical field, you are likely to find yourself in situations where you have more detailed information in your head than that of your audience. Your goal is to bring them with you rather than talking over their heads. But how to do that without talking down to the audience? Curie provides us with a great framework.

The overall tone in this speech is that Curie sees herself on the same level as the audience. She is neither talking down or up — quite an accomplishment for somebody who does not like speaking in public. Another tactic that Curie demonstrates is the use of signposts to mark transitions in content. Given that the subject matter is rather dense, these are a useful and generous addition.

In the full version of the speech, Curie draws our attention to what the speech has delivered with phrases such as 'I have so far considered ...' and 'I have shown ...'. She also notes, for our benefit, where she's headed next with phrases such as 'I shall now describe ...'. Finally, she uses a clear, 'To conclude I should like to emphasise ...' to indicate we are now about to hear her conclusions.

It was at this time in my life that each penny came to be worth the same as every other penny, despite whose head was on it – thus teaching me an important lesson: in high finance, aesthetic considerations soon drop by the wayside.

Margaret Atwood

Margaret Atwood

Writer

B: *18 November 1939, Ottawa, Canada*

Payback: Debt and the shadow side of wealth

When: *12 October 2008*

Where: *Massey Lecture: St. Johns Newfoundland (lecture 1)*

Audience: *Live auditorium audience and CBC Radio broadcast*

Like many of us, Margaret Atwood wanted to know more about money and debt — what money is, how debt works and what forces are at play in the sometimes mysterious inner-workings of the economy. Unlike most of us, Atwood turned her flight of fancy into a five-part lecture series and then a book— *Payback* — which offer a fresh perspective on the topic.

Margaret Atwood is a futurist as much as a talented author and Canadian national treasure. Some of her novels, including the wildly popular *The Handmaid's Tale*, present a dystopian view that Atwood extrapolates from real-life events. Her attention is captured by a broad range of topics — from climate change to women's rights, and totalitarianism to the female relationship dynamic. In *Payback*, her focus is an imaginative look at the concept of debt and how it is represented in mythology, religion, history and literature.

This is a lecture series — not a ten-minute YouTube clip — delivered as part of the CBC Radio Massey Lecture Series. (These are an annual series of lectures delivered by writers, thinkers and scholars, and attended by those with an interest in contemporary topics, thinkers and ideas.) The extract included here comes from the first in a series of five lectures delivered in St Johns Newfoundland — a maritime province in Canada — in front of a full auditorium and also broadcast on CBC Radio across Canada.

To get the full effect, you need to settle in and listen. Luckily, the sound recordings are readily available, so you can hear insights from Margaret Atwood herself — worth the investment of your time. The experience is at once hypnotic and deeply disturbing. Her voice perfectly punctuates the characteristic Atwood wit, which you might have missed if you have only thus far been exposed to her fiction writing.

Her timing for these lectures on the concept of debt couldn't have been better. They were delivered at a time when debt — the financial kind — was on everyone's minds: October 2008, the peak of the global financial crisis.

The first lecture in the series is called 'Ancient Balances', and it will take you to places you never thought you would go in the study of finance. The excerpt provided here is a transcription of the first ten minutes or so of the first lecture — enough to see Margaret Atwood's brilliance with language applied to this most ordinary yet beguiling subject: money.

<u>WHAT</u> SHE SAID

Canadian nature writer Ernest Thompson Seton had an odd bill presented to him on his twenty-first birthday. It was a record kept by his father of all the expenses connected with young Ernest's childhood and youth, including the fee charged by the doctor for delivering him. Even more oddly, Ernest is said to have paid it. I used to think that Mr Seton Snr was a jerk but now I'm wondering, what if he was, in principle, right? Are we in debt to anyone or anything for the bare fact of our existence? If so, what do we owe, and to whom or to what, and how should we pay?

The motive for this lecture series is curiosity — mine. And my hope is that the writing of it will help me to explore a subject I know little about but which for this reason intrigues me. That subject is debt.

Payback is not about debt management or sleep debt or the national debt or about managing your monthly budget or about how debt is actually a good thing because you can borrow money and then make it grow, or about shopaholics and how to figure out that you are one. Bookstores and the internet abound in such materials. Nor is it about the more lurid forms of debt — gambling debts and mafia revenges, karmic justice whereby bad deeds trigger reincarnation as a beetle, or melodramas in which moustache-twirling creditors use non-payment of the rent to force unwanted sex on beautiful women. Though it may touch on these.

Instead, it's about debt as a human construct — thus an imaginative construct — and how this construct mirrors and magnifies both voracious human desire and ferocious human fear.

Writers write about what worries them, says Alistair McLeod; also about what puzzles them, I'd add. The subject of payback is one of the most worrisome and puzzling things I know — that peculiar nexus where money, narrative or story and religious belief intersect, often with explosive force.

The things that puzzle us as adults begin by puzzling us as children, or this has certainly been the case for me. In the late 1940s society in which I grew up, there were three things you were never supposed to ask questions about. One of them was money, especially how much of it anyone made. The second was religion. To begin a conversation on that subject would lead directly to the Spanish Inquisition, or worse. The third was sex. I lived among the biologists and sex, at least as practised by insects, was something I could look up in the textbooks that were lying around the house. The ovipositor was no stranger to me.

So the burning curiosity children experience vis-à-vis the forbidden was focused, for me, on the other two taboo areas: the financial and the devotional. At first, these appeared to be distinct categories. There were the things of God, which were unseen. Then there were the things of Caesar, which were all too material. They took the form of golden calves, of which we didn't have many in Toronto at that time, and also the form of money, the love of which was the root of all evil. But, on the other hand, stood the comic book character Scrooge McDuck, much read about by me, who was a hot-tempered, tight-fisted and often devious billionaire named after Charles Dickens' famous redeemed miser, Ebenezer Scrooge. The Plutocratic McDuck had a large money bin full of gold coins, in which he and his three adopted nephews splashed around as if in a swimming pool. Money, for Uncle Scrooge and the young duck triplets, was not the root of all evil but a pleasurable plaything. Which of these views was correct?

We kids of the 1940s did usually have some pocket money and although we weren't supposed to talk about it or have an undue love of it, we were expected to learn to manage it at an early age. When I was eight years old, I had my first paying job. I was already acquainted with money in a more limited way — I got five cents a week allowance, which bought a lot more tooth decay then than it does now. The pennies not spent on candy I kept in a tin box that had once held Lipton tea. It had a brightly coloured Indian design, complete with elephant, opulent veiled lady, men in turbans, temples and domes, palm trees and a sky so blue it never was. The pennies had leaves on one side and Kings' heads on the other and were desirable to me according to their rarity and beauty. King George VI, the reigning monarch, was common currency and thus low ranking on my snobby little scale, and also he had no beard or moustache. But there were still some hairier George V's in circulation and, if you were lucky, a really fur-faced Edward VII or two.

I understood these pennies could be traded for goods such as ice cream cones, but I did not think them superior to the other units of currency used by my fellow children — cigarette packaged aeroplane cards, milk bottle tops, comic books and glass marbles of many kinds. Within each of these categories, the principle was the same: rarity and beauty increased value. The rate of exchange was set by the children themselves, though a good deal of haggling took place.

All of that changed when I got a job. The job paid 25 cents an hour, a fortune, and consisted of wheeling a baby around in the snow. As long as I brought the baby back, alive, and not too frozen, I got the 25 cents. It was at this time in my life that each penny came to be worth the same as every other penny, despite whose head was on it — thus teaching me an important lesson: in high finance, aesthetic considerations soon drop by the wayside. Worse luck.

99

<u>HOW</u> SHE DID THAT

Explore new perspectives of common ideas

In this lecture series, Margaret Atwood set herself an ambitious goal: to encourage people to take a fresh look at money — something that governs our lives in many ways that maybe we don't understand as well as we think we do. Even if you're an economist or work in the financial sector, Atwood will take you to places in the world of money that you have never been to before. She is successful in making us think about money and debt very differently.

She begins with a thorough set-up. Given that this is a lengthy five-part lecture series, taking some time at this stage is necessary to ensure people stay for the whole journey. But for all its thoroughness, this introduction is anything but boring. This is partly because Atwood has a superior way with words. With her touch, a humble tin for storing money becomes an artefact imbued with meaning: 'It had a brightly coloured Indian design, complete with elephant, opulent veiled lady, men in turbans, temples and domes, palm trees and a sky so blue it never was.'

Margaret Atwood also spends a good amount of time at the beginning of her first lecture telling you what her talk is not about. In doing so, she takes us on an adventurous romp through other titles you might find in the bookstore, before finally and succinctly stating what she intends to cover: 'it's about debt as a human construct — thus an imaginative construct — and how this construct mirrors and magnifies both voracious human desire and ferocious human fear.'

To develop the Atwood eye, cast around for subjects that are so ubiquitous to your life or your profession that they escape detailed analysis. What could be missing from this analysis? How could you re-examine concepts, explore perceptions or challenge assumptions to elucidate new meaning? Take your lead from Atwood: establish clarity about what you intend to talk about and what is outside your scope.

Give the subject the time it deserves

Not everything has to be a sound bite. Chronic societal attention deficit disorder means the opportunities to develop complex arguments are rare. The Massey lectures are one of these rare opportunities. Atwood delivers five lectures in total, of nearly an hour each. That people are still open to long-form content is encouraging. Indeed, most people are willing to go with you on an intellectual adventure, so long as something is in it for them. That could be the payoff of learning or being entertained.

Atwood uses this long format to develop her thoughts, deep and wide. The breadth of the subject is roughly divided using the format of the five lectures, each with their own theme. The depth that she goes to within each is quite impressive. At no point does the information seem overwhelming and it is possible to dip in and out, to let your attention wander and then to rejoin, without losing the gist.

You might be able to determine how long a presentation or series should be, based on what you need to achieve. Or perhaps you are in a situation where the parameters are already established. Start by clarifying how long you have to speak and determine the appropriate purpose — and then gather the content. You might need to hone your view, considering what topic you can do justice to in the time provided. Perhaps you can go wide and give a broad overview of a subject. Or using the time you have to go deep might suit your purposes better — exploring layers of detail and bringing your audience with you to a new level of specialist knowledge.

Present the way that best suits you

If you are more comfortable with writing than speaking, you may want to do what Atwood does here. She is not speaking from bullet points; she is reading her prepared speech. Every word is prearranged and in its place. Of course, the benefit of this approach is that you won't accidentally say something you don't intend. You will be in control and able to manage any jitters that might arise.

This is Atwood's typical approach. Her prepared speeches are usually written in prose and then read. This is not because she is not capable or quick-witted enough to speak off the cuff. I could cite several examples of her in interview or panel discussions when she is every bit as articulate as she is here. Perhaps her appreciation for language or her long career as a writer is the reason she prefers to write her speeches ahead of time.

For most of us, this would be a daunting, maybe unachievable task. The amount of work involved in writing five hours' worth of content is huge. And then there is the preparation time to consider. Even if you present with the benefit of notes, you still need to prepare. Margaret Atwood shows that it is possible to be fully present despite having a written speech. Just ensure you practise so you don't sound too wooden.

The point is to choose the method that suits you best. So long as you are aware of and have allowed for the time required, go ahead and write out your speech if that's your preference. Better that than electing not to speak at all.

Opening hearts
and minds

All change begins at the individual level.

Before a team changes direction, before a society advances, before a law is changed, there must be a shift of some kind that one human experiences — this is the inflection point. This change can be activated through the power of speech. Words that make people feel something have hit on the right message, delivered by the right person at the right time to inspire change. Each of the four speakers featured in this chapter were themselves an integral part of the message they delivered.

A kind of alchemy comes into play with speeches like these. It's not magic, but it may seem like it. When Eleanor Roosevelt addressed the United Nations in 1948, it was to mark the agreement that had been brokered in the formulation of the Universal Declaration of Human Rights. In the wake of the atrocities of World War II, her words helped to galvanise a general commitment to prevent such violations in the future. In her speech, she only obliquely spurns the opposition voices, preferring to keep her focus on the ethics of voting in favour of the Declaration and the momentum that has been created.

Sometimes a group of people will change their minds in an instant ... and sometimes the shift will take years. And sometimes you must create the opportunity for yourself. When Nancy Astor delivered her first speech to the UK parliament, she would have been acutely aware that no woman had ever taken this step or delivered such a speech. You can imagine the prejudice she needed to overcome. Her speech was about telling the assembly how they might think differently but, more than that, it was about showing them how she intended to perform in the job for which she had been elected.

How does the sixteen-year-old Malala Yousafzai attract and hold the attention of the world as she advocates for the education of girls? When you take a closer look at her speech included in this chapter, you will see how she managed to move people and how you can make her techniques your own. I don't mean you should simply copy what she did, but you can learn from her understanding of the inflection point in history and draw from your own personal experience to inspire others. Malala's speech reminds us that our emotional selves are inextricably connected to our thinking selves.

Malala does so much more than recount her personal story — although her captivating retelling is woven through the fabric of her speech. She manages to show us a path to finding the better part of our own nature. She presents us with an example of how one girl could rise above violence and take the higher road.

At times you will need to find a way for your voice to stand out among the cacophony of noise that surrounds a particular subject. This was the case for Naomi Klein offering her perspective on climate change. Faced with so much noise, misinformation, disbelief and confusion in the public arena, she found a way for her speech to cut through. We can look to speakers such as Klein to remind us that moral conviction is a tactic of persuasion that our audiences will see, hear and feel.

Most speakers underestimate the power they have to make people feel something — especially in a professional setting. They tend to limit the impact of their speech before they even create it and they grossly misjudge the role of emotional resonance in human decision-making.

We stand today at the threshold of a great event, both in the life of the United Nations and in the life of mankind. This Universal Declaration of Human Rights may well become the international Magna Carta of all men everywhere.

Eleanor Roosevelt

Eleanor Roosevelt

Former First Lady of the United States, human rights advocate and journalist

B: *11 October 1884, New York City, NY, United States*

D: *7 November 1962, New York City, NY, United States*

On the adoption of the Universal Declaration of Human Rights

When: *9 December 1948*

Where: *Paris, France*

Audience: *United Nations General Assembly*

Eleanor Roosevelt was once called 'the archetype of the twentieth-century woman'. Archetypical perhaps, but she was anything but ordinary. She is remembered fondly in modern popular culture. Her quotes adorn T-shirts, mugs and endless social media posts. But she was broadly criticised in her day. In addition to filling the role of first lady during the 12-year term in office of her husband, Franklin Delano Roosevelt, she was a prolific columnist, lecturer and activist. Hers was the struggle shared with other intellectually ambitious women of her day — but, in her case, played out in the public arena.

Perhaps her most notable achievement and one of global significance was her role in bringing the Universal Declaration of Human Rights into existence — as Chairperson of the drafting committee of the Declaration. Eleanor Roosevelt was deeply affected by the events of World War II and used the postwar sentiment as momentum to forge this significant path. The Declaration proclaims the inalienable rights everyone is inherently entitled to as a human being — regardless of race, colour, religion, sex, language, political or other opinion, national or social origin, property, birth or other status.

In her role as Chairperson, Roosevelt used her prestige and credibility when working behind the scenes to smooth out disagreements and achieve consensus — at a time of increasing tensions between the emerging superpowers of the Soviet Union and the United States. Then she led from the front with this address to the United Nations General Assembly in Paris in 1948. The address extracted here provides glimpses of the woman she must have been to have spearheaded the initiative.

Roosevelt delivered her speech on 9 December 1948. The Declaration was accepted by the General Assembly the following day. Of the 58 members of the United Nations at the time, 48 voted in favour, none against, eight abstained, and two did not vote.

WHAT SE SAID

"

Mr President, fellow delegates.

The long and meticulous study and debate of which this Universal Declaration of Human Rights is the product means that it reflects the composite views of the many men and governments who have contributed to its formulation. Not every man nor every government can have what he wants in a document of this kind. There are, of course, particular provisions in the Declaration before us with which we are not fully satisfied. I have no doubt this is true of other delegations, and it would still be true if we continued our labours over many years.

... I should like to comment briefly on the amendments proposed by the Soviet delegation. The language of these amendments has been dressed up somewhat, but the substance is the same as the amendments which were offered by the Soviet delegation in committee and rejected after exhaustive discussion. Substantially the same amendments have been previously considered and rejected in the Human Rights Commission. We in the United States admire those who fight for their convictions, and the Soviet delegation has fought for their convictions. But in the older democracies, we have learned that sometimes we bow to the will of the majority. In doing that, we do not give up our convictions. We continue sometimes to persuade, and eventually we may be successful. But we know that we have to work together and we have to progress. So, we believe that when we have made a good fight, and the majority is against us, it is perhaps better tactics to try to cooperate.

... In giving our approval to the Declaration today, it is of primary importance that we keep clearly in mind the basic character of the document. It is not a treaty; it is not an international agreement. It is not and does not purport to be a statement of law or of legal obligation. It is a Declaration of basic principles of human rights and freedoms, to be stamped with the approval of the

General Assembly by formal vote of its members, and to serve as a common standard of achievement for all peoples of all nations.

We stand today at the threshold of a great event, both in the life of the United Nations and in the life of mankind. This Universal Declaration of Human Rights may well become the international Magna Carta of all men everywhere. We hope its proclamation by the General Assembly will be an event comparable to the proclamation of the Declaration of the Rights of Man by the French people in 1789, the adoption of the Bill of Rights by the people of the United States, and the adoption of comparable declarations at different times in other countries.

At a time when there are so many issues on which we find it difficult to reach a common basis of agreement, it is a significant fact that 58 states have found such a large measure of agreement in the complex field of human rights. This must be taken as testimony of our common aspiration first voiced in the Charter of the United Nations to lift men everywhere to a higher standard of life and to a greater enjoyment of freedom. Man's desire for peace lies behind this Declaration. The realisation that the flagrant violation of human rights by Nazi and Fascist countries sowed the seeds of the last world war has supplied the impetus for the work which brings us to the moment of achievement here today.

... This Declaration is based upon the spiritual fact that man must have freedom in which to develop his full stature and through common effort to raise the level of human dignity. We have much to do to fully achieve and to assure the rights set forth in this Declaration. But having them put before us with the moral backing of 58 nations will be a great step forward.

As we here bring to fruition our labours on this Declaration of Human Rights, we must at the same time rededicate ourselves to the unfinished task which lies before us. We can now move on with new courage and inspiration to the completion of an international covenant on human rights and of measures for the implementation of human rights.

In conclusion, I feel that I cannot do better than to repeat the call to action by Secretary Marshall in his opening statement to this Assembly:

> Let this third regular session of the General Assembly approve by an overwhelming majority the Declaration of Human Rights as a standard of conduct for all; and let us, as Members of the United Nations, conscious of our own shortcomings and imperfections, join our effort in good faith to live up to this high standard.

99

<u>HOW</u> SHE DID THAT

Acknowledge what has been achieved

This speech is an accompaniment to a more formal process of approval through the UN channels. Eleanor Roosevelt is seeking consensus in the assembly, in both formal agreement by way of the vote, and informal goodwill and the overall sentiment of consensus.

Her opening remarks set the perfect tone:

> The long and meticulous study and debate of which this Universal Declaration of Human Rights is the product means that it reflects the composite views of the many men and governments who have contributed to its formulation

These opening remarks imply the work has been done and agreements are in place. She then sweeps away any lingering reservations by telling the assembly, as if it is self-evident, that full agreement on every point and sub-point from myriad governments and representatives involved is, of course, impossible. She indicates that what they have built together is both remarkable and pragmatic — and as good as they're going to get it.

Show positive resilience

Eleanor Roosevelt's words do not pull a veneer of false positivity over the work that must have happened behind the scenes. She openly addresses the proposed amendments put forward by the Soviet delegation. She tactfully recognises their position and then swiftly despatches them — arguing 'when we have made a good fight, and the majority is against us, it is perhaps better tactics to try to cooperate'.

By calling out the dissenting voice, you claim the opportunity to frame the terms of the issue. Then you can provide your counterargument so as to swat away your opposition like an annoying fruit fly. It is a crafty technique and one Roosevelt may have picked up in her time observing and participating in the political arena.

Take a closer look at the language she uses here when discussing the Soviet amendments. It is not accusatory. In fact, it is quite gentle and you may have to listen (or read) twice to pick up the nuance in her voice. In the following, note the repetition of the word 'we' and appreciate how she puts herself in the shoes of the Soviets (emphasis added for effect):

> But in the older democracies *we* have learned that sometimes *we* bow to the will of the majority. In doing that, *we* do not give up *our* convictions. *We* continue sometimes to persuade, and eventually *we* may be successful. But *we* know that *we* have to work together and *we* have to progress. So, *we* believe that when *we* have made a good fight, and the majority is against *us*, it is perhaps better tactics to try to cooperate.

That is a lot of putting herself (and the free world) on the side of the Soviets, when the reality was quite the opposite.

Too often in modern communication, leaders try too hard to sell an idea or a new direction. They get so carried away with the need for positivity that they step over any counterarguments. The problem is that people can usually sense a snow job. The lesson deftly displayed by Roosevelt is that your proposal will actually appear stronger when your audience can see you have considered the alternatives and are not afraid to discuss other possibilities.

Of course, leadership ultimately means a direction must be chosen. Roosevelt is careful not to let the dissenting opinion linger in the air. She quickly picks up her now fortified thesis with the following: 'In giving our approval to the Declaration today, it is of primary importance that we keep clearly in mind the basic character of the document.' And in doing so, her tone returns to one of positivity and achievement.

Appeal to a higher purpose

At the heart of this speech is an appeal to ethics. The Universal Declaration of Human Rights has been designed, debated and delivered because it is the right thing to do. Eleanor Roosevelt appeals to the higher ideals of the assembled delegates and looks to recognise their collective efforts. She states:

> This Declaration is based upon the spiritual fact that man must have freedom in which to develop his full stature and through common effort to raise the level of human dignity.

By elevating its purpose to the spiritual level and linking it with the goal of raising the level of human dignity, Roosevelt creates an unarguable platform.

All people in the world continue to benefit from the effect of Roosevelt's superior powers of persuasion.

I know that it was very difficult for some Hon. Members to receive the first lady MP into the House ... It was almost as difficult for some of them as it was for the lady MP herself to come in.

Nancy Astor

Nancy Astor

First female member of the British House of Commons

B: 19 May 1879, Danville, Virginia, United States

D: 2 May 1964, Grimsthorpe, United Kingdom

Maiden speech

When: 24 February 1920

Where: London, England

Audience: British House of Commons

Lady Nancy Astor was the first woman to sit in the British House of Commons, serving from 1919 to 1945. Her maiden speech (now known as a 'first speech' or 'inaugural speech') was delivered on 24 February 1920 to the otherwise all-male House of Commons, led by Prime Minister David Lloyd George, leader of the Liberal Party.

More than a hundred years later, we can still extract some lessons in eloquence from this brave woman of conviction. The overarching lesson has less to do with her rhetorical prowess and more with her character and tenacity. Parliament (in the UK and in Australia and elsewhere) is an inhospitable environment for many women in the current climate; just imagine the vipers' nest it would have been for Astor in 1920. Winston Churchill later admitted that they 'tried to freeze' Astor out. But she kept turning up, speaking her mind and fighting for her beliefs. You may not agree with her politics — in fact, many of her views are quite objectionable to the modern ear — but you have to admire her grit.

The historical significance of this speech comes in part from Nancy Astor having been the first woman to be elected to the UK House of Commons. But the power and significance of the speech comes from so much more than this. The words stand on their own. Astor's message is only enhanced when you know the history and circumstances. The resilience she must have had to withstand the barbs of the crossbenches is admirable. But her ability to push forward and address a matter she believed to be critical to the wellbeing of her constituents in Plymouth Sutton is admirable.

In the extracts of the speech provided here, Lady Nancy Astor gives us a wonderful lesson in tenacity and eloquence.

<u>WHAT</u> SHE SAID

" I shall not begin by craving the indulgence of the House. I am only too conscious of the indulgence and the courtesy of the House. I know that it was very difficult for some hon. Members to receive the first lady MP into the House. [HON. MEMBERS: 'Not at all!'] It was almost as difficult for some of them as it was for the lady MP herself to come in. Hon. Members, however, should not be frightened of what Plymouth sends out into the world. After all, I suppose when Drake and Raleigh wanted to set out on their venturesome careers, some cautious person said, 'Do not do it; it has never been tried before. You stay at home, my sons, cruising around in home waters.'

I have no doubt that the same thing occurred when the Pilgrim Fathers set out. I have no doubt that there were cautious Christian brethren who did not understand their going into the wide seas to worship God in their own way. But, on the whole, the world is all the better for those venturesome and courageous west country people, and I would like to say that I am quite certain that the women of the whole world will not forget that it was the fighting men of Devon who dared to send the first woman to represent women in the Mother of Parliaments. Now, as the west country people are a courageous lot, it is only right that one of their representatives should show some courage, and I am perfectly aware that it does take a bit of courage to address the House on that vexed question, drink.

… Do we want the welfare of the community, or do we want the prosperity of the trade? Do we want national efficiency, or do we want national inefficiency? That is what it comes to. So I hope to be able to persuade the House. Are we really trying for a better world, or are we going to slip back to the same old world before 1914? I think that the Hon. Member is not moving with the times.

… He talks about the restrictions. I maintain that they brought a great deal of good to the community. There were two gains. First, there were the moral gains. I should like to tell you about them. The convictions of drunkenness among women during the war were reduced to one-fifth after these vexatious restrictions were brought in. I take women, because, as the hon. Member has said, most of the men were away fighting.

… I do not think the country is really ripe for prohibition, but I am certain it is ripe for drastic drink reforms. [HON. Members: 'No!']

I know what I am talking about, and you must remember that women have got a vote now and we mean to use it, and use it wisely, not for the benefit of any section of society, but for the benefit of the whole. I want to see what the Government is going to do …

<u>HOW</u> SHE DID THAT

Be brave

The subject of Astor's first speech in parliament was alcohol. She sought to bring about restrictions on the sale of the 'demon drink'. It is hard to imagine a less popular topic, given the times and the audience, but she felt strongly about this matter. She set aside any lingering need to be liked and bravely made her case.

In the speech, she acknowledges her own bravery, saying, 'I am perfectly aware that it does take a bit of courage to address the House on that vexed question, drink'. She goes on to construct a persuasive argument, lining up a choice for her fellow members and making an appeal to the moral high ground:

> Do we want the welfare of the community, or do we want the prosperity of the trade? Do we want national efficiency, or do we want national inefficiency? That is what it comes to. So I hope to be able to persuade the House. Are we really trying for a better world, or are we going to slip back to the same old world before 1914?

Astor's tenacity and belief on this issue were not about making a splash. She followed through on her words. Astor's first bill — the first bill introduced into British parliament by a woman — sought to restrict the sale of alcohol to persons under the age of 18. The law was eventually passed and stands to this day.

Go forth with humour

Nancy Astor was famous for her wit. She kept company with the likes of playwright and activist George Bernard Shaw (who once referred to Astor as 'a recklessly unladylike lady'). It is true that Nancy Astor could never have achieved the success that she did without her substantial wealth and existing power; however, the real secret to her enduring success was her ability to engage. She could and would enter into a verbal joust with the best of them. As we can see in the rhetoric of many women throughout history seeking to make their point, a little bit of humour goes a long way. It's not about softening the message so much as coating it in a candy shell.

Astor uses humour to good effect throughout the full version of her first speech (see Sources for details); for example:

> The War Office and the Admiralty both commended the Liquor Control Board for having greatly gained that for which it was set up. No one would call the War Office or the Admiralty pussyfoots. There are several among them, but you can hardly look upon them as prejudiced pussyfoots.

Astor repeatedly demonstrates an awareness that her admission to the parliamentary 'club' meant that she needed to acknowledge the written and unwritten rules of engagement — as she does throughout this speech. She seems to be saying, 'I will play your game and win the odd point with humour, but I will always return to what really matters'. She does just this when moving in to make her argument, again in the full version of the speech:

> We, the women, know, and the men know, thousands of us in the country who work amongst the slums, and in prisons and hospitals, we know where John Barleycorn, as you are pleased to call him, leads to. It is not to Paradise. It promises Heaven, and too often it leads to Hell. I will not go on, because it would not be quite fair; but I do beg hon. Members to think of these things, and when they are talking about freedom, to think of the children.

Start as you mean to continue

With this speech and many more delivered throughout her long tenure in public office, Nancy Astor was driven by a desire to make a change in the world. In her own words when reflecting on her calling, she said,

> I wanted the world to get better and I knew that it couldn't get better if it was going to be ruled by men. As a matter of fact, I think it is amazing how well the men did for two thousand years considering they did it alone.

I like to think her inaugural speech was brilliantly crafted to strike just the right note of challenge and discord to shake up the parliament of the day. She set the tone here for how she meant to continue — as a politician who was wily, fiery and quite funny. The effect was to ruffle some very significant feathers. In a later interview, Astor recalled Churchill telling her:

> When you entered the House of Commons, I felt as if a woman had entered my bathroom and I had nothing to protect myself with except a sponge.

To this criticism carrying a hidden compliment, Astor quipped back, 'Would it never occur to you that your appalling appearance might have been protection enough?'

So here I stand, one girl among many.

I speak not for myself, but for all girls and boys.

I raise up my voice — not so that I can shout, but so that those without a voice can be heard.

Malala Yousafzai

Malala Yousafzai

Education activist

B: *12 July 1997, Mingora, Pakistan*

One girl among many

When: *12 July 2013*

Where: *New York City*

Audience: *United Nations General Assembly*

Malala Yousafzai, often referred to simply as Malala, lives in the hearts of many as a symbol of hope. She represents a gentle but unyielding commitment to the best of humanity, refusing to capitulate even in the wake of a barbaric attack.

Education activist Malala marked her sixteenth birthday in July of 2013 with her first high-level public appearance — in front of the United Nations General Assembly in New York. This special event to mark Youth Takeover Day was opened by the Secretary General Ban Ki-moon and attended by dignitaries plus invited activists and education specialists. Malala used this appearance to make an international appeal for the importance of education and the rights of girls.

Malala was shot in the face by a Taliban gunman for the crime of going to school and her growing activism in this area. A girl seeking an education and daring to speak out about her life was all that triggered this attack. Her personal strength in surviving and moving on with her life is admirable. Her ability to turn this vicious attack into a platform from which she will attempt to improve the world is remarkable. The ability for someone so young to speak out with such bravery and compassion is truly exceptional.

In the speech extracted here, she is respectful of the forum of the United Nations, clearly humbled by the fact that she is holding the attention of so many powerful people. However, she is also unwavering in her stance and careful to shift the attention away from her personal experience to the greater mission she has set for herself.

Malala speaks with calm commitment and a respectful sense of purpose, providing many lessons for anyone wanting to generate attention for their mission. More importantly, this speech is emblematic of a generation of girls needing to be heard by the world. If we all can listen, the future will certainly brighten.

WHAT SHE SAID

"... Today, it is an honour for me to be speaking again after a long time. Being here with such honourable people is a great moment in my life.

I don't know where to begin my speech. I don't know what people would be expecting me to say. But, first of all, thank you to God for whom we all are equal and thank you to every person who has prayed for my fast recovery and a new life. I cannot believe how much love people have shown me. I have received thousands of good wish cards and gifts from all over the world. Thank you to all of them. Thank you to the children whose innocent words encouraged me. Thank you to my elders whose prayers strengthened me.

... There are hundreds of human rights activists and social workers who are not only speaking for human rights, but who are struggling to achieve their goals of education, peace and equality. Thousands of people have been killed by the terrorists and millions have been injured. I am just one of them.

So here I stand, one girl among many.

I speak not for myself, but for all girls and boys.

I raise up my voice — not so that I can shout, but so that those without a voice can be heard.

Those who have fought for their rights:

Their right to live in peace.

Their right to be treated with dignity.

Their right to equality of opportunity.

Their right to be educated.

Dear friends, on the 9th of October 2012, the Taliban shot me on the left side of my forehead. They shot my friends too. They thought that the bullets would silence us. But they failed. And then, out of that silence came thousands of voices. The terrorists thought that they would change our aims and stop our ambitions but nothing changed in my life except this: weakness, fear and hopelessness died. Strength, power and courage was born. I am the same Malala. My ambitions are the same. My hopes are the same. My dreams are the same.

Dear sisters and brothers, I am not against anyone. Neither am I here to speak in terms of personal revenge against the Taliban or any other terrorist group. I am here to speak up for the right of education of every child. I want education for the sons and the daughters of all the extremists, especially the Taliban.

... Honourable Secretary-General, peace is necessary for education. In many parts of the world, especially Pakistan and Afghanistan, terrorism, wars and conflicts stop children to go to their schools. We are really tired of these wars. Women and children are suffering in many parts of the world in many ways. In India, innocent and poor children are victims of child labour. Many schools have been destroyed in Nigeria. People in Afghanistan have been affected by the hurdles of extremism for decades. Young girls have to do domestic child labour and are forced to get married at early age. Poverty, ignorance, injustice, racism and the deprivation of basic rights are the main problems faced by both men and women.

... Dear sisters and brothers, now it's time to speak up.

So today, we call upon the world leaders to change their strategic policies in favour of peace and prosperity.

We call upon the world leaders that all the peace deals must protect women and children's rights. A deal that goes against the dignity of women and their rights is unacceptable.

We call upon all governments to ensure free compulsory education for every child all over the world.

We call upon all governments to fight against terrorism and violence, to protect children from brutality and harm.

We call upon the developed nations to support the expansion of educational opportunities for girls in the developing world.

We call upon all communities to be tolerant — to reject prejudice based on caste, creed, sect, religion or gender. To ensure freedom and equality for women so that they can flourish. We cannot all succeed when half of us are held back.

We call upon our sisters around the world to be brave — to embrace the strength within themselves and realise their full potential.

Dear brothers and sisters, we want schools and education for every child's bright future. We will continue our journey to our destination of peace and education for everyone. No-one can stop us. We will speak for our rights and we will bring change through our voice. We must believe in the power and the strength of our words. Our words can change the world.

Because we are all together, united for the cause of education. And if we want to achieve our goal, then let us empower ourselves with the weapon of knowledge and let us shield ourselves with unity and togetherness.

Dear brothers and sisters, we must not forget that millions of people are suffering from poverty, injustice and ignorance. We must not forget that millions of children are out of schools. We must not forget that our sisters and brothers are waiting for a bright peaceful future.

So let us wage a global struggle against illiteracy, poverty and terrorism and let us pick up our books and pens. They are our most powerful weapons.

One child, one teacher, one pen and one book can change the world.

Education is the only solution. Education first.

<u>HOW</u> SHE DID THAT

Form an emotional connection

To appreciate the power of a speech, we need to place it in time and space. Looking back on an event like this and trying to form a true sense of what was happening in the room can be difficult. But with Malala Yousafzai's address to the United Nations, we have the benefit of video evidence of the assembly, in addition to the transcript. Her speech is well crafted but perhaps the most captivating evidence of Malala's emotional resonance is in how her emotions are mirrored in the reactions of her audience. It is moving to witness the affection on the faces of the crowd, and especially the barely contained pride in the face of her father.

As Malala bravely proceeds through her address, we can forget that she is just 16 years old. As we observe the reactions of the audience throughout, true affection and admiration are mirrored back. The expressions, spontaneous applause and nods of agreement are not staged. All are evidence of emotional resonance. This is the holy grail of speechmaking — difficult to achieve for even the most practised orators.

Why is it so difficult for a speaker to strike the right chord, and achieve the poignant effect Aristotle would have described as pathos? Sometimes we get in our own way by preparing and carefully rehearsing our speech. With the best intentions, we can create a situation where we fail to connect with the people in the room. Nothing is wrong with preparation; in fact, for a situation like this, it is essential. However, once you have done all you can do, you need to consciously change gears. Create some space between your time to refine and practise, and your time to perform. Remember every speech is a conversation. You must feel the presence of the other people in the room and try to speak *to* them, not *at* them.

Aim high and be memorable

Malala uses this speech as a platform to make a global plea for human dignity, equality and education for all. This is not the forum for ten-point plans or policy analysis; instead, the occasion calls for a high-minded, optimistic, aspirational appeal to humankind's better nature. Her purpose is lofty and ambitious — some might say idealistic and impossible. But none of that matters. Her purpose is to set the bar high.

Malala constructs her speech in such a way that her audience is empowered. She implores her listeners to be brave. We are given a reasonable basis on which to base that bravery. If we stand up and raise our united voices, we will succeed in the end, because the enemies of freedom are intimidated by free speech and 'the pen is mightier than the sword'.

Malala is not asking her audience to pick up arms against the terrorists. The fight she means to foment is one of courageous conviction. Her real enemies are fear and ignorance, not the armed Taliban insurgents. The best weapon against this insidious enemy is reading, writing and, indeed, speaking out. And this is a battle we can all wage.

Even if you are never invited to speak before the United Nations, you might find yourself in a situation that allows for an appeal to principles and ethics. You may need to urge people to be brave and do what might be hard, just because it is right. You will need to appeal to your audience's higher selves. Start with a generous assumption that, no matter how deeply buried, everybody has this side to themselves. Then look to Malala for beautiful inspiration.

Embody bravery

Malala's message is admirable. Her conviction is strong. Her personal sacrifice and resilience are undeniable. But the most powerful aspect of her message is her ability to rise above even the most despicable of human behaviour — the terrorists who tried to take her life. In the full version of the speech (see Sources), she shows she can rebound from the terror when she says, 'Even if there is a gun in my hand and he stands in front of me, I would not shoot him.' This is a personal demonstration of her commitment to peace and progress.

She also delves into the psyche of the terrorists in the full version of the speech, offering us her explanation: 'The power of education frightens them. They are afraid of women. The power of the voice of women frightens them.'

The words are impressive in their own right. That they are delivered by one so young who has, herself, experienced the most terrifying experience firsthand is phenomenal.

Why are people so moved by Malala's words? It has to do with the glimpses we get into her character. The story of her personal experience precedes her. We know before she speaks that she has credibility born of tragedy. We know she is the best person to tell her story. We convey upon Malala the scope to extrapolate meaning from her experience. Consider your own experience — what is the story only you can tell?

Our challenge is less to save the Earth from ourselves, and more to save ourselves from an Earth that if pushed too far has ample power to rock, burn and shake us off completely.

Naomi Klein

Naomi Klein

Journalist, activist and author

B: *8 May 1970, Montreal, QC, Canada*

This changes everything

When: *18 October 2014*

Where: *Bioneers Annual Conference, San Rafael, California*

Audience: *1500 conference delegates, various backgrounds*

The subject of climate change is a fraught business, with so many voices adding to what continues to be framed as a debate — scientific, militant, political, moderate and mystical. How, then, might someone such as journalist Naomi Klein add to the conversation?

Not in baby steps. In this speech, Klein challenges globalisation, capitalism and the titans of consumerism, which all sounds like intellectual danger territory. Perhaps she has grown accustomed to contentious debates in her work as an investigative journalist, author and activist. She, after all, coined the term 'disaster capitalism' and has taken aim at all the seemingly unchallengeable forces that she sees as culpable in the fight for climate change.

Perhaps Klein learned her 'uppity ways' at home. Born in Montreal, Canada, Klein's parents were American Vietnam War draft-dodgers — self-proclaimed hippies and activists in their own sets of issues and drives for progress. Klein's version of teenage rebellion was to embrace designer labels and consumerism — that is, until she saw the light. Unwilling or unable to let hypocrisy, poor decision-making and lazy thinking pass her by, Klein has written and spoken out on a range of topics, taking aim at the powers that be.

She is an award-winning journalist and bestselling author of eight critically acclaimed books. Well respected across several domains, she has a credible platform from which to agitate.

In November 2014, Naomi Klein delivered this speech at the Bioneers Annual Conference in San Rafael, California, to an audience likely predisposed to learning more and taking action on matters of social advancement and climate change. Her talk shared its title with her latest book at the time: *This Changes Everything*.

True to form, Klein pulls no punches—as the extracts provided here show. Clear-eyed and straight-talking, this is a welcome strident female voice that cuts through the noise.

<u>WHAT</u> SHE SAID

This is a photograph from the day in 2007 when Richard Branson, the impresario behind the Virgin Empire, launched his Virgin Earth challenge — a 25-million-dollar prize that would go to the first person to invent a technological solution to the problem of global warming.

Specifically, the task was to build some kind of gizmo to suck large amounts of carbon out of the air and sequester it without countervailing harmful effects. Now, 25 million dollars for a single prize is a lot of money. It is the largest pot of money for any scientific award out there, and I want to just take a little closer look at this picture. So you see Branson over there with that big grin on his face, gleefully tossing the planet in the air as if it were a beach ball. And there's Al Gore over there looking a little unsure about whether this is a good idea.

So I wanted to show this to you because I feel like this frozen moment is the perfect snapshot for the first incarnation of the climate movement. The one that failed. An extremely wealthy and powerful man, with the whole world literally in his hands, promising to save the fragile blue planet on our behalf.

...To paraphrase Arundhati Roy: the goal for this set is to change without having to change at all. So there's no doubt that if you are one of the big winners of our current system, there's a powerful appeal in that. If you think that the only problem with our economic model is the small matter of rising sea levels, then you're looking for a fix that is going to leave the status quo pretty much unchanged.

If, however, you are part of the vast majority of the people on this planet who know that this system is failing — with or without climate change — then you may have a very different approach.

So I've also begun to think that there is another problem with this picture besides all of that, and that has to do with that pale blue sphere that Branson is tossing skywards.

For more than 40 years, the view of the Earth from space has been the environmental movement's unofficial logo. It's featured on countless T-shirts, pins, bumper stickers, and if you have one on one of your bags at the moment don't feel bad. It's the thing that we're supposed to protect at UN climate conferences. It's the thing we're called upon to save every Earth Day — as if the planet were an endangered species or a starving child far away or a pet in need of our love and care. And that conception of the planet as needy child or animal is, I think, just as dangerous as that idea born in the 1600s that the Earth was an inert machine and that we humans were its engineers, called upon by God to exert total mastery.

…Our challenge is less to save the Earth from ourselves, and more to save ourselves from an Earth that if pushed too far has ample power to rock, burn and shake us off completely.

…One person who saw it coming was Kurt Vonnegut, who saw a lot coming. He wrote in 1969: 'Earth is such a pretty blue and pink and white pearl in the pictures NASA sent to me. It looks so clean. You can't see all the hungry angry Earthlings down there, and the smoke and the sewage and the trash and the sophisticated weaponry.' In other words, seen from space there are no people down there.

It's worth remembering this point. It's worth remembering that before this point American environmentalism had mostly been intensely local. An earthy thing; a lowercase earth thing, not an uppercase Earth thing. It was Henry David Thoreau musing on the rows of white bush beans by Walden Pond. It was Edward Abbey ranging through the Red Rocks of southern Utah. It was Rachel Carson down in the dirt with DDT contaminated worms. It was vividly descriptive prose, naturalist sketches and eventually photography and film seeking to awaken and inspire love for specific places — and, by extension, places like them around the world.

...The best news is that the time of astronauts' eyeview environmentalism is appearing to be coming to a close. And a new movement is rising to take its place. One deeply rooted in specific geographies but networked globally as never before.

...Though often described as anti–fossil fuel, this is, in fact, a pro-water movement. One grounded in a ferocious love of place. And as you'll be hearing from my dear friend Clayton Thomas Muller next, many of these movements are led by indigenous people using their land and title rights to block planet-destabilising projects.

Increasingly, they are also inspired and being transformed by an indigenous world view that is reviving long-buried traditions of humility before nature, and the deep knowledge that we are not above the world but of it — the antithesis of the hubris of the would-be planet hackers. This movement is telling new stories to replace the techno-escape fantasies — that this planet is our only home and that what comes around goes around and, most importantly, what goes up stays up for a very long time.

...This is just the beginning because local fights are morphing into guiding principles. No new carbon frontiers from the Arctic to the Amazon. No new sacrifice zones. We can power our lives without poisoning anyone. Justice and reparations for the communities that have already suffered the most in the old model. The polluter must pay to clean up this mess. The bill cannot be passed on to the most vulnerable. The time of privatised profits and socialised gains is coming to a close.

This is a movement of many movements and though utterly undetectable from outer space, it is beginning to shake the fossil fuel companies to their very core.

<u>HOW</u> SHE DID THAT

Elevate the debate

What Naomi Klein does not do in this speech is make an attempt to dumb down the climate change debate. She does not veer into the advertiser's domain of catchphrases and she avoids hackneyed soapbox demands. Although she is a journalist, she steps around opportunities for sound bites. She does not insult the intelligence of her audience; instead, she elevates the debate — and her speech is all the better for it.

Making assumptions about the level of knowledge of your audience is a delicate business. Of course, ensuring your audience understands the content of your speech is important, and this may require a spot of teaching. After all, you might not be speaking to people with the same detailed knowledge of your pet subject. However, your audience will recoil if you speak to them like they are kindergarten students. All too often, this is the preachy, teacherly tone we hear from activists.

This speech takes place on a sufficiently intellectual plane to cause the thinking listener to lean in. When referencing the impact of an indigenous worldview, Klein tells us this is 'the deep knowledge that we are not above the world but of it — the antithesis of the hubris of the would-be planet hackers'. A well-placed reminder of where we fit among the custodians of the land.

This speech traverses scientific facts, cultural paradigms, globalisation, popular culture, the cult of business titans, literary visionaries and much more. It is a heady tour of Klein's brain — all that she has discovered and come to know about the current reality — eloquently delivered.

Invoke voices outside your field

In this speech, Naomi Klein invokes the voice of beloved American author Kurt Vonnegut. Although she mentions several figures that are relevant to climate change — and some currently alive — she channels the voice of the deceased but somewhat revered author to serve as the source of reason. If you are familiar with Vonnegut, you might now conjure an image of him shaking his head at our petty mumbling.

This is a clever persuasion tactic, firmly grounded in the secular realm. Klein clearly understands the collective sentiments of her audience and chooses a creative point of reference to bring a touch of visionary literary mystique to her otherwise factual and strident talk.

She tells us, 'One person who saw it coming was Kurt Vonnegut, who saw a lot coming'. Vonnegut fans, and I am one, now have their interests well and truly piqued. Kurt did have so many pithy, wise comments to make in his time, but Klein focuses on her theme:

> He wrote in 1969: 'Earth is such a pretty blue and pink and white pearl in the pictures NASA sent to me. It looks so clean. You can't see all the hungry angry Earthlings down there, and the smoke and the sewage and the trash and the sophisticated weaponry.'

Klein follows this up with three more literary references, then links to photography and film, and then beautifully connects the scientific factual world to the spiritual dimension. If somebody else said it better — and if their words managed to move you — then why not use those words?

Sometimes, speakers think they must stay in the realm of the technical. If you are delivering a presentation on a product, strategy direction or technical solution, quoting a poet or a novelist might seem strange to you. But that might be just the beacon needed to awaken your audience. We all have lives and interests that span the earthly and ethereal domains. You can elevate your message with subtle links to the arts, spirituality or philosophy, and find a way to influence beyond the purely rational.

Set yourself up for success with a hook

Every speech, regardless of the receptivity of the audience, needs to begin with some kind of hook. In her live presentation at the Bioneers conference (see Sources), Klein opens with a short video clip that outlines the key concepts in her book.

This is a simple but effective technique. How can you use a video, piece of music, quote or anecdote to do the work for you? Your hook must be relevant to the purpose of your talk and it must capture the attention of your audience.

The use of a creative hook can make a big difference if you are one of several speakers at a conference-style event. More than just capturing attention and adding interest, you are effectively creating space between the person who spoke before you and your opening remarks. In all likelihood, your audience will need a few moments to squirm and fidget before they settle. By using a video or other device, you will be able to capture and redirect attention, while also highlighting your credibility beyond your own presentation.

4

Beckoning the waves of feminism

This study of speeches by women has revealed that many a powerful address was delivered in support of the women's movement.

The lessons embedded in the speeches of this chapter are not limited to women's struggle for equality, however; they can be extrapolated to any circumstance in which you are looking to challenge the status quo, build a movement and, you know—change the world.

Something about women's voices raised up in support of all women feels especially powerful. This is not intended to be a mini gender studies module or even an in-depth look at the feminist movement. Instead, this chapter explores four stand-out examples of women who have succeeded in paving the way for other women. You can extract the lessons of persuasion that these speeches deliver and, hopefully, be inspired to do more — because the fight is far from over.

The words of Mary Wollstonecraft are truly groundbreaking. You might consider *A Vindication of the Rights of Woman*, published in 1792, as the first ripple that preceded the first wave of feminism. Her deep resolve to challenge the conventions of society and her astounding intellect came together to outline a 'utopian dream' that women go back to, again and again, when they need renewed guidance.

Suffragette Emmeline Pankhurst was a skilled rhetorician, and she shows us how oratorical skill, and a lifelong practice of making speeches, could be put to extraordinarily good use in the service of winning the vote for women movement. A justification for militancy seems like a topic that would not be well received, but Pankhurst delivers such a well-spoken and persuasive address that she commands attention. Embedded in her message, in this speech and many others, is the idea that a change in the distribution of power will never be politely granted. For Pankhurst, those who find themselves on the wrong side of the divide must prepare to fight and to take, because equality will not be given.

Some of the colourful figures of second-wave feminism are more familiar to us. Women in the 1960s and '70s who picked up the struggle for women's rights found the game had changed. Political organisation and protests in support of the civil rights movement in many ways left women behind and that 'raised the rebel' in many. The impatient and impassioned words of Betty Friedan in her speech included here encouraging women, once again, to march gives us a flavour for how much had changed, and yet how much still had to happen.

Audre Lorde's voice is an important one, not only for her advancement of the cause but also as a warning against staying silent. As she asks so beautifully, 'What are the tyrannies you swallow day by day and attempt to make your own, until you will sicken and die of them, still in silence?'

In a way, every speech and speaker featured in this book is a contributor to the advancement of the feminist movement. The individual voices are as unique as a fingerprint, each a reflection of a distinctive idea. But the collection can be heard as a choir of liberation.

These may be termed Utopian dreams — thanks to that Being who impressed them on my soul, and gave me sufficient strength of mind to dare to exert my own reason, till, becoming dependent only on him for the support of my virtue, I view, with indignation, the mistaken notions that enslave my sex.

Mary Wollstonecraft

Mary Wollstonecraft

Writer and philosopher

B: *27 April 1759, London, United Kingdom*

D: *10 September 1797, London, United Kingdom*

I have a dream

When: *1792*

Where: *England*

Audience: *Presented through various forums*

Nearly two centuries before Martin Luther King Jr delivered his iconic speech, English writer and philosopher Mary Wollstonecraft also had a dream. Her dream imagined a future state where the conventions that define us and divide us might fall away. For Wollstonecraft, the dream was about a society in which women were valued for their equal wisdom and virtue — no longer the property and servants of man.

Mary Wollstonecraft may have been the original feminist rebel writer. She wrote her famous tome *A Vindication of the Rights of Woman* (from which this extract comes) and continued to generally speak up and disrupt the patriarchy in a well-reasoned, philosophical sort of way.

Although no recordings of Wollstonecraft's speeches exist, we know she formulated many of her ideas through discussion and debate as well as through articles and pamphlets — used at the time to set out a summary of one's position on a matter. Joseph Johnson recruited Wollstonecraft to write articles for the *Analytical Review* and invited her to participate in lively discussions with contemporaries such as Thomas Paine. *A Vindication of the Rights of Woman* came about as a response to her opposition of other, male, thinkers of the day.

In London, Wollstonecraft also began associating with the group the Rational Dissenters, later known as Unitarians, which included political radicals and proponents of independence movements. Unlike her rival, Edmund Burke, as a woman Wollstonecraft did not have the platform for formal speechmaking. Instead, she mounted her case in these less formal forums.

She was not, however, just a bookish-feminist. Her posthumously published memoirs revealed a rather salacious life (including love affairs and illegitimate children). Hers was certainly not the path of a demurring eighteenth-century lady obsessed with little more than the power struggles of the parlour room.

As with many of the feminists who would follow her, speaking out on the rights of women, Wollstonecraft was an advocate of equal education for boys and girls. This plea is far from obsolete — as the story and words of Malala Yousafzai (refer to the previous chapter) so painfully highlight.

Now, centuries later, Wollstonecraft's dream is still held up as a future state ideal, despite the enormous gains made by the feminist movement. Her influence lives on in the minds of enlightened thinkers who go back to her words again and again.

<u>WHAT</u> SHE SAID

These may be termed Utopian dreams—thanks to that Being who impressed them on my soul, and gave me sufficient strength of mind to dare to exert my own reason, till, becoming dependent only on him for the support of my virtue, I view, with indignation, the mistaken notions that enslave my sex.

I love man as my fellow; but his sceptre, real, or usurped, extends not to me, unless the reason of an individual demands my homage; and even then the submission is to reason, and not to man. In fact, the conduct of an accountable being must be regulated by the operations of its own reason; or on what foundation rests the throne of God? It appears to me necessary to dwell on these obvious truths, because females have been insulated, as it were; and, while they have been stripped of the virtues that should clothe humanity, they have been decked with artificial graces that enable them to exercise a short-lived tyranny. Love, in their bosoms, taking place of every nobler passion, their sole ambition is to be fair, to raise emotion instead of inspiring respect; and this ignoble desire, like the servility in absolute monarchies, destroys all strength of character. Liberty is the mother of virtue, and if women be, by their very constitution, slaves, and not allowed to breathe the sharp invigorating air of freedom, they must ever languish like exotics, and be reckoned beautiful flaws in nature.

As to the argument respecting the subjection in which the sex has ever been held, it retorts on man. The many have always been enthralled by the few; and monsters, who scarcely have shewn any discernment of human excellence, have tyrannised over thousands of their fellow-creatures. Why have men of superior endowments submitted to such degradation? For, is it not universally acknowledged that kings, viewed collectively, have ever been inferior, in abilities and virtue, to the same number of men taken from the common mass of mankind — yet, have they not, and are they not still treated with a degree of reverence that is an insult to reason? China is not the only country where a living man has been made a God. Men have submitted to superior strength to enjoy with impunity the pleasure of the moment — women have only done the same, and therefore till it is proved that the courtier, who servilely resigns the birthright of a man, is not a moral agent, it cannot be demonstrated that woman is essentially inferior to man because she has always been subjugated.

Brutal force has hitherto governed the world, and that the science of politics is in its infancy, is evident from philosophers scrupling to give the knowledge most useful to man that determinate distinction.

I shall not pursue this argument any further than to establish an obvious inference, that as sound politics diffuse liberty, mankind, including woman, will become more wise and virtuous.

99

<u>HOW</u> SHE DID THAT

Dare to question

As far as feminism is understood as an intellectual advancement of humankind, Mary Wollstonecraft may be viewed as its founder.

In the world of enlightenment philosophers that Wollstonecraft operated within, she dared to question society's conventions and hierarchies far more than any of her contemporary thinkers. She challenged the rules that governed society in a world that treated her horribly — a world that would have seen her destroyed for her views.

Mary Wollstonecraft refused to accept the strictures that would limit her full participation in humanity. Her commitment was born of a terrible childhood in which she saw her father treat her mother so brutally that it caused a fundamental questioning of the assumed natural law. Her questioning led her to conjure a dream — a dream of a future in which women were capable of full intellectual participation and not treated like slaves or adornments.

The lesson here is to question everything. Wollstonecraft challenged tradition, and particularly the conservatism wrapped up in the views of Edmund Burke (who had published *A Vindication of Natural Society* in 1756) and other leading thinkers of the time. Wollstonecraft was brave in her propensity to not only challenge the prevailing wisdom of the day, but doing so as a woman, with a limited voice and no public platform. Contemporary figures recognised her intelligence and engaged with her in discussion.

How do the philosophical clashes of the enlightenment era affect how we operate in the world today? You might have to think about the received wisdom under which you, your team or your organisation operates and whether some of the unwritten rules need to be challenged. Calling out the flawed logic of behaving in a particular way — simply because that is how it has always been done — might help you to lead a change in perspective. This in turn may create a new fertile ground for innovation.

Look beyond self

When speaking for a fundamental shift in paradigm, to be considered at all you must include a holistic view of the system you seek to deconstruct. When Wollstonecraft advocates for the elevation of women — suggesting that they be educated and emancipated — she also must consider how this change might affect the rest of society (namely, men).

Wollstonecraft recognises and speaks to the limitations of her modern convention for both boys and girls. Conditioning that begins at a young age also creates for boys a pre-packaged set of beliefs and expectations that might not help them fully actualise. This conditioning is limiting for everybody.

A similar sentiment is echoed by Betty Friedan many decades later. She observed that the actions of free-thinking boys in the 1970s who grew their hair long were, in part, outward symbols of resistance to the expectations that were thrust upon them. Feminists today still argue against these conventions and conditioning, and the damage they do to men as well as women.

If you are looking to disrupt the norm take heed of Wollstonecraft's advice. Especially when challenging the status quo, consider the benefits that such a challenge might create for those with existing privilege. Be a systems thinker and include everyone in your vision for how you want the world to be. This is not about manipulating those with privilege; this is the hard work of progress.

This sane wisdom can be applied if your purpose is something other than gender equality. If you are proposing any change, cast around to ensure you understand and can speak to all the impacts the change may have. Pay particular attention to any people or groups who stand to lose.

Lay the groundwork for the long game

A Vindication of the Rights of Woman is, as Wollstonecraft herself says, a utopian dream. So early in the women's rights process does she appear on the scene that concrete solutions for the problems she identifies were yet unformed.

Wollstonecraft was proposing a new way of thinking. She was the alpha trailblazer — but somebody has to be. Hers is not a treatise about rights. She does not propose new ways of dealing with property, divorce or even the notion of suffrage. And yet she lays the groundwork for all of these advancements, understanding that before the possibility can be revealed this thinking has to happen. She lays this groundwork early in the book:

> My own sex, I hope, will excuse me, if I treat them like rational creatures, instead of flattering their fascinating graces...

As always, when framing your speech make sure you know what you are trying to achieve. What do you want your audience to think, feel or do? Resist the urge to do everything all at once. It takes time — sometimes years or even decades — to shift collective thought patterns. But remember the big shifts are the cumulative result of lots of small changes, which can be inspired by your words.

More meetings were held, and larger, for Woman Suffrage than were held for votes for men, and yet the women did not get it. Men got the vote because they were and would be violent.

Emmeline Pankhurst

Emmeline Pankhurst

British and American suffragette

B: 15 July 1858, Manchester, United Kingdom

D: 14 June 1928, London, United Kingdom

Why we are militant

When: 1913

Where: New York City, USA

Audience: Suffrage groups

Emmeline Pankhurst was a significant player in the British and then American suffragette movement. She is remembered for her activism and for achieving significant outcomes on behalf of women. But to really grasp the strength of character that this woman must have had, imagine what life would have been like for her at the turn of the twentieth century.

In most parts of the world, women did not have the vote. (Women in New Zealand gained the vote in 1893, and in Australia gained the right to vote and sit for parliament in 1901.) Women had few rights under British law. Despite years of activism in the UK, Pankhurst was barely successful in being heard, let alone having her arguments considered in parliament.

She was a woman of action as well as words. In 1903, Pankhurst founded the Women's Social and Political Union (WSPU), an all-women suffrage advocacy organisation dedicated to 'deeds not words'. Interestingly, because she delivered a number of speeches in support of the cause, she is remembered as much for her words as for her deeds — so well crafted they were.

Pankhurst travelled constantly, including to the United States, where she continued her struggle, agitating for women's right to vote. Pankhurst made the speech included here in New York City in October 2013. She shows she has quickly located the pulse points of American culture and uses her newfound understanding to make her message resonate. Her comparison of British versus American lawmaking and power structures, and her mention of American independence from the British, seek to activate the revolutionary spirit she saw in the New World, and aim it at the rights women would claim.

Her purpose in the speech extracted here was to heighten support for the suffragist movement. She wanted to portray it less as a concept of progress and more as a militant uprising — in other words, less evolution, more revolution.

WHAT SHE SAID

"

I know that in your minds there are questions like these; you are saying, 'Woman Suffrage is sure to come; the emancipation of humanity is an evolutionary process, and how is it that some women, instead of trusting to that evolution, instead of educating the masses of people of their country, instead of educating their own sex to prepare them for citizenship, how is it that these militant women are using violence and upsetting the business arrangements of the country in their undue impatience to attain their end?'

Let me try to explain to you the situation.

Although we have a so-called democracy, and so-called representative government there, England is the most conservative country on Earth. Why, your forefathers found that out a great many years ago. If you had passed your life in England as I have, you would know that there are certain words which certainly, during the last two generations, certainly till about ten years ago, aroused a feeling of horror and fear in the minds of the mass of the people. The word revolution, for instance, was identified in England with all kind of horrible ideas. The idea of change, the idea of unsettling the established order of things was repugnant.

…The extensions of the franchise to the men of my country have been preceded by very great violence, by something like a revolution, by something like civil war. In 1832, you know we were on the edge of a civil war and on the edge of revolution, and it was at the point of the sword — no, not at the point of the sword — it was after the practice of arson on so large a scale that half the city of Bristol was burned down in a single night, it was because more and greater violence and arson were feared that the Reform Bill of 1832 was allowed to pass into law. In 1867, John Bright urged the people of London to crowd the approaches to the Houses of Parliament in order to show their determination, and he said that if they did that no Parliament, however obdurate, could resist their just demands. Rioting went on all over the country, and as the result of that rioting, as the result of that unrest, which resulted in the pulling down of the Hyde Park railings, as a result of the fear of more rioting and violence the Reform Act of 1867 was put upon the statute books.

…Meanwhile, during the '80s, women, like men, were asking for the franchise. Appeals, larger and more numerous than for any other reform, were presented in support of Woman's Suffrage. Meetings of the great corporations, great town councils and city councils, passed resolutions asking that women should have the vote. More meetings were held, and larger, for Woman Suffrage than were held for votes for men, and yet the women did not get it. Men got the vote because they were and would be violent. The women did not get it because they were constitutional and law-abiding. Why, is it not evident to everyone that people who are patient where mis-government is concerned may go on being patient!

…Now, gentlemen, in your heart of hearts you do not believe that. You know perfectly well that there never was a thing worth having that was not worth fighting for. You know perfectly well that if the situation were reversed, if you had no constitutional rights and we had all of them, if you had the duty of paying and obeying and trying to look as pleasant, and we were the proud citizens who could decide our fate and yours, because we knew what was good for you better than you knew yourselves, you know perfectly well that you wouldn't stand it for a single day, and you would be perfectly justified in rebelling against such intolerable conditions.

…We know the joy of battle. When we have come out of the gates of Holloway at the point of death, battered, starved, forcibly fed as some of our women have been — their mouths forced open by iron gags — their bodies bruised, they have felt when the prison bars were broken and the doors have opened, even at the point of death, they have felt the joy of battle and the exultation of victory.

People have said that women could never vote, never share in the government, because government rests upon force. We have proved that is not true. Government rests not upon force; government rests upon the consent of the governed; and the weakest woman, the very poorest woman, if she withholds her consent cannot be governed.

They sent me to prison, to penal servitude for three years. I came out of prison at the end of nine days. I broke my prison bars. Four times they took me back again; four times I burst the prison door open again. And I left England openly to come and visit America, with only three or four weeks of the three years' sentence of penal servitude served. Have we not proved, then, that they cannot govern human beings who withhold their consent?

And so we are glad we have had the fighting experience, and we are glad to do all the fighting for all the women all over the world. All that we ask of you is to back us up. We ask you to show that although, perhaps, you may not mean to fight as we do, yet you understand the meaning of our fight; that you realise we are women fighting for a great idea; that we wish the betterment of the human race, and that we believe this betterment is coming through the emancipation and uplifting of women.

99

<u>HOW</u> SHE DID THAT

Use evocative language

What would make you agree that militancy is justified? Let's say you are opposed to violence. Can you imagine a set of circumstances in which you would bypass that principle and accept that violent intervention is worthwhile? This is a thought experiment that may have helped Pankhurst in selecting the right examples to strengthen her argument. Then she selected language that evokes the feelings associated with the physical impact of battle, presumably in an attempt to engender the anger she herself feels:

> We know the joy of battle. When we have come out of the gates of Holloway at the point of death, battered, starved, forcibly fed as some of our women have been — their mouths forced open by iron gags — their bodies bruised, they have felt when the prison bars were broken and the doors have opened, even at the point of death, they have felt the joy of battle and the exultation of victory.

When you need to shift people's attitudes and encourage them to support solutions that they would not otherwise, you may need extreme measures and evocative language. The best route might be the emotional one. Put yourself in the shoes of your audience and imagine how they are likely to react. Now consider what set of circumstances might make them change their mind. Then select the right tone and examples that bring a scene to life. You will need to provoke a limbic response — the part of the brain that responds to intense emotions of fear and anger — in order to shake a rationally held position.

Emmeline Pankhurst understood a jolting address was necessary. She needed to provoke anger—or at least sympathy—if everyone in her audience, and particularly the men, were ever to agree. The lesson from Pankhurst is to choose words that trigger emotion, in hopes of bypassing a more analytical rational response.

Emphasise with the power of three

A well-seasoned speaker and practitioner of rhetoric, Pankhurst displays a great deal of oratorical flair. The Aristotelian concept of tricolon (the rule of three) is used throughout, strengthened with repetition to further emphasise meaning—as shown by these examples from the full version of the speech (see Sources):

> …The only justification for violence, the only justification for damage to property, the only justification for risk to the comfort of other human beings…

> …good fathers, good husbands and good brothers…

> …You are full of sympathy with men in Russia. You are full of sympathy with nations that rise against the domination of the Turk. You are full of sympathy with all struggling people striving for independence.

This ancient technique is commonly adopted by crafty communicators — in writing and speaking. It adds emphasis and introduces rhythm and flow. Try playing with this technique to emphasise the principle you mean to communicate.

Create the counterargument

Like many persuasive speakers, Emmeline Pankhurst seems to be the sort who shines in opposition. She fires up when she has something to brace against. So, she first posits the claim of her opposition and then goes about refuting this claim. Pankhurst does this several times in the full version of this address, personifying her opponent with direct (though made-up quotes):

> When we were patient, when we believed in argument and persuasion, they said, 'You don't really want it because, if you did, you would do something unmistakable to show you were determined to have it.'

Once you see the trick, you will no doubt notice this technique used by litigators, politicians and agitators the world over. The technique has several benefits. Firstly, you avoid a direct attack on an actual person, which may be dangerous. Secondly, you can craft the counterargument in a way that best suits your persuasive needs. And, most importantly, you whip up the environment of contention, maybe even aggression, to best suit your purpose, style and occasion.

Emmeline Pankhurst, it now seems, was not just an instrumental player in the suffragette movement on two continents, she was also an exceptional, highly skilled public speaker.

I propose that the women who are doing menial chores in the offices cover their typewriters and close their notebooks, the telephone operators unplug their switchboards, the waitresses stop waiting, cleaning women stop cleaning, and everyone who is doing a job for which a man would be paid more — stop.

Betty Friedan

Betty Friedan

Feminist, writer and activist

B: *4 February 1921, Peoria, IL, United States*

D: *4 February 2006, Washington, D.C., United States*

Call to women's strike for equality

When: *20 March 1970*

Where: *New York City*

Audience: *Members of the National Organization for Women (NOW)*

In August 1970, 50 years after American women were awarded the right to vote, Betty Friedan, author of the seminal feminist tome *The Feminine Mystique*, organised the Women's Strike for Equality to continue the fight.

Friedan's initial call for the strike came a few months earlier. On 20 March 1970, Friedan was scheduled to deliver the farewell address to the fourth annual convention of NOW (the National Organization for Women). Rather than deliver the polite, reflective, congratulatory address that might be expected, Friedan used the power of the podium to rally her supporters.

Her speech, reproduced in full here, called for women to step away from their menial, underpaid and unrecognised tasks and take to the streets — or, in what became a slogan for the strike, 'Don't iron while the strike is hot!'

Friedan was impatient with the progress of women's rights in the preceding 50 years. She was a seminal figure of second-wave feminism. She was brave, she was political and she was vocal. Now, another 50-plus years in the future, we can look back on the progress we have made and evaluate our level of satisfaction. With Ms Friedan's words ringing out through history, we may find renewed inspiration in her zeal.

The *New York Times* obituary for Friedan noted that she was 'famously abrasive', and recently her character was brought to life in the miniseries *Mrs America*. She was obviously a force to be reckoned with. Her elocutions stand out for their passion and vitriol. She could hold the stage for long periods, launching herself from argument to example to principle and around again. Always in service of the cause, her voice was her weapon and she wielded it willingly and often.

<u>WHAT</u> SHE SAID

"

Our movement toward true equality for all women in America in fully equal partnership with men has reached a point of critical mass. All of us this past year have learned in our gut that sisterhood is powerful. The awesome power of women united is visible now and is being taken seriously, as all of us who define ourselves as people now take action in every city and state, and together make our voices heard.

It is our responsibility to history, to ourselves, to all who will come after us, to use this power now, in our own lives, in the mainstream of our society, not in some abstract future, when the apocalypse comes. There is an urgency in this moment. We face recession in this country, and repression, with the babies overproduced in the postwar era of the feminine mystique moving into the job market; with inflation eating up all our dollars; with men taking over even those professions that used to be female, as automation replaces blue-collar work. And in this era of recession, if we are going to compete for jobs with men, as we must to support ourselves and our families, there is bound to be more resistance than we have yet encountered. We are going to have to show that we meant it, and use our economic power to break through the barriers of sex discrimination once and for all, if women are not again to be the first fired, the last hired, as they have been in all other economic depressions.

As we visibly become the fastest-growing movement for drastic social change in the country, it would be naïve not to recognise that there are, and will be, many trying to destroy our strength, to divide and divert us. I have said from the beginning that the enemy is not man or men, though individual men among bosses, politicians, priests, union leaders, husbands and educators must be concretely confronted as enemies. Men are fellow victims; ours is a two-sex revolution.

The rage women have so long taken out on themselves, on their own bodies, and covertly on their husbands and children, is exploding now. I understand the conditions that cause the rage, the impotence that makes women so understandably angry, but if we define that rage as sexual, if we say that love and sex and men and even children are the enemy, not only do we doom ourselves to live lives less rich and human, but we doom our movement to political sterility. For we will not be able to mobilise the power of that great majority of women who may have been oversold on love as the end of life, but nevertheless have a right to love; who may be overdefined as sex objects, but nevertheless cannot be asked to suppress their sexuality. Nor will we be able to use the political power of the men who are able to love women and, perhaps even more importantly, to identify with them as people. We will not be able to use their power to help us break through sex discrimination and to create the new social institutions that are needed to free women, not from childbearing or love or sex or even marriage, but from the intolerable agony and burden those become when women are chained to them.

I would warn you that those societies where women are most removed from the full action of the mainstream are those where sex is considered dirty and where violence breeds. If we confront the real conditions that oppress men now as well as women and translate our rage into action, then and only then will sex really be liberated to be an active joy and a receiving joy for women and for men, when we are both really free to be all we can be. This is not a war to be fought in the bedroom, but in the city, in the political arena.

I do not accept the argument that to use this power to liberate ourselves is to divert energies to stop repression and the war in Vietnam and the crisis in the cities. Our movement is so radical a force for change that as we make our voices heard, as we find our human strength in our own interests, we will inevitably create a new political force with allies and a common humanistic frontier, with new effectiveness against the enemies of war and repression that affect us all as human beings in America. Either that energy so long buried as impotent rage in women will become a powerful force for keeping our whole society human and free, or it will be manipulated in the interests of fascism and death.

I therefore propose that we accept the responsibility of mobilising the chain reaction we have helped release, for instant revolution against sexual oppression in this year, 1970. I propose that on Wednesday, August 26, we call a twenty-four-hour general strike, a resistance both passive and active, of all women in America against the concrete conditions of their oppression. On that day, fifty years after the amendment that gave women the vote became part of the Constitution, I propose we use our power to declare an ultimatum on all who would keep us from using our rights as Americans. I propose that the women who are doing menial chores in the offices cover their typewriters and close their notebooks, the telephone operators unplug their switchboards, the waitresses stop waiting, cleaning women stop cleaning, and everyone who is doing a job for which a man would be paid more — stop. Every woman pegged forever as assistant, doing jobs for which men get the credit — stop. In every office, every laboratory, every school, all the women to whom we get word will spend the day discussing and analysing the conditions which keep us from being all we might be. And if the condition that keeps us down is the lack of a childcare centre, we will bring our babies to the office that day and sit them on our bosses' laps. We do not know how many will join our day of abstention from so-called women's work, but I expect it will be millions. We will then present concrete demands to those who so far have made all the decisions.

And when it begins to get dark, instead of cooking dinner or making love, we will assemble, and we will carry candles symbolic of the flame of that passionate journey down through history — relit anew in every city — to converge the visible power of women at City Hall — at the political arenas where the larger options of our life are decided. If men want to join us, fine. If politicians, if political bosses, if mayors and governors wish to discuss our demands, fine, but we will define the terms of the dialogue. And by the time those twenty-four hours are ended, our revolution will be a fact.

<u>HOW</u> SHE DID THAT

Be opportunistic

Betty Friedan saw herself as a revolutionary. Patience was never her strong suit. She was anxious for change and somewhat disappointed, with every gain, that more could not be achieved. Any opportunity to take action or speak out in support of the women's movement was seized, or even hijacked if necessary, and fully leveraged. Such was the level of commitment from Friedan — who would never reconcile herself to the status quo.

As mentioned, Friedan could have delivered a more reflective farewell address for the NOW conference. But she didn't. Perennially dissatisfied, she wanted more for women and she used the opportunity to demand it — and to rally other women to her cause.

So often the speeches that disrupt are the ones we remember. Grasping the protocols expected when speaking at different sorts of events is useful, but power also comes from knowing when to break the rules. If you have a cause — if you need to challenge the way things are typically done — maybe you need to lead the way by countering expected norms of behaviour.

If you find yourself in front of an audience you are seeking to influence, don't let somebody else or the unwritten rules of convention set your agenda. Radical ideas sometimes need to be voiced in radical ways.

Let the words flow

Not everything that Betty Friedan ever said was as eloquent or as memorable as this particular piece. But she always chose to speak when she had the chance. She was often unscripted, willing to let herself go and think 'out loud', formulating her witticisms on the fly.

This kind of extemporaneous public speaking is not for everybody. After all, so many things could go wrong. Most of us need at least a rough outline of what we plan to say. But what we can learn from Betty Friedan is that brilliance can sometimes be conjured in the moment. Speaking often is its own form of preparation. We learn by doing.

Can you try to be a little more open, enough to see and seize your moment and enough to allow the words to flow? Maybe you will surprise yourself with some Friedan-esque remarks that capture the hearts of your would-be supporters.

Go against the grain

'Famously abrasive' is probably an apt description of Betty Friedan's public persona. Maybe she cultivated the image with pride or perhaps she just couldn't help herself. An interminable dissenter who is unwilling to go along to get along — you can imagine the collective eye-roll when Friedan's name is added to the agenda. None of that matters when evaluated against her legacy.

We need the abrasive ones. We must have, among us, voices that are consistently dissatisfied because of their commitment to faster progress towards a better outcome. We need to pay more attention to the dissenters if there is to be change. Like a tiny pebble in your shoe, Friedan's words slowly but surely abrade to the point of annoyance, finally demanding your attention — exactly as she intends.

What are the tyrannies you swallow day by day and attempt to make your own, until you will sicken and die of them, still in silence?

Audre Lorde

Audre Lorde

Poet, speaker and activist

B: *18 February 1934, New York City, NY, United States*

D: *17 November 1992, Saint Croix, Virgin Islands, United States*

The Transformation of Silence

When: *28 December 1977*

Where: *Lesbian and Literature panel of Modern Language Association conference, Chicago*

Audience: *MLA Conference attendees*

The words of Audre Lorde have a timeless quality. Her message is as relevant today as it was in the 1970s. Listening to her now, filtered through our modern understanding of the world, we are in awe of her strength and conviction. When many were bustling in the shadows, Lorde was externally focused, using the platform built on her creative success to highlight the need for change. Lorde speaks out on the need to speak out. In doing so, she exposes the insidious danger of silence.

Lorde described herself as a *Black, feminist, lesbian, poet, mother warrior*. Throughout her career, she proudly claimed her multi-dimensional identity, continually asserting her right to be counted. Her poetry explores these themes with bravery. Lorde once said,

> Poetry is the way we help give name to the nameless so it can be thought ... As they become known to and accepted by us, our feelings and the honest exploration of them become sanctuaries and spawning grounds for the most radical and daring ideas.

Evidence of her poetry can be found in Lorde's many works of prose, and indeed her speeches. Her mastery of language, imagery and rhythm imbue her words with an ethereal quality that is at once beguiling and direct. Her voice is clear and intelligent. She speaks to invite contemplation and discussion, not to incite opposition. Yet she broaches controversial subjects that often cause division.

In December 1977, Lorde delivered the speech extracted here at the Lesbian and Literature panel of Modern Language Association conference in Chicago. This is a striking example of her unique style and her stalwart commitment to speaking out on speaking out.

WHAT SHE SAID

I have come to believe over and over again that what is most important to me must be spoken, made verbal and shared, even at the risk of having it bruised or misunderstood. That the speaking profits me, beyond any other effect. I am standing here as a Black lesbian poet, and the meaning of all that waits upon the fact that I am still alive, and might not have been. Less than two months ago, I was told by two doctors, one female and one male, that I would have to have breast surgery, and that there was a 60 to 80 per cent chance that the tumour was malignant. Between the telling and the actual surgery, there was a three-week period of the agony of an involuntary reorganisation of my entire life. The surgery was completed, and the growth was benign.

But within those three weeks, I was forced to look upon myself and my living with a harsh and urgent clarity that has left me still shaken but much stronger. This is a situation faced by many women, by some of you here today. Some of what I experienced during that time has helped elucidate for me much of what I feel concerning the transformation of silence into language and action. In becoming forcibly and essentially aware of my own mortality, and of what I wished and wanted for in my life, however short it might be, priorities and omissions became strongly etched in a merciless light, and what I most regretted were my silences. Of what had I ever been afraid? To question or to speak as I believed would have meant pain, or death. But we all hurt in so many different ways, all the time, and pain will either change or end. Death, on the other hand, is the final silence. And that might be coming quickly, now, without regard for whether I had ever spoken what needed to be said, or only betrayed myself into small silences, while I planned someday to speak, or waited for someone else's words. And I began to recognise a source of power within myself that comes from the knowledge that while it is most desirable not to be afraid, learning to put fear into a perspective gave me great strength.

I was going to die, if not sooner then later, whether or not I had ever spoken myself. My silences had not protected me. Your silence will not protect you. But for every real word spoken, for every attempt I had ever made to speak those truths for which I am still seeking, I had made contact with other women while we examined the words to fit a world in which we all believed, bridging our differences. And it was the concern and caring of all those women which gave me strength and enabled me to scrutinise the essentials of my living.

The women who sustained me through that period were Black and white, old and young, lesbian, bisexual and heterosexual, and we all shared a war against the tyrannies of silence. They all gave me a strength and concern without which I could not have survived intact. Within those weeks of acute fear came the knowledge — within the war we are all waging with the forces of death, subtle, and otherwise, conscious or not — I am not only a casualty, I am also a warrior. What are the words you do not have yet? What do you need to say? What are the tyrannies you swallow day by day and attempt to make your own, until you will sicken and die of them, still in silence? Perhaps for some of you here today, I am the face of one of your fears. Because I am a woman, because I am Black, because I am myself — a Black woman warrior poet doing my work — come to ask you, are you doing yours?

And, of course, I am afraid — you can hear it in my voice — because the transformation of silence into language and action is an act of self-revelation and that always seems fraught with danger. But my daughter, when I told her of our topic and my difficulty with it, said, 'Tell them about how you're never really a whole person if you remain silent, because there's always that one little piece inside of you that wants to be spoken out, and if you keep ignoring it, it gets madder and madder and hotter and hotter, and if you don't speak it out one day it will just up and punch you in the mouth.'

On the cause of silence, each one of us draws her own fear — fear of contempt, of censure, or some judgment, or recognition, of challenge, of annihilation. But most of all, I think, we fear the visibility without which we also cannot truly live. Within this country where racial difference creates a constant, if unspoken, distortion of vision, Black women have on one hand always been highly visible, and so, on the other hand, have been rendered invisible through the depersonalisation of racism. Even within the women's movement, we have had to fight, and still do, for that very visibility which also renders us most vulnerable, our Blackness. For to survive in the mouth of this dragon we call America, we have had to learn this first and most vital lesson — that we were never meant to survive. Not as human beings. And neither were most of you here today, Black or not. And that visibility which makes you most vulnerable is also our greatest strength. Because the machine will try to grind us into dust anyway, whether or not we speak. We can sit in our corners mute forever while our sisters and ourselves are wasted, while our children are distorted and destroyed, while our Earth is poisoned, we can sit in our safe corners as mute as bottles, and still we will be no less afraid.

... And it is never without fear; of visibility, of the harsh light of scrutiny and perhaps of judgment, of pain, of death. But we have lived through all of those already, in silence, except death. And I remind myself all the time now, that if I was to have been born mute or had maintained an oath of silence my whole life long for safety, I would still have suffered, and I would still die. It is very good for establishing perspective.

And where the words of women are crying to be heard, we must each of us recognise our responsibility to seek those words out, to read them and share them and examine them in their pertinence to our lives. That we not hide behind the mockeries of separations that have been imposed upon us and which so often we accept as our own: for instance, 'I can't possibility teach Black women's writing — their experience is so different than mine,' yet how many years have you spent teaching Plato and Shakespeare and Proust? Or another: 'She's a white woman, what could she possibly have to say to me?' Or, 'She's a lesbian, what would my husband say, or my chairman?' Or again, 'This woman writes of her sons and I have no children.' And all the other endless ways in which we rob ourselves of ourselves and each other.

We can learn to work and speak when we are afraid in the same way we have learned to work and speak when we are tired. For we have been socialised to respect fear more than our own needs for language and definition, and while we wait in silence for that final luxury of fearlessness, the weight of that silence will choke us. The fact that we are here and that I speak these words is an attempt to break that silence and bridge some of those differences between us, for it is not difference which immobilises us, but silence. And there are so many silences to be broken.

<u>HOW</u> SHE DID THAT

Play with poetic language

The language, speech patterns and cadence of this speech combine to enhance the performance. As a poet, Lorde is obviously adept at using words to create images. She uses the metaphor of her words being 'bruised', connecting us to the pain that can come from speaking up, before engaging with the pain that inevitably follows from silence. Further visceral reactions are triggered by the use of the 'tyrannies you swallow' until you become 'sick and die' from them. She reminds us that our continued silence will certainly 'choke' us. Our pain receptors are switched on, forcing a bodily response as we absorb her words.

If you listen to a recording of this speech, or just speak the words aloud, you will likely notice its musical notes. We hear a series of staccato sentences mixed in with longer melodious expressions. Her cadence seems to reflect the complexity beneath the harsh reality of discrimination, the stereotypes that keep women silent and fearful.

These are subtle practices that you can explore as you develop your own communication style. Play around with the use of rhythm, pace and metaphor, as a poet might, to make your presentation soar.

Engage the audience with a question

Although a lot of personal reflection is included in this speech, the central intent is to turn the tables on the audience. Even now, all these decades later, we are struck by Lorde's challenge to consider the rhetorical question: 'What are the tyrannies you swallow day by day and attempt to make your own, until you will sicken and die of them, still in silence?' Lorde makes the point that inaction, although understandable and bred from fear, is — in a way — complicitous. She urges us, still, to fight the fear, which doesn't save us anyway. 'My silences had not protected me. Your silence will not protect you.'

Lorde shares with us her responsibility to inaction, for silence. She does not accuse without accepting responsibility, but neither does she let her audience off the hook. This is a skilful technique for handling a challenging topic.

Lorde goes on to challenge any resistance we might have to fully appreciate her point of view. As is common with her work, she brings her own identity and image into the message. No doubt, Aristotle himself would have been impressed with the claim of credibility, to character or ethos that accompanies this query:

> Perhaps for some of you here today, I am the face of one of your fears. Because I am a woman, because I am Black, because I am myself — a Black woman warrior poet doing my work — come to ask you, are you doing yours?

She gives us nowhere to hide, having called out any prejudices we might harbour.

Finish strong

Of all the lessons we can take from Audre Lorde's speech from 1977, the most impactful might be the importance of a strong finish. Hers is both powerful and relevant. There is no sense in making a flourish for the sake of it, but if you have an opportunity to raise the stakes, ending with something thought-provoking or challenging can be a useful option.

Remember a 'mic-drop' closing is not enough if the moment of drama is disconnected from the central point — which is so often the case. Here you have a challenge, but Lorde provides some answers. Lorde gathers up the crumbs she scattered through her speech and presents us with the ultimate challenge — the only solution — which, in fact lies with us, her audience. She transfers the onus for change onto us. No longer allowing passive observers, her intention is to inspire action.

Great speechmakers know to link their conclusion to the energy and evidence they have built throughout their speech. Your finish shouldn't feel tacked on or gratuitous. Instead, use pace and pause at the right moment to strike the perfect chord — and leave the audience in a state slightly transformed compared to when you began.

Demanding
respect

Sometimes persuasion is slow and steady — change takes years, decades or even centuries to really yield results.

And then other times change can happen in a moment. Sometimes a speaker will find themselves at just the right point in time to take a stand. Demanding respect often happens in reaction to something — an event, a provocation or an injustice acts as the spark in the powder keg.

Though not necessarily an angry outburst, a heightened emotional resonance often marks the type of speech where you draw the line. And this sort of address produces certain after-effects. Who was the target? How do you see them react? There might be a widening of the eyes, a straightening of the spine, and hopefully a moment of retreat. Definitely you will have captured their attention.

These are words that exist outside what is expected — either it is atypical in the circumstances or out of character for the speaker. These are words that pull the audience up with a sharp tug. Consider the impact of Julia Gillard's words on then Australian Opposition leader, Tony Abbott, and others on his side of the House. They seem slightly shocked, a tiny bit afraid. That is exactly the desired result.

Because of the amped-up nature of these moments, they should only happen occasionally. The power to shock and demand should be used sparingly. If outrage is the modus operandi every day, it will lose its power.

The ancient Greek philosopher Aristotle, among the first to document the workings of persuasion, identified something he called *kairos* — the critical or opportune context and timing for a speech. Timing is everything. What made Sylvia Rivera grab the microphone and demand the crowd 'quiet down' at a New York rally in the 1970s? Because it was the right place and right time *and* because of her commitment to change. Maybe some other substances were at play too; nonetheless, her timing was what mattered.

'The lady's not for turning' moment delivered by Margaret Thatcher happened within the context of a much longer, more conventional political speech. But this moment — with an out-of-character reaction and tone, in contrast — stands out and lives on. Not exactly emotive but noteworthy in a Thatcher sort of way, this speech drew a line in the sand and indicated to her colleagues and would-be opponents exactly where her boundary was to be.

The American ex-slave and suffragist Sojourner Truth also stole the moment and the spotlight when she delivered her legendary 'Ain't I a woman?' speech. Personal conviction and a touch of outrage fuelled her passion and helped to create her eloquent address. We can only imagine how her words landed for the men in the room.

Making demands can be a tricky business. The potential for it to backfire is high. You might need to 'keep your powder dry' as you wait for just the right set of conditions and just the right audience before you take aim and fire.

I will not be lectured about sexism and misogyny by this man. I will not.

Julia Gillard

Julia Gillard

Former Prime Minister of Australia

B: *29 September 1961, Barry, United Kingdom*

Misogyny speech

When: *9 October 2012*

Where: *Australian Parliament*

Audience: *House of Representatives*

One thing is for sure — there will be times in your life when you are provoked; when you are moved to anger by the words of another. If you are a politician, however, you would need to brace yourself, for these instances are the norm, rather than the exception.

For most people, words spoken with emotion come out slightly muddled. The 'mic-drop' of our dreams might in reality be born as a frustrated, inarticulate, garbled verbal spray. All the more reason to be in awe of the now-famous 'Misogyny speech' delivered by then Australian Prime Minister Julia Gillard, on 9 October 2012 in the Australian House of Representatives in Canberra, the nation's capital.

The trigger came in the form of an accusation of sexism from Tony Abbott. Abbott was a long-term political rival of comparatively conservative views. When he later became prime minister himself, Abbott notably added the portfolio of Minister for Women to his own, rather full plate — a telling indication of his regard for feminism. Throughout her career, and especially as prime minister, Gillard had endured a string of slurs concerning her gender and her non-married status. She was notoriously unrufflable — not that her stable demeanour did much to deter her critics.

But on this occasion a line was crossed. To be accused of sexism in a comic attempt to turn the tables struck a chord somehow. Beyond absurd, this accusation, imbued with all its lack of respect, demanded one mighty rebuke. Perhaps the final spark to the powder keg of emotions was Abbott's accusation that every day Gillard allowed the supposed sexism to continue was 'another day of shame for a government which should already have died of shame' (a repetition of broadcaster Alan Jones's widely denounced comments about the prime minister's late father). We all have trigger points, but we don't always know where they are exactly, until we feel the anger rise.

The brilliance of Gillard's speech is her ability to speak coherently while clearly containing emotion. Her words are propelled by anger. Anyone in the chamber that day would have been able to feel the fervour of her address. Her speech (extracted here), delivered to Members of Parliament and aimed squarely at the Leader of the Opposition, now has a life of its own, separate from the controversy in parliament that immediately preceded it. Her words, pace, delivery and personal investment make this speech one for the history books.

<u>WHAT</u> SHE SAID

66 Thank you very much Deputy Speaker and I rise to oppose the motion moved by the Leader of the Opposition, and in so doing I say to the Leader of the Opposition: I will not be lectured about sexism and misogyny by this man. I will not. And the Government will not be lectured about sexism and misogyny by this man. Not now, not ever.

The Leader of the Opposition says that people who hold sexist views and who are misogynists are not appropriate for high office. Well I hope the Leader of the Opposition has got a piece of paper and he is writing out his resignation. Because if he wants to know what misogyny looks like in modern Australia, he doesn't need a motion in the House of Representatives; he needs a mirror. That's what he needs.

Let's go through the Opposition Leader's repulsive double standards, repulsive double standards when it comes to misogyny and sexism. We are now supposed to take seriously that the Leader of the Opposition is offended by Mr Slipper's text messages, when this is the Leader of the Opposition who has said, and this was when he was a minister under the last government — not when he was a student, not when he was in high school — when he was a minister under the last government.

He has said, and I quote, in a discussion about women being under-represented in institutions of power in Australia, the interviewer was a man called Stavros. The Leader of the Opposition says, 'If it's true, Stavros, that men have more power generally speaking than women, is that a bad thing?'

And then a discussion ensues, and another person being inter-viewed says, 'I want my daughter to have as much opportunity as my son'. To which the Leader of the Opposition says, 'Yeah, I completely agree, but what if men are, by physiology or temperament, more adapted to exercise authority or to issue command?'

…This is the man from whom we're supposed to take lectures about sexism. And then of course it goes on. I was very offended personally when the Leader of the Opposition, as Minister for Health, said, and I quote, 'Abortion is the easy way out'. I was very personally offended by those comments. You said that in March 2004, I suggest you check the records.

I was also very offended on behalf of the women of Australia when in the course of this carbon pricing campaign, the Leader of the Opposition said 'What the housewives of Australia need to understand as they do the ironing…' Thank you for that painting of women's roles in modern Australia.

And then, of course, I was offended too by the sexism, by the misogyny of the Leader of the Opposition catcalling across this table at me as I sit here as Prime Minister, 'If the Prime Minister wants to, politically speaking, make an honest woman of herself…', something that would never have been said to any man sitting in this chair. I was offended when the Leader of the Opposition went outside in the front of Parliament and stood next to a sign that said 'Ditch the witch'.

I was offended when the Leader of the Opposition stood next to a sign that described me as a man's bitch. I was offended by those things. Misogyny, sexism, every day from this Leader of the Opposition. Every day in every way, across the time the Leader of the Opposition has sat in that chair and I've sat in this chair, that is all we have heard from him.

And now, the Leader of the Opposition wants to be taken seriously. Apparently he's woken up after this track record and all of these statements, and he's woken up and he's gone, 'Oh dear, there's this thing called sexism, oh my lords, there's this thing called misogyny. Now who's one of them? Oh, the Speaker must be because that suits my political purpose.'

Doesn't turn a hair about any of his past statements, doesn't walk into this Parliament and apologise to the women of Australia.

Doesn't walk into this Parliament and apologise to me for the things that have come out of his mouth. But now seeks to use this as a battering ram against someone else.

Well this kind of hypocrisy should not be tolerated, which is why this motion from the Leader of the Opposition should not be taken seriously.

…Well can I indicate to the Leader of the Opposition the Government is not dying of shame, my father did not die of shame, what the Leader of the Opposition should be ashamed of is his performance in this Parliament and the sexism he brings with it.

…He could change a standard himself if he sought to do so. But we will see none of that from the Leader of the Opposition because on these questions he is incapable of change. Capable of double standards, but incapable of change. His double standards should not rule this Parliament.

Good sense, common sense, proper process is what should rule this Parliament. That's what I believe is the path forward for this Parliament, not the kind of double standards and political game-playing imposed by the Leader of the Opposition now looking at his watch because apparently a woman's spoken too long.

I've had him yell at me to shut up in the past, but I will take the remaining seconds of my speaking time to say to the Leader of the Opposition I think the best course for him is to reflect on the standards he's exhibited in public life, on the responsibility he should take for his public statements, on his close personal connection with Peter Slipper, on the hypocrisy he has displayed in this House today.

And on that basis, because of the Leader of the Opposition's motivations, this Parliament today should reject this motion and the Leader of the Opposition should think seriously about the role of women in public life and in Australian society — because we are entitled to a better standard than this.

<u>HOW</u> SHE DID THAT

Control and weaponise anger

Julia Gillard is undoubtedly mad — in fact, she is incensed — when delivering this speech. But she is also in control, articulate and evenly paced.

By this point, the Australian public and her fellow parliamentarians were used to an even-keel sort of speaking style from Gillard. In fact, most of the time Gillard spoke in a tone that did little to rouse emotions. Hers was a leadership style of pragmatism, negotiation and conciliation, which was very effective in the minority government she led. But, on this occasion, all bets were off. Her words and her delivery coalesce to make her central point — 'enough!'

Perhaps the use of emotion is so striking in this speech because it was so uncharacteristic of Gillard's typical style. While the expected heckling ensued from the Opposition, perhaps the slightest — oh so satisfying — glimmer of fear can also be spotted in the eyes of her target. Certainly, a noticeably altered mood descended on the House that day.

For many of us, remaining in control and maintaining something like coherence is difficult when we are angry or upset. Perhaps you have experienced a loss of composure when overcome by frustrations. The next time this happens, take a step back, channel Julia Gillard in the moment, and then step back into the fray with carefully chosen words fuelled by your genuine emotion.

Know when to take a stand

In communication, timing is everything. This is an ancient precept of rhetorical technique. As mentioned, Aristotle wrote of a concept called *kairos*, meaning the rhetorician's ability to appreciate the context and timing when framing a speech. The Romans even created a god — Occasio — to denote the critical importance of appreciating the right occasion and opportunity. Well, the god Occasio was smiling on the Australian Prime Minister on this day in October 2012, as she delivered a perfectly timed shot across the bow.

The Prime Minister took aim at the misogyny she herself and other women had experienced. She provided specific examples mixed with general assertions and claimed the higher ground. Her conviction was compelling and contagious.

This speech will live on to inspire a new generation of female leaders and politicians.

Be yourself, but a little bit extra

Speeches of this sort are not and should not be a daily occurrence. This is a speech that draws a line. Its construction and delivery reflect the character of the speaker, but a little bit extra.

At this moment, Julia Gillard amped up her normal parliamentary style. No stranger to adversarial question time, she ignores the hecklers from the Opposition. She raises her voice a little to drown out the jibes, thus signalling that she means to make this point and the House had better listen. This particular environment can be a viper's nest of barbs and heckles. In an attempt to intimidate, the Opposition insults are often barely veiled personal attacks.

The fact that Julia Gillard allowed herself to get so fired up and spoke with more animation than usual is what makes this speech historically significant. A sort of oratorical flow state is on show. Gillard hits her stride, the words come forth and she exhibits the perfect intensity of emotion to emphasise her meaning.

Good speakers are well prepared but also adept at being fully in the moment. Think of the performance aspect of your speech. Actors need to channel and control their emotions to convey the right tone on stage or on camera. Make sure the audience gets a shared sense of what you are feeling.

The people are trying to do something for all of us, and not men and women that belong to a white middle class white club. And that's what you all belong to!

Sylvia Rivera

Sylvia Rivera

Gay rights activist

B: *2 July 1951, New York City, NY, United States*

D: *19 February 2002, New York City, NY, United States*

Y'all better quiet down

When: *24 June 1973*

Where: *New York City*

Audience: *Gay pride Christopher Street Liberation Day Rally*

By anyone's definition, Sylvia Rivera had a tough life. Born in New York City, she was abandoned by her father when she was an infant and lost her mother to suicide when she was only three years old. Her flamboyant personality, which began to emerge in grade school, alienated her from her remaining family. Rivera ended up living on the streets at the age of ten and worked as a child prostitute.

A rebirth of sorts happened for Rivera when she was taken in by a community of New York City drag queens and given the name 'Sylvia'. She went on to fight for gay rights and for the inclusion of trans people into the gay rights movement.

A victim of systemic poverty and racism, Sylvia Rivera continually found herself at the bottom of society's hierarchy. She had to scrap just to survive. Her identity, her nature and public persona are inseparable from her manner of speaking. Her struggle for recognition fostered a rebellious adversarial approach. She simply refused to conform and now embodies the dissenting voice and spirit of her lifelong cause.

On a warm day in New York City back in 1973, the gay pride Christopher Street Liberation Day Rally was starting to lose its way. This worked-up group of protesters was rapidly descending into a decentralised mob. The crowd was threatening to implode with heckles and cat calls. 'Mob rule' was imminent. Then Sylvia Rivera grabbed the microphone. She didn't so much 'address the crowd' as scream at them to settle down, get over themselves, and recognise the seriousness of what is at stake for gay people.

<u>WHAT</u> SHE SAID

"

Y'all better quiet down. I've been trying to get up here all day for your gay brothers and your gay sisters in jail.

…Have you ever been beaten up and raped and jailed? Now think about it. They've been beaten up and raped.

…The women have tried to fight for their sex changes or to become women … they do not write women, they do not write men, they write 'STAR' because we're trying to do something for them.

I have been to jail. I have been raped. And beaten. Many times! By men, heterosexual men that do not belong in the homosexual shelter. But do you do anything for them? No. You tell me to go and hide my tail between my legs. I will not put up with this shit. I have been beaten. I have had my nose broken. I have been thrown in jail. I have lost my job. I have lost my apartment for gay liberation and you all treat me this way? What the fuck's wrong with you all? Think about that!

…I believe in the gay power. I believe in us getting our rights, or else I would not be out there fighting for our rights. That's all I wanted to say to you people … come and see the people at Star House.

…The people are trying to do something for all of us, and not men and women that belong to a white middle class white club. And that's what you all belong to!

REVOLUTION NOW!

Gimme a 'G'! Gimme an 'A'! Gimme a 'Y'! Gimme a 'P'! Gimme an 'O'! Gimme a 'W'! Gimme an 'E! Gimme an 'R'! Gay power! Louder!

GAY POWER!

"

<u>HOW</u> SHE DID THAT

Bring order to chaos

If you find yourself in a situation where mayhem is brewing, could you be the one to grab the mic as Rivera did that summer day in 1973? If not, the alternative might be chaos and infighting — not only a waste of everyone's time but also a step backwards for your cause.

Rivera recognised the signs of impending pandemonium and decided a circuit breaker was required. She was ready and willing to step up.

You might not find yourself having to wrangle an out-of-control mob in your day-to-day job (or perhaps you do). Maybe you're just faced with a rowdy group of co-workers. Regardless, your power can derive from your willingness to bring order to chaos. When you sense the devolving chatter and you know the centre cannot hold, maybe you have found your opportunity to lead the group back to a more productive, civil and collaborative place.

Sometimes one brave soul needs to shout out, to emphasise the fact that all this squabbling is useless, selfish and destructive to the cause. Rivera was just the street fighter to take control: 'Y'all better quiet down!'

Speak from the heart

The world of impromptu speaking is a dangerous game — made even more perilous if you are fuelled by emotion, particularly anger. But the result of seizing the moment can be cathartic — for the audience and the speaker alike.

Clearly, this short passage was not a prepared speech. Rivera's words were spat out at the crowd. They were barely articulate anger bombs fired at everyone present. So disappointed was she with the counterproductive behaviour of the crowd, she was willing to shock them into compliance.

You can't get much more shocking than lines such as this: 'I have been to jail. I have been raped. And beaten. Many times!'

The circumstances that justify an outburst like this would be extremely rare. But if you ever find yourself in such a situation, Rivera's words provide a wonderful lesson. Surely the discrimination, pain and horror she suffered overshadow the challenges most of us will face in our lifetimes. And, yet, rather than let her past consume her, she used her anger to fuel her words that changed the behaviour of a crowd. Her embodied emotion, so uncomfortable and yet so compelling, changed the trajectory of events that afternoon.

Shift the energy

Just screaming at the crowd and putting them in their place would not have been enough to change the game. What Sylvia Rivera managed to do at the rally was to channel the energy of the crowd towards a positive collective goal.

After her cathartic rant, she did not drop the mic and walk away. If she had, that might have produced far less useful outcomes. It would have been satisfying, sure, but not helpful to the cause. Instead, she gathered up what must have been a sea of stunned faces and led them all in a chant — 'GAY POWER'. With all its fist-pumping, fight-song, rally energy she seized their attention, sparked their emotions and changed their behaviour.

There is a lesson here. If you are going to challenge the crowd and attempt to shock them into a new way of thinking and acting, you had better then lead the way. Give me a 'G'! (You know the rest ...)

To those waiting with bated breath for that favourite media catchphrase the 'U' turn, I have only one thing to say. 'You turn if you want to. The lady's not for turning.' I say that not only to you but to our friends overseas, and also to those who are not our friends.

Margaret Thatcher

Margaret Thatcher

Former UK Prime Minister

B: 13 October 1925, Grantham, United Kingdom

D: 8 April 2013, London, United Kingdom

The lady's not for turning

When: 10 October 1980

Where: Brighton, United Kingdom

Audience: Conservative Party members

In October 1980, Margaret Thatcher delivered a lengthy (40-minute) speech to the Conservative Party Conference in Brighton, UK. She had a lot to say to her fellow party members and provided much to analyse, but this phrase lives on in infamy: 'the lady's not for turning'. A twist on *The Lady's Not for Burning*, a 1948 play by Christopher Fry about a witchcraft trial, perhaps this phrase is so memorable because it is rather enigmatic and, therefore, interesting.

The mention of former British prime minister Margaret Thatcher's name will provoke a reaction from most people who have even a little bit of political awareness. This was certainly true in the time she was in power but seems to have evolved into an even deeper legacy of divisiveness. Ideology notwithstanding, Thatcher's attainment of the top job and the years she held her position were unprecedented, and they remain a standout achievement for a woman in leadership.

Thatcher was known as a committed conservative. Her policies were almost always polarising, but we all knew, and still know, what she stood for. The 'Iron Lady' rarely indulged concepts of the left and remained steadfast in her convictions throughout her tenure and her lifetime.

When Thatcher delivered the speech extracted here, she had been in power for about a year and, in that time, unemployment had risen from 1.5 to 2 million people. In addition to facing opposition from the Labour Party and the public, she was also fending off criticism from within her own party. Some conservatives opposed Thatcher's radical free-market policies. She was under fire.

In this speech — particularly her declaration of strength — Thatcher signals her commitment to the policy she has set in motion. Indeed, most of the speech is about arguing for and defending her strategy. These are words intended to demand the respect she deserves, and encourage her allies to hold the line.

<u>WHAT</u> SHE SAID

66

Most of my Cabinet colleagues have started their speeches of reply by paying very well deserved tributes to their junior ministers. Now at Number 10, I have no junior ministers — there's just Denis [Thatcher] and me, and I could not do without him. I am, however, very fortunate in having a marvellous deputy who is wonderful in all places at all times in all things — Willie Whitelaw.

…When I am asked for a detailed forecast of what will happen in the coming months or years, I remember Sam Goldwyn's advice: 'Never prophesy, especially about the future.' Nevertheless — Nevertheless —

[Heckler interjects.]

Never mind — it's wet outside. I expect they wanted to come in. You cannot blame them; it is always better where the Tories are. And you — and perhaps they — will be looking to me this afternoon for an indication of how the Government sees the task before us and why we are tackling it the way we are.

…It was Anthony Eden who chose for us the goal of a 'property-owning democracy'. But for all the time that I've been in public affairs that has been beyond the reach of so many who were denied the right to the most basic ownership of all — the homes in which they live. They wanted to buy. Many could afford to buy. But they happened to live under the jurisdiction of a Socialist council, which would not sell and did not believe in the independence that comes with ownership. Now Michael Heseltine has given them the chance to turn a dream into reality. And all this, Mr Chairman, and a lot more, in seventeen months. The Left continues to refer with relish to the death of capitalism. Well, if this is the death of capitalism, I must say it is quite a way to go.

But all this will avail us little unless we achieve our prime economic objective: the defeat of inflation. Inflation destroys nations and societies as surely as invading armies do. Inflation is the parent of unemployment. It is the unseen robber of those who have saved. No policy which puts at risk the defeat of inflation — however great its short-term attraction — can be right. Our policy for the defeat of inflation is, in fact, traditional. It existed long before Sterling M3 embellished the Bank of England Quarterly Bulletin, or 'monetarism' became a convenient term of political invective.

... If I could press a button and genuinely solve the unemployment problem, do you think that I would not press that button this instant? Does anyone imagine that there is the smallest political gain in letting this unemployment continue, or that there is some obscure economic religion which demands this level of unemployment as part of its ritual?

... So what can stop us from achieving this? What then stands in our way? The prospect of another winter of discontent? I suppose it might.

But I prefer to believe that certain lessons have been learnt from experience, that we are coming slowly, painfully, to an autumn of understanding. And I hope that it will be followed by a winter of commonsense. If it is not, we shall not be diverted from our course.

To those waiting with bated breath for that favourite media catchphrase the 'U' turn, I have only one thing to say. 'You turn if you want to. The lady's not for turning.' I say that not only to you but to our friends overseas, and also to those who are not our friends.

... I have always known that that task was vital. Since last week it has become even more vital than ever. We close our Conference in the aftermath of that sinister Utopia unveiled at Blackpool. Let

Labour's Orwellian nightmare of the Left be the spur for us to dedicate with a new urgency our every ounce of energy and moral strength to rebuild the fortunes of this free nation.

If we were to fail, that freedom could be imperilled. So let us resist the blandishments of the faint hearts; let us ignore the howls and threats of the extremists; let us stand together and do our duty. And we shall not fail.

99

<u>HOW</u> SHE DID THAT

Handle the hecklers

Early in Margaret Thatcher's speech, she faced an interruption from the floor. This came from a protester who had breached security and entered the hall, shouting 'Power to the workers. Tories out!'

Thatcher used this as an opportunity to ad lib a retort:

> Never mind — it's wet outside. I expect they wanted to come in. You cannot blame them; it is always better where the Tories are. And you — and perhaps they — will be looking to me this afternoon for an indication of how the Government sees the task before us and why we are tackling it the way we are.

Her response shows a certain level of comfort in her position at the podium. While her speech was no doubt fully prepared, such off-the-cuff refutations are a sign of oratorical skill.

Thatcher was no comedian but this technique of pausing midstream to directly engage with a heckler is something you might see in a comedy club. Sometimes you can gain more ground by facing off than by raising your voice over the dissenters and refusing to be interrupted. Thatcher saw an opening for a joke and she took it.

Choose your moment. If interruptions persist, you may need to take them on directly. Look out for opportunities to win support and release the tension with a touch a humour.

Use metaphor

Typically, Margaret Thatcher is light on the use of metaphor. And this speech is no exception. Her persona is pragmatic and her rhetoric is generally aligned to that identity. However, Thatcher indulges sparingly in this particularly effective rhetorical flourish, which certainly enhances the speech.

She refers to the potential for 'another winter of discontent' but then disputes this metaphor, going on to say,

> But I prefer to believe that certain lessons have been learnt from experience, that we are coming slowly, painfully, to an autumn of understanding. And I hope that it will be followed by a winter of commonsense. If it is not, we shall not be diverted from our course.

This is a deft, if slightly out of character, use of rhetorical flair. The lesson here is to make the most of your chosen metaphor. Thatcher combines here seasonal metaphor with a literary allusion and adds a bit of poetry. And in her characteristic thoroughness, she satisfyingly closes the loop. This small flourish makes the speech memorable.

Recognise the contribution of others

In highlighting the successes of the party, Margaret Thatcher is diligent in mentioning those involved by name. She begins by thanking her husband, Denis Thatcher, and mentions her deputy, Willie Whitelaw. In the full version of the speech (see Sources), she also mentions the budget created by Geoffrey Howe, and then goes on to share the limelight with multiple players, including Jim Prior, Keith Joseph, David Howell, John Nott and Norman Fowler. She also acknowledges Michael Heseltine, Anthony Eden, Lord Carrington — and the list goes on.

This speech is just one example of hundreds delivered by Thatcher in her many years in politics. It is a good example of her 'speechcraft' — in which she uses the podium, as all politicians must, to reiterate and reinforce her platform, to whip up support among her own party and knock back her opponents.

Observing the arc of Thatcher's poise and presence is also interesting. If you were to watch the speeches from her early years in politics, you would see a very different style. A similar commitment to learning and practising the craft will benefit you and what you seek to achieve, now and in the long term.

If there is one message that echoes forth from this conference, it is that human rights are women's rights. And women's rights are human rights.

Hillary Clinton

Hillary Clinton

Politician, diplomat and lawyer

B: *26 October 1947, Chicago, IL, United States*

Women's rights are human rights

When: *5 September 1995*

Where: *Beijing, China*

Audience: *17000 participants, including government delegates, NGOs and media*

In September 1995, Hillary Clinton delivered an impassioned yet rational plea before the United Nations Fourth World Conference for Women in Beijing, China. In front of more than 17000 participants, including government delegates, NGOs and media, Clinton spoke in support of women's rights on a global scale. We are all familiar with Clinton's achievements and, of course, her momentous loss in the US presidential race in 2016. More than 20 years before all that, a younger, feistier First Lady Clinton appeared before the United Nations — literally ready to take on the world. She spoke with the conviction of being on the side of what is right and she shows none of the encumbrances of knowing a campaign was on the horizon — at least, not her own.

You have probably heard Clinton speak many times — usually as a campaigner. When running for office — including the highest possible office — an undertone of supplication can often be detected. The speech extracted here highlights the fact that the solicitous voice does not come as naturally to Hillary as it clearly did for her husband. She is more comfortable speaking out when she does not have to worry about winning votes. Here she is forthright, unapologetic and rational. She shows no solicitation, no need to be liked, and no discomfort.

It's not that her emotion is lacking. Clinton clearly cares about her subject and she craftily includes emotional appeals throughout — in the examples she uses and the images she evokes. The emotional appeal is balanced with the other two components of argumentation — logos (rational argumentation) and ethos (the character of the speaker). The alchemy of all three elements, delivered with aplomb, make this speech remarkable.

<u>WHAT</u> SHE SAID

I would like to thank the Secretary General of the United Nations for inviting me to be part of the United Nations Fourth World Conference on Women. This is truly a celebration — a celebration of the contributions women make in every aspect of life: in the home, on the job, in their communities, as mothers, wives, sisters, daughters, learners, workers, citizens and leaders.

...By gathering in Beijing, we are focusing world attention on issues that matter most in the lives of women and their families: access to education, healthcare, jobs and credit, the chance to enjoy basic legal and human rights and participate fully in the political life of their countries.

There are some who question the reason for this conference. Let them listen to the voices of women in their homes, neighbourhoods and workplaces.

There are some who wonder whether the lives of women and girls matter to economic and political progress around the globe. Let them look at the women gathered here and at Huairou — the homemakers, nurses, teachers, lawyers, policymakers and women who run their own businesses.

It is conferences like this that compel governments and peoples everywhere to listen, look and face the world's most pressing problems.

...Over the past 25 years, I have worked persistently on issues relating to women, children and families. Over the past two and a half years, I have had the opportunity to learn more about the challenges facing women in my own country and around the world.

I have met new mothers in Jojakarta, Indonesia, who come together regularly in their village to discuss nutrition, family planning and baby care.

I have met working parents in Denmark who talk about the comfort they feel in knowing that their children can be cared for in creative, safe and nurturing after-school centres.

I have met women in South Africa who helped lead the struggle to end apartheid and are now helping build a new democracy.

I have met with the leading women of the Western Hemisphere who are working every day to promote literacy and better healthcare for the children of their countries.

I have met women in India and Bangladesh who are taking out small loans to buy milk cows, rickshaws, thread and other materials to create a livelihood for themselves and their families.

I have met doctors and nurses in Belarus and Ukraine who are trying to keep children alive in the aftermath of Chernobyl.

...The great challenge of this conference is to give voice to women everywhere whose experiences go unnoticed, whose words go unheard. Women comprise more than half the world's population. Women are 70 per cent of the world's poor, and two-thirds of those who are not taught to read and write.

Women are the primary caretakers for most of the world's children and elderly. Yet much of the work we do is not valued — not by economists, not by historians, not by popular culture, not by government leaders.

...As an American, I want to speak up for women in my own country — women who are raising children on the minimum wage, women who can't afford healthcare or childcare, women whose lives are threatened by violence, including violence in their own homes.

…We also must recognise that women will never gain full dignity until their human rights are respected and protected.

Our goals for this conference, to strengthen families and societies by empowering women to take greater control over their own destinies, cannot be fully achieved unless all governments — here and around the world — accept their responsibility to protect and promote internationally recognised human rights.

The international community has long acknowledged — and recently affirmed at Vienna — that both women and men are entitled to a range of protections and personal freedoms, from the right of personal security to the right to determine freely the number and spacing of the children they bear.

No-one should be forced to remain silent for fear of religious or political persecution, arrest, abuse or torture.

Tragically, women are most often the ones whose human rights are violated.

…I believe that, on the eve of a new millennium, it is time to break our silence. It is time for us to say here in Beijing, and the world to hear, that it is no longer acceptable to discuss women's rights as separate from human rights.

…It is a violation of human rights when babies are denied food, or drowned, or suffocated, or their spines broken, simply because they are born girls.

It is a violation of human rights when women and girls are sold into the slavery of prostitution.

It is a violation of human rights when women are doused with gasoline, set on fire and burned to death because their marriage dowries are deemed too small.

It is a violation of human rights when individual women are raped in their own communities and when thousands of women are subjected to rape as a tactic or prize of war.

It is a violation of human rights when a leading cause of death worldwide among women ages 14 to 44 is the violence they are subjected to in their own homes.

It is a violation of human rights when young girls are brutalised by the painful and degrading practice of genital mutilation.

It is a violation of human rights when women are denied the right to plan their own families, and that includes being forced to have abortions or being sterilised against their will.

If there is one message that echoes forth from this conference, it is that human rights are women's rights. And women's rights are human rights.

... Let this conference be our — and the world's — call to action.

And let us heed the call so that we can create a world in which every woman is treated with respect and dignity, every boy and girl is loved and cared for equally, and every family has the hope of a strong and stable future.

Thank you very much.

God's blessings on you, your work and all who will benefit from it.

<u>HOW</u> SHE DID THAT

Show personal conviction

Hillary Clinton has always leveraged the power of her position, as would be expected given her political pedigree. In 1995, her power derived from being the First Lady of the United States. She knew to use this as her platform to address the assembly. Her right to be at the podium and speak for women globally and for her own country was obvious. She was comfortable and capable of challenging the status quo at this international level.

This speech leaves no traces of obsequiousness or compliance. She does not pander to special interest groups or otherwise indicate any other form of political point scoring. In this address, Clinton consistently exhibits an absolute commitment to her ideals.

This topic would presumably present some danger of sounding preachy. Clinton does not allow this to happen. She never blames men for the worldwide issue of global gender inequality. Doing so would cause the powers that be to switch off from the message. She does not put the blame on less-developed nations, but uses examples from around the world. In fact, she explicitly takes accountability for the changes that need to happen in the United States.

Argue logically

The tone of this speech leans towards the rational. We see evidence of Clinton's legal training in her ability to structure a logical argument — for example, when she says, 'We also must recognise that women will never gain full dignity until their human rights are respected and protected.' She lays out the prerequisites to progress, breaks down the barriers and makes short work of dismissing cultural or religious impediments to equality.

She goes on to mention precedent — rights previously recognised by international bodies — and then juxtaposes the contradiction with current experiences around the world. As she highlights, 'Tragically, women are most often the ones whose human rights are violated'. She then lists these violations and provides specific examples, building out her case. Then she circles back to the crux of the argument: 'human rights are women's rights. And women's rights are human rights.'

What she creates is a cogent, unmistakable case — well argued, well structured and clearly articulated.

Use repetition

Several rhetorical devices are used in this speech, but the most notable is the repetition — used here to great effect, to emphasise her central thesis, rather than just a flourish. 'Anaphora' is the term for the repetition of a word or phrase at the beginning of successive sentences. Hillary Clinton employs this technique twice in her address.

She places herself on the world stage and signals her own experiences that are directly relevant to her argument. With the phrase 'I have met ...' she delivers her list of six groups of women, assembling them here as the joint protagonist of her cause.

Towards the climax of her speech, Clinton uses the power of repetition again, this time with her use of the phrase 'It is a violation of human rights when ...' to preface seven statements that highlight some of the most serious examples of violations of the rights of women. It is impossible to miss the emphasis.

If you need to deliver a speech that references moral or ethical principles, consider the techniques so aptly demonstrated by Clinton in this speech. Through repetition of an introductory word or phrase, you will underscore your point again and again. You can also build momentum with each successive phrase towards your eventual crescendo. That is the power of words when they are arranged in just the right way.

Arguing
a position

To be convincing, an argument must not only present a rational position with supporting evidence, but also consider and concede or refute any potential counterarguments.

The synthesised position must then be explained in such a way as to persuade the rational, critical evaluator.

The presentation of a rational argument often involves situations of some formality. In the speeches featured in this chapter, the situations include the US Supreme Court, a congressional committee, a joint session of the US Congress and a plea in defence of birth control delivered at a conference in New York. The benefit of a formal environment is that the audience is forewarned; they should have a general idea of what is happening and their role in evaluating your argument. Because they already have some level of awareness, you can start slightly ahead of where you might with a general audience.

The challenge of a more formal speaking environment is that your audience is primed to critically evaluate your presentation. This is not to suggest that they will necessarily be negative, but they will be analytical. They are likely to be listening more closely than they might in another context, so you need to be tighter with your case.

In her argument to the US Supreme Court, before she was appointed to the bench herself, Ruth Bader Ginsburg presented a compelling case in the matter of Frontiero *v*. Richardson. RBG, as she came to be known, reminds us of the mechanics of a good case — lay out the requirements of what must be proved, and then prove it. You don't need to get caught up in extemporaneous and distracting matters that might make the case more of a challenge than it needs to be.

In a blistering oratorical masterpiece, Barbara Jordan shows us how gravitas and logic can combine for one of the most compelling arguments in history. Her presentation of the Articles of Impeachment during the Watergate scandal is a true masterclass on how to mount a compelling case.

The use of classical rhetorical technique and influence tactics can be seen at work beneath the surface of Margaret Sanger's speech on the morality of birth control from 1921. A practised speaker, having defended her position many times over, she knows where the counterarguments are and how to head them off at the pass.

And when Chancellor of Germany Angela Merkel addressed the US Congress and Senate members in 2009, she cleverly signalled the virtues of American democracy and culture as the foundation of her argument.

These successful speeches show something that is often taken for granted: the 'human factor' is very much at the heart of their success. Though logic may be the top note, persuasion by means of emotional resonance is the not-so-secret ingredient.

Sex like race is a visible, immutable characteristic bearing no necessary relationship to ability.

Ruth Bader Ginsburg

Ruth Bader Ginsburg

US Supreme Court Justice and lawyer
B: 15 March 1933, New York City, NY, United States
D: 18 September 2020, Washington, D.C., United States

Argument in Frontiero v. Richardson
When: 17 January 1973
Where: Washington DC
Audience: US Supreme Court

There is so much to admire about Ruth Bader Ginsburg—the notable RBG. Her international fame has been astounding. Something about the quiet strength of the late US Supreme Court justice captivated people all over the world, from different backgrounds and systems of belief.

Her life story is an inspiring accumulation of accomplishments, made all the more impactful when you understand how 'regular' her day-to-day life was. She was also a wife, mother and grandmother. She was not a fan of the spotlight. Her first child was born while she was attending law school. I'm sure the challenges of domestic life would have been difficult, but for RBG they seem to be part of the tapestry of her existence. Time and again, she just got on with it and kept showing up. Working tirelessly, she rose to the highest position possible in her field, with her ethics and ideals intact.

Her legacy as the noteworthy RBG is replete with stories of accomplishment throughout her legal career. When she was sworn in as a US Supreme Court Justice in 1996, Bill Clinton remarked that

Bader Ginsburg had already made her mark on constitutional law by successfully fighting for the 'equal treatment for women and men before the law'.

Clinton was referring to the landmark case of Frontiero *v*. Richardson, held before the nine justices of the US Supreme Court in 1973, which addressed military benefits that were being paid differently on the basis of sex. At the time RBG, representing the American Civil Liberties Union as *amicus curiae* (or 'friend of the court'), was permitted by the Court to argue in favour of Frontiero. (The Court found in favour of Frontiero.)

Her words from this landmark case, extracted here, will live on.

<u>WHAT</u> SHE SAID

66

Mr Chief Justice and may it please the Court.

Amicus views this case as kin to Reed v. Reed 404 US. The legislative judgment in both derives from the same stereotype.

The man is or should be the independent partner in a marital unit.

The woman with an occasional exception is dependent, sheltered from bread-winning experience.

Appellees stated in answer to interrogatories in this case that they remained totally uninformed on the application of this stereotype to serve as families — that is, they do not know whether the proportion of wage-earning wives of servicemen is small, large or middle size.

What is known is that by employing the sex criterion, identically situated persons are treated differently.

The married serviceman gets benefits for himself, as well as his spouse regardless of her income.

The married servicewoman is denied medical care for her spouse and quarter's allowance for herself as well as her spouse even if, as in this case, she supplies over two-thirds the support of the marital unit.

For these reasons, amicus believes that the sex-related means employed by Congress fails to meet the rationality standard.

It does not have a fair and substantial relationship to the legislative objective so that all similarly circumstanced persons shall be treated alike.

Nonetheless, amicus urges the Court to recognise in this case what it has in others; that it writes not only for this case and this day alone, but for this type of case.

...To provide the guidance so badly needed and because recognition is long overdue, amicus urges the Court to declare sex a suspect criterion.

This would not be quite the giant step appellee suggests.

...Appellees concede that the principle ingredient involving strict scrutiny is present in the sex criterion.

Sex like race is a visible, immutable characteristic bearing no necessary relationship to ability.

Sex like race has been made the basis for unjustified or at least unproved assumptions concerning an individual's potential to perform or to contribute to society.

But appellees point out that although the essential ingredient rendering a classification suspect is present, sex-based distinctions, unlike racial distinctions, do not have an especially disfavoured constitutional history.

It is clear that the core purpose of the Fourteenth Amendment was to eliminate invidious racial discrimination.

But why did the framers of the Fourteenth Amendment regard racial discrimination as odious?

Because a person's skin colour bears no necessary relationship to ability, similarly as appellees concede a person's sex bears no necessary relationship to ability.

Moreover, national origin and alienage have been recognised as suspect classifications, although the newcomer to our shores were not the paramount concern of the nation when the Fourteenth Amendment was adopted.

But the main thrust of the argument against recognition of sex as a suspect criterion centres on two points.

First, women are a majority.

Second, legislative classification by sex does not, it is asserted, imply the inferiority of women.

With respect to the numbers argument, the numerical majority was denied even the right to vote until 1920.

Women today face discrimination in employment as pervasive and more subtle than discrimination encountered by minority groups.

In vocational and higher education, women continue to face restrictive quotas no longer operative with respect to other population groups.

Their absence is conspicuous in Federal and State Legislative, Executive, and Judicial Chambers in higher civil service positions and in appointed posts in federal, state, and local government.

Surely, no-one would suggest that race is not a suspect criterion in the District of Columbia because the black population here outnumbers the white.

Moreover, as Mr. Justice Douglas has pointed out most recently in Hadley against Alabama 41 Law Week 3205, Equal Protection and Due Process of law apply to the majority as well as to the minorities.

Do the sex classifications listed by appellees imply a judgment of inferiority?

Even the Court below suggested that they do.

That court said it would be remiss if it failed to notice lurking in the background the subtle injury inflicted on servicewomen, the indignity of being treated differently so many of them feel.

Sex classifications do stigmatise when as in Goesaert against Cleary 235 US, they exclude women from an occupation thought more appropriate to men.

The sex criterion stigmatises when it is used to limit hours of work for women only. Hours regulations of the kind involved in Muller against Oregon, though perhaps reasonable on the turn-of-the-century conditions, today protect women from competing for extra remuneration, higher-paying jobs, promotions.

The sex criterion stigmatises when as in Hoyt against Florida 368 US, it assumes that all women are preoccupied with home and children and, therefore, should be spared the basic civic responsibility of serving on a jury.

These distinctions have a common effect.

They help keep woman in her place, a place inferior to that occupied by men in our society.

Appellees recognise that there is doubt as to the contemporary validity of the theory that sex classifications do not brand the female sex as inferior.

But they advocate a hold the line position by this Court unless and until the equal rights amendment comes into force.

Absent the equal rights amendment, appellees assert, no close scrutiny of sex-based classifications is warranted.

This Court should stand pat on legislation of the kind involved in this case.

Legislation making a distinction, servicewomen regard as the most frozen equity, the greatest irritant and the most discriminatory provision relating to women in the military service.

But this Court has recognised that the notion of what constitutes equal protection does change.

Proponents as well as opponents of the equal rights amendment believe that clarification of the application of equal protection to the sex criterion is needed and should come from this Court.

Proponents believe that appropriate interpretation of the Fifth and Fourteenth Amendments would secure equal rights and responsibilities for men and women.

But they also stressed that such interpretation was not yet discernible and in any event the amendment would serve an important function in removing even the slightest doubt that equal rights for men and women is fundamental constitutional principle.

In asking the Court to declare sex a suspect criterion, amicus urges a position forcibly stated in 1837 by Sara Grimke, noted abolitionist and advocate of equal rights for men and women.

She spoke not elegantly, but with unmistakable clarity.

She said, 'I ask no favour for my sex. All I ask of our brethren is that they take their feet off our necks.'

In conclusion, amicus joins appellants in requesting that this Court reverse the judgment entered below and remand the case with instructions to grant the relief requested in appellants complaint.

Thank you.

<u>HOW</u> SHE DID THAT

Set pragmatic goals

Behind this historic appeal was a very clever, very clear, strategic intent. Ruth Bader Ginsburg's goal was to persuade the court to recognise gender as a 'suspect classification' — that is, a distinction that requires a standard of 'strict scrutiny' to uphold. The 'suspect classification' has precedent in the court's earlier ruling about race discrimination.

When attempting to persuade an audience, zeroing in on the shift you are trying to achieve is important. Ask yourself, what is the current belief? What are the grounds for the current position? What do I need to prove to effect the shift? Then research other similar cases, find ways to attack those underlying assumptions and gather your research.

Obviously, Ginsburg was operating in the domain of legal precedent, which interestingly can occasionally bypass principles of commonsense or even moral and ethical justifications. Perhaps the first lesson here is one of pragmatism. Can you argue your point without taking on an ethical argument — with all its permutations and potential for polarisation? Is there an easier path?

In this argument before the US Supreme Court, Bader Ginsburg pulls back from proposing a giant leap forward. She urges the all-male court that their ruling would be logical — a kind of tidying up of inconsistent rulings made by various lower courts. When urging the declaration of sex as a suspect criterion she qualifies it: 'This would not be quite the giant step appellee suggests'.

Ginsburg shows us that your perhaps myopically defined purpose should be the yard stick by which you determine what to include and what to leave out; what to downplay and what to emphasise. As a highly accomplished woman, she surely would have had a strong and personally held belief that the central argument of this case — namely, the unequal treatment of women before the law—was morally and ethically wrong. However, she favoured the even-tempered, perhaps more 'winnable' legal argument.

Confirm you are the best person to speak

As a woman and a feminist, Ruth Bader Ginsburg had a stake (though not a legal vested interest) in this case. Certainly, no legal ramifications come from this argument being made by a female lawyer. No notations or footnotes were included on this in the eventual ruling or judgement papers — as is right and proper. At the same time, separating the speaker from the message is impossible. The fact that this argument was put before the highest court in the land by a female would not have gone unnoticed — and not just any female. RBG was a highly accomplished lawyer and professor, and one of only nine women in her class of 500 at Harvard.

Her very presence is an unspoken argument in favour of gender parity.

If you are delivering a speech that relies on rational argument, you don't need to put yourself in the story. You do not need to share your personal history. You do not need to disclose personal details. But you must not ignore the fact that you are making an appeal to other human beings. We, all of us, make decisions based on rational *and* emotional grounds. We are not necessarily aware of the subconscious and all the layers of subjectivity at play — but come into play they do.

Consider your position as the speaker and all that can be left unsaid, regarding your credibility, personal stake and embodied beliefs. Consider, also, the timing of the address. What may have been acceptable 20 years ago, or even five years ago, might now raise the hackles of a good portion of your audience. We now see real commitment to diversity — in panel discussions, for example, as women have expressed their frustration with an all-male (and white) collection of experts. Perhaps you will need to change your approach, or choose somebody else to speak if you are not the right person.

Add a touch of drama

The final remark of the argument comes in the form of a quote. Ruth Bader Ginsburg reaches back into history to provide an 1837 quote from the abolitionist Sarah Grimke. Having already established the link between sex discrimination and race discrimination throughout her statement, her argument benefits from this colourful, memorable quote: 'I ask no favour for my sex. All I ask of our brethren is that they take their feet off our necks.'

The more restrained you are in your presentation, the greater the impact of such a move. Bader Ginsburg was true to form with her rather reserved, factual, even-keel delivery style. So her foray into the mildly dramatic punctuated her delivery perfectly.

Consider your own style. Do you, like Ginsburg, tend toward steadiness in your delivery? Perhaps you could try spicing up your content with a quote, anecdote or fact that is slightly antithetical. It will stand out in contrast to the rest of your speech. Or maybe you tend towards the dramatic. In that case, you might want to channel RBG from time to time to create moments of meaning.

If the impeachment provision in the Constitution of the United States will not reach the offenses charged here, then perhaps that eighteenth-century Constitution should be abandoned to a twentieth-century paper shredder!

Barbara Jordan

Barbara Jordan

Politician, lawyer and educator
B: 21 February 1936, Houston, TX, United States
D: January 17, 1996, Austin, TX, United States

Articles of Impeachment during Watergate
When: 24 July 1974
Where: Washington D.C., United States
Audience: US House Judiciary Committee, and broadcast on televison

Throughout her career marked by firsts, Barbara Jordan was known for the power of her voice. As a student debater, teacher, lawyer and, ultimately, legislator, she learned to value the importance of good oratory — and Jordan was better than most. But she was far more than a mouthpiece. The woman of substance that she was behind the voice made her a legend in Texas and across the United States.

Her list of achievements is long. The first Black woman to be elected to the Texas Senate (in 1966). The first African-American US congresswoman in the deep south (elected to represent Texas in the House of Representatives in 1972). The first woman of colour to deliver a keynote address at a Democratic National Convention (in 1976 — another of her oratorical legacies).

A lot was going on for politicians in the US (and elsewhere) in 1974 — the end of the Vietnam War, the Equal Rights Amendment and ongoing battles for civil rights everywhere. Then the Watergate scandal reached its boiling point with the resignation of senior White House officials and the impending impeachment of President Richard Nixon.

The situation was looking much worse for Nixon after US congresswoman Jordan delivered this scathing speech to the very crowded chamber at the House Judiciary Committee. These proceedings were also televised during prime time, so Jordan's words also reached a massive television audience who were tuned in to developments on the Watergate scandal.

Her 'Articles of Impeachment', extracted here, is a thirteen-minute power play of a speech that argues for no less than the defence of the American Constitution.

Texas Governor Ann Richards spoke at Barbara Jordan's funeral in 1996, saying,

> No matter what else was going on, when you were with Barbara you could never quite shake the feeling that you were in the presence of somebody that was truly great.

The American people may have concurred as they watched this prime-time televised speech, extracted here, on 24 July 1974. Nixon resigned on 8 August.

<u>WHAT</u> SHE SAID

Thank you, Mr Chairman.

Mr Chairman, I join my colleague Mr Rangel in thanking you for giving the junior members of this committee the glorious opportunity of sharing the pain of this inquiry. Mr Chairman, you are a strong man, and it has not been easy but we have tried as best we can to give you as much assistance as possible.

Earlier today, we heard the beginning of the Preamble to the Constitution of the United States: 'We, the people'. It's a very eloquent beginning. But when that document was completed on the 17th of September in 1787, I was not included in that 'We, the people'. I felt somehow for many years that George Washington and Alexander Hamilton just left me out by mistake. But through the process of amendment, interpretation and court decision, I have finally been included in 'We, the people'.

Today I am an inquisitor. An hyperbole would not be fictional and would not overstate the solemnness that I feel right now. My faith in the Constitution is whole; it is complete; it is total. And I am not going to sit here and be an idle spectator to the diminution, the subversion, the destruction, of the Constitution.

'Who can so properly be the inquisitors for the nation as the representatives of the nation themselves?' 'The subjects of its jurisdiction are those offenses which proceed from the misconduct of public men.' And that's what we're talking about. In other words, [the jurisdiction comes] from the abuse or violation of some public trust.

It is wrong, I suggest, it is a misreading of the Constitution for any member here to assert that for a member to vote for an article of impeachment means that that member must be convinced that the President should be removed from office. The Constitution doesn't say that. The powers relating to impeachment are an essential check in the hands of the body of the Legislature against and upon the encroachments of the Executive. The division between the two branches of the Legislature, the House and the Senate, assigning to the one the right to accuse and to the other the right to judge. The Framers of this Constitution were very astute. They did not make the accusers and the judges the same person.

We know the nature of impeachment. We've been talking about it awhile now. It is chiefly designed for the President and his high ministers to somehow be called into account. It is designed to 'bridle' the Executive if he engages in excesses. 'It is designed as a method of national inquest into the conduct of public men.' The Framers confided in the Congress the power if need be, to remove the President in order to strike a delicate balance between a President swollen with power and grown tyrannical, and preservation of the independence of the Executive.

The nature of impeachment: a narrowly channelled exception to the separation-of-powers maxim. The Federal Convention of 1787 said that. It limited impeachment to high crimes and misdemeanours and discounted and opposed the term 'maladministration'. 'It is to be used only for great misdemeanours,' so it was said in the North Carolina ratification convention. And in the Virginia ratification convention: 'We do not trust our liberty to a particular branch. We need one branch to check the other.'

... The drawing of political lines goes to the motivation behind impeachment; but impeachment must proceed within the confines of the constitutional term 'high crime[s] and misdemeanours'. Of the impeachment process, it was Woodrow Wilson who said that 'Nothing short of the grossest offenses against the plain law of the land will suffice to give them speed and effectiveness. Indignation so great as to overgrow party interest may secure a conviction; but nothing else can.'

Common sense would be revolted if we engaged upon this process for petty reasons. Congress has a lot to do: appropriations, tax reform, health insurance, campaign finance reform, housing, environmental protection, energy sufficiency, mass transportation. Pettiness cannot be allowed to stand in the face of such overwhelming problems. So today we are not being petty. We are trying to be big, because the task we have before us is a big one.

... At this point, I would like to juxtapose a few of the impeachment criteria with some of the actions the President has engaged in. Impeachment criteria: James Madison, from the Virginia ratification convention. 'If the President be connected in any suspicious manner with any person and there be grounds to believe that he will shelter him, he may be impeached.'

We have heard time and time again that the evidence reflects the payment to defendants money. The President had knowledge that these funds were being paid and these were funds collected for the 1972 presidential campaign. We know that the President met with Mr Henry Petersen 27 times to discuss matters related to Watergate, and immediately thereafter met with the very persons who were implicated in the information Mr Petersen was receiving. The words are: 'If the President is connected in any suspicious manner with any person and there be grounds to believe that he will shelter that person, he may be impeached.'

Justice Story: 'Impeachment' is attended — 'is intended for occasional and extraordinary cases where a superior power acting for the whole people is put into operation to protect their rights and rescue their liberties from violations.' We know about the Huston plan. We know about the break-in of the psychiatrist's office. We know that there was absolute complete direction on September 3rd when the President indicated that a surreptitious entry had been made in Dr Fielding's office, after having met with Mr Ehrlichman and Mr Young. 'Protect their rights.' 'Rescue their liberties from violation.'

The Carolina ratification convention impeachment criteria: those are impeachable 'who behave amiss or betray their public trust'. Beginning shortly after the Watergate break-in and continuing to the present time, the President has engaged in a series of public statements and actions designed to thwart the lawful investigation by government prosecutors. Moreover, the President has made public announcements and assertions bearing on the Watergate case, which the evidence will show he knew to be false. These assertions, false assertions, impeachable, those who misbehave; those who 'behave amiss or betray the public trust'.

James Madison again at the Constitutional Convention: 'A President is impeachable if he attempts to subvert the Constitution.' The Constitution charges the President with the task of taking care that the laws be faithfully executed, and yet the President has counselled his aides to commit perjury, wilfully disregard the secrecy of grand jury proceedings, conceal surreptitious entry, attempt to compromise a federal judge, while publicly displaying his cooperation with the processes of criminal justice. 'A President is impeachable if he attempts to subvert the Constitution.'

If the impeachment provision in the Constitution of the United States will not reach the offenses charged here, then perhaps that eighteenth-century Constitution should be abandoned to a twentieth-century paper shredder!

Has the President committed offenses, and planned, and directed, and acquiesced in a course of conduct which the Constitution will not tolerate? That's the question. We know that. We know the question. We should now forthwith proceed to answer the question. It is reason, and not passion, which must guide our deliberations, guide our debate, and guide our decision.

<u>HOW</u> SHE DID THAT

Cultivate gravitas

Speaking the Truth with Eloquent Thunder is the title of a book of Barbara Jordan's speeches, edited by Max Sherman. This is a perfect description of Jordan's exceptional speaking ability. Jordan possessed more than oratorical skill — she packed her words full of substance as well.

The moment Barbara Jordan begins to speak, we are struck with an almost hypnotic compulsion to listen. She has gravitas. This is one of the most highly prized yet elusive qualities that anyone seeking to improve their public speaking should seek to foster. The quality of gravitas can and should vary according to the speaker. It is like beauty — difficult to define, but we know it when we see it.

Jordan's expression of gravitas manifests here after years of professional achievement. Her ability to turn a phrase, use her voice to propel a message and emphasise a point with perfect weight and inflection have been honed over years of experience. Besides her enviable eloquence, Jordan stood for something. This too is a source of gravitas. She took a stand for ethics in government and the military, and she consistently defended democratic values.

How do you cultivate your own version of gravitas? The first step is to develop self-awareness. As a university debater, Barbara Jordan would have been exposed to feedback and experienced wins and losses, helping her to acknowledge her strengths and weaknesses. Secondly, you must construct an image of how you want to be perceived. You can look to people you admire for inspiration, but the persona you create must be authentically you. How would that version of you speak in a range of situations? Work to align the way people perceive you with your vision by planning for and reflecting on each speaking opportunity.

Present a rational argument

Barbara Jordan's address to the House Judiciary Committee takes the form of a clear, well-argued, rational contention. She anchors her thesis to the constitutionality of Nixon's behaviour. For constitutional arguments to find a foothold, they must reference the framer's intentions — Jordan carefully brings the founders into her address, thus attaching her argument to the very intentions of those who devised and defined American democracy.

Jordan defines the terms of what she intends to submit — that is, the nature of impeachment — which she goes on to explain as 'a narrowly channelled exception to the separation-of-powers maxim', limited to 'high crimes and misdemeanours'. So, she sets the bar and then goes about reaching it. Listening to her laying out the terms of her argument and articulating her positions is a dizzying adventure. It would be difficult to rebut such a tightly controlled rationale.

Presenting a set of impeachment criteria, she carefully presents specific evidence that demonstrates that each criterion has been met, making her proposition for impeachment all but unassailable. In case the House Committee (or the television audience) misses the breadcrumbs she has carefully laid, she signposts her tactic; 'At this point, I would like to juxtapose a few of the impeachment criteria with some of the actions the President has engaged in.'

To develop your own skills of rational persuasion, you will need to first decide if you are making an *inductive* or *deductive* argument. An inductive argument presents evidence that supports your conclusion, whereas a deductive argument presents evidence to support an observable fact. In other words, if the premises are correct, the conclusion of a deductive argument is certain while the truth of the conclusion of an inductive argument is probable, based upon the evidence given.

Once you've decided the conclusion you're hoping for, you can then define your terms and choose your facts accordingly. While keeping an eye on the audience's current level of understanding, you build your case by introducing relevant evidence. Cross-check your content with your initial purpose and make sure your language and examples allow your audience to see, and agree with, your thought pattern and you'll be on your way to a Jordan-level argument.

Speak with passion

This is interesting and perhaps controversial but, in my opinion, this speech is permeated with passion. Why controversial? Because Barbara Jordan herself at the conclusion of this address says, 'It is reason, and not passion, which must guide our deliberations, guide our debate, and guide our decision'.

Not only does her style convey commitment akin to passionate belief but, on several occasions, she allows flourishes that introduce an unmistakable quality of pathos, evoking an emotional response. The first and most striking is her inspired opening. In referencing the preamble to the constitution, she plays on the hallowed phrase, 'We the people', reminding the committee 'when that document was completed on the 17th of September in 1787, I was not included in that "We, the people".'

And then she presents this phrase with a touch of dramatic flair: 'Today I am an inquisitor'. In the recorded version of this speech, you can hear her grandiose emphasis on the fourth syllable '*TOR*'. The whole affair is as serious and formal as it gets, but she makes the proceedings sound almost biblical. Jordan also uses this dramatic flair to highlight her personal commitment to the Constitution: 'My faith in the Constitution is whole; it is complete; it is total' with a pleasing demonstration of rhetorical tricolon. This type of flair is not necessarily required in a purely rational legal argument, but is certainly powerful.

At one point, she obliquely refers to Nixon as 'a President swollen with power and grown tyrannical'. Not only is her language sophisticated, but with only a handful of words she also manages to evoke a particularly effective reaction of disgust.

The slightly hidden but nonetheless essential learning from Jordan's speech is to remember that pathos always matters. Even in the most ostensibly rational of circumstances — such as presenting a legal argument — we need to trust the speaker *and* we need to feel something. Look for opportunities to create emotional resonance in order to win both the hearts and minds of your audience.

We claim that woman should have the right over her own body and to say if she shall or if she shall not be a mother, as she sees fit.

Margaret Sanger

Margaret Sanger

Women's rights activist and social reformer
B: *14 September 1879, Corning, NY, United States*
D: *6 September 1966, Tucson, AZ, United States*

The morality of birth control

When: *18 November 1921*
Where: *New York City, NY, United States*
Audience: *Approximately 2000 people*

Margaret Sanger is often referred to as the mother of planned parenthood in the United States. Her views, like so many of the voices we hear in this book, are controversial, even today. Many would cause backlash now — especially given our polarised political environment. In the 1920s she caused a furore when she spoke about a woman's right to decide her own reproductive future.

Jailed eight times for her efforts, Sanger kept showing up and kept speaking up. She suffered constant social abuse and vilification. Her marriage dissolved. And yet, she kept going. Through all of this, she got better and better at formulating her arguments and standing up for her beliefs.

Not a lot of women in the interwar years would have proclaimed themselves to be a feminist or social reformer, let alone a sex educator. And yet, Sanger displayed notable bravery in her steady, unwavering proclamations.

The speech extracted here was delivered to a packed house in Park Theatre, New York City, in November 1921. One week prior, Sanger had been arrested when attempting to deliver her planned address so curiosity was mounting. Over 2000 people filled the theatre with many more clamouring to get in.

No recording of this remarkable speech remains, but Sanger gave a number of interviews throughout her life, notably with Mike Wallace in 1957 — and a video recording of this interview is available. In this recording, we see glimpses of her level-headed conviction. She is impressive in her commitment and lack of resentment.

Sanger founded the American Birth Control League, which later became the Planned Parenthood Federation of America. She worked tirelessly through this body and other grassroots initiatives to make a marked impact on the reproductive health of women. She was also instrumental in securing funding for the research and development of the contraceptive pill and continued her lobbying efforts throughout her life by speaking publicly, lobbying government and engaging the media.

<u>WHAT</u> SHE SAID

We know that every advance that woman has made in the last half century has been made with opposition, all of which has been based upon the grounds of immorality. When women fought for higher education, it was said that this would cause her to become immoral and she would lose her place in the sanctity of the home. When women asked for the franchise it was said that this would lower her standard of morals, that it was not fit that she should meet with and mix with the members of the opposite sex, but we notice that there was no objection to her meeting with the same members of the opposite sex when she went to church. The church has ever opposed the progress of woman on the ground that her freedom would lead to immorality.

We ask the church to have more confidence in women. We ask the opponents of this movement to reverse the methods of the church, which aims to keep women moral by keeping them in fear and in ignorance, and to inculcate into them a higher and truer morality based upon knowledge. And ours is the morality of knowledge. If we cannot trust woman with the knowledge of her own body, then I claim that two thousand years of Christian teaching has proved to be a failure.

We stand on the principle that birth control should be available to every adult man and woman. We believe that every adult man and woman should be taught the responsibility and the right use of knowledge. We claim that woman should have the right over her own body and to say if she shall or if she shall not be a mother, as she sees fit.

We further claim that the first right of a child is to be desired. While the second right is that it should be conceived in love, and the third, that it should have a heritage of sound health.

Upon these principles the Birth Control Movement in America stands.

<u>HOW</u> SHE DID THAT

Echo past triumphs

Sanger effectively places her message in the line-up of other achievements of the women's movement to date. She mentions the hard-fought right to education and the right to vote. In both instances, common beliefs and incorrect assumptions about inevitable moral degradation are broken down and shown to be baseless.

This is a savvy technique of persuasion. The audience is led to believe that the right to birth control naturally follows the other triumphs of female rights in society — and arguments against birth control are as equally baseless. This alone is a contentious point — or at least it would have been in 1921 — but Sanger deftly sweeps it up with other accomplishments of her gender.

This technique broadly adheres to a tactic of persuasion known as 'consistency and commitment', identified by American researcher Robert Cialdini. This tactic makes use of people's tendency to behave in a manner that matches their past decisions or behaviours, and feel comfortable in doing so. You may be able to increase the chances of an agreement by tacking your request on to something that has already been accepted — get your foot in the door, so to speak.

Your argument is along the lines of, 'Since you already agree with *xyz*, you must also believe in *abc*.' This is a technique that in the wrong hands could become manipulative. But Sanger gives us an example of how it is used to push open the door once a glimmer of light has emerged through the crack.

Name and rebut your opponents

When arguing a contentious position, creating your own version of the opposition can be quite useful. You can then portray, with your own spin, the counterarguments they are likely to make. And now, suddenly, you have the upper hand. You not only control the premise of the counterargument, but also give yourself adequate time and all the benefits of pre-planning in order to respond.

Some of the best and most strident speakers only really shine when they have an opponent to push against. This is a technique you will observe in many interviews and speeches by the somewhat controversial Canadian academic and writer Jordan Peterson, for example.

Sanger casts the church in the role of her opponent: 'The church has ever opposed the progress of woman on the ground that her freedom would lead to immorality.' She then takes aim and fires her rebuttal. Look out for this technique among other savvy persuaders, including many politicians. The value of this move is that you can even animate an otherwise uncontentious matter by concocting something to brace against. You can invite people in and then ask them to choose a side, now that you have created a contest.

Be inclusive

Margaret Sanger probably didn't feel that the reproductive rights of men needed her strident support. She was clearly advocating for the rights of women. By including the rights of men in her plea, she was again using a crafty technique of fending off opposing arguments. Her language signalled that her message was not 'anti-men'. Instead, she was mounting a case that birth control 'should be available to every adult man and woman'.

By identifying the group with the power, and sweeping them up as your de facto supporters, you might just be able to repel at least some of the enemies you might disturb when putting forward a radical point of view.

Sanger shows us an argument for inclusivity is strengthened by reinforcing the whole. It's not women's rights as such, but equal rights for men and women. Semantics perhaps, but don't miss the opportunity for subtle persuasion.

Where there used to be a dark wall, a door suddenly opened, and we all walked through it out into the streets, into the churches, across borders. Each and every one was suddenly given a chance to build something new, to help shape things, to dare a new beginning. I, too, saw a new beginning.

Angela Merkel

Angela Merkel

Chancellor of Germany (2005–2021)

B: *17 July 1954, Hamburg, Germany*

Speech to US Congress

When: *3 November 2009*

Where: *Washington DC*

Audience: *US Congress (joint session)*

In November 2009 the German Chancellor, Angela Merkel, delivered a speech to a joint session of the US Congress in Washington. She spoke in her native German, with English translation. Her appearance came almost exactly two decades after the fall of the Berlin Wall, at a time when the US, Germany and the world were facing a very different set of challenges.

The preliminaries have an air of formality. You can sense the shared reverence in the chamber. The atmosphere seems charged with historical significance — which Merkel correctly reads and leverages to great effect.

It eventually becomes clear that Merkel's intention is to state her position and generate support for the key issues of the day — climate change, the situation in Afghanistan (in the full version of the speech — see Sources) and free trade. She knew that opening with this would not serve her. She leads, instead, with Germany's troubled recent past, and then moves to shared values and all that the United States stands for. Look out for the pro-Western sentiments so strongly held by somebody who grew up under the restrictive, sometimes hopeless, East German regime when it was part of the German Democratic Republic. Like many of her generation — those who knew life before and after the fall of the Berlin Wall—ideology is strong. Conviction is held on a deeply personal level.

Merkel speaks eloquently of the relationship between the two countries and the way forward. She inspires several standing ovations but she is neither obsequious nor theatrical. Merkel manages to convey repeated compliments and recognise shared values in a straightforward, levelling manner. This speech is one to watch, not only for its historical political significance but also for its masterful construction and delivery.

<u>WHAT</u> SHE SAID

Madam Speaker, Mr Vice President, distinguished Members of Congress: Thank you for the great honour and privilege to address you today, shortly before the twentieth anniversary of the fall of the Berlin Wall. I am the second German Chancellor on whom this great honour is bestowed. Konrad Adenauer was the first when, in 1957, he addressed both Houses of Congress, albeit one after the other. Our lives could not have been more different. In 1957, I was a small child of three years. I lived in Brandenburg together with my parents, a region that at the time belonged to the German Democratic Republic, the part of Germany that was not free. My father worked as a Protestant pastor. My mother, who had studied English and Latin to become a teacher, was not allowed to work in her chosen profession in the GDR.

... In only a few days will mark the 9th of November. On the 9th of November, 1989, the Berlin Wall fell. The 9th of November, 1938, however, also left an indelible mark on German and European history. On this day, the National Socialists pillaged and destroyed synagogues, set fire to them and killed innumerable people. It was the beginning of what later turned into the break with civilisation that was the Shoah. I cannot stand before you today without remembering the victims of that very day and of the Shoah. There is one guest in the audience today who personally experienced the horrors of Germany under National Socialism.

... In my wildest dreams, I would not have thought this possible 20 years ago, before the fall of the wall, for at the time it was beyond my imagination to ever even travel to the United States, let alone stand here before you one day. The land of unlimited opportunity was, for me for a long time, impossible to reach. The wall, barbed wire and the order to shoot at those who tried to leave limited my access to the free world. Therefore, I had to rely on films and books, some of which were smuggled by relatives from the West, to gain an impression of the United States. What did I see, and what did I read? What was it I was passionate about? I was passionate about the American Dream, the possibility for each and every one to be successful, to actually make it in life through one's own personal effort. And like many other teenagers, I was passionate about jeans of a particular brand that you could not get in the GDR, which my aunt kindly sent me regularly from the West. I was passionate about the vast American landscapes that seemed to breathe the very spirit of freedom and independence.

…I think of John F Kennedy who won the hearts of the Berliners when, during his visit in 1963 after the wall had been built, he reached out to the desperate citizens of Berlin by saying, 'Ich bin ein Berliner'.' I think of Ronald Reagan who, far earlier than most, clearly saw the sign of the times and, standing in front of the Brandenburg Gate already in 1987, called out, 'Mr Gorbachev, open this gate. Mr Gorbachev, tear down this wall.'

…Ladies and gentlemen, to put it in just one sentence, I know — we Germans know — how much we owe to you, our American friends, and we shall never — I, personally shall never, ever — forget this. The common quest for freedom released incredible forces all over Europe: the trade union Solidarność in Poland, the reformers around Václav Havel in Czechoslovakia, the first opening of the Iron Curtain in Hungary, and the demonstrations in the GDR every Monday. Where there used to be a dark wall, a door suddenly opened, and we all walked through it out into the streets, into the churches, across borders. Each and every one was suddenly given a chance to build something new, to help shape things, to dare a new beginning. I, too, saw a new beginning.

…Now today's generation needs to prove that it is able to meet the challenges of the twenty-first century and that, in a sense, we are able to tear down the walls of today. What does this mean? Well, it means we create freedom and security. It means we create prosperity and justice, and it means protecting our planet. And here again, America and Europe are called upon in a very special way to do that, even after the end of the Cold War. Therefore, what is important is to see to it that we tear down walls in the minds of people, walls that separate different concepts of life that make it difficult time and again for us to understand each other all over the world.

… [F]reedom is the very essence of our economy and our society. Man can only be creative when he's free, but what is also clear is that freedom does not stand alone. It is the freedom in responsibility and freedom to show and shoulder responsibility. For this, the world needs an underlying order.

… To achieve prosperity and justice, we have to do everything to prevent such a crisis in the future. This also means not giving in to the temptation of protectionism. This is why the Doha negotiations and the framework of WTO are so important. The success of the Doha Round would send a very important message of openness for global trade, particularly in the current crisis. And, just as much, the Transatlantic Economic Council can fulfil an important task in preventing the race for subsidies and giving incentives to reduce barriers to trade between Europe and America. Please, do let us jointly work for a global economic order that is in the interest of both America and Europe.

<u>HOW</u> SHE DID THAT

Use value signalling

Freedom ... the American Dream ... independence ... prosperity.

More than just recurring themes in Merkel's address, these are the core values of American political culture. For many, these are the ultimate virtues that make America what it is. The US is a patriotic nation, and happy to publicly espouse its first principles. Angela Merkel seems to grasp the Zeitgeist of the nation and the emblematic chamber that is her audience. She manages to hit on each virtue repeatedly during her address to the United States Congress. This is value signalling on a global scale. She communicates the fact that she, and by extension, Germany, share these values. What a way to build trust.

This speech is a fine example of how you can quickly create fondness with your audience. Praise is usually a sound method of engendering partiality. Observe how this is amplified when the compliments are genuine and personal.

The truthfulness of this message notwithstanding, this is a tactic of influence. Merkel uses the platform of affinity as a springboard to articulate her policy opinions on a broad range of topics, including (in the full version of the speech) Afghanistan, Israel and climate change.

The lesson here is to warm up your audience before attempting to generate consensus. What Angela Merkel teaches us is that this can be done in a way that does not feel icky. Make sure you identify compliments that are true and that you actually believe. Frame them in a manner that is appropriate to the occasion and your own communication style. Once you have created this connection, build your argument from your newly created foundation of collegiality.

Identify a personal connection

Angela Merkel tends toward a more rational, even-tempered communications style. Compared with, say, Jacinda Ardern or Oprah

Winfrey, Merkel is, well ... more Germanic. This does not preclude her from sharing something of her personal circumstance.

We hear about her childhood in Brandenburg and gain a tiny glimpse of what life might be been like behind the Iron Curtain. Merkel shares her memories of the wall coming down, the ancillary events across Europe and (in the full version of the speech) her first trip to the United States. With a few brushstrokes, we are shown her *Weltanschauung* — her world view. This is all the more effective and endearing because of her otherwise formal manner.

If you have ever felt some resistance in sharing your personal experiences, perhaps this address with be an inspiration for you. You don't need to overshare, you don't need to dwell on the emotional component and you don't need to venture into territory that makes you in any way uncomfortable — after all, we are not all emotive empathetic types.

Name drop judiciously

Another adroit bond-inducing tactic on display here is the strategic referencing of heroes past. Angela Merkel masterfully brings past American heroes into the room. And not just any room — the US Congress. She evokes first the voice of John F Kennedy and then Ronald Reagan.

Knowing she is addressing an audience consisting of both Democrats and Republicans, she hedges her bet. She mentions JFK first, reminding us of the historic *'Ich bin ein Berliner'* speech delivered at the height of the Cold War. Then, just in case any Republicans in the chamber do not credit the words of the Democrat, even one of this stature, she quotes Ronald Reagan. She carefully chooses a non-contentious, yet no less dramatic quote with, 'Mr Gorbachev, open this gate. Mr Gorbachev, tear down this wall.'

When we examine the persuasive techniques embedded in Merkel's address to the US Congress, all those standing ovations are not too surprising. This speech is a masterclass in influence, deftly executed in a manner of authenticity and personal commitment.

7

Inspiring action

Speeches that inspire action operate at the break-point moments in history.

While they might contain aspects of other intentions — opening hearts and minds, for example, or personal experience — the overwhelming tone is one of action. They are imperative, authoritative and commanding — they demand you move your feet.

In each of the four speeches featured in this chapter, you can observe a high level of personal commitment. The speakers themselves demonstrate through their words and their tone they have put themselves on the line. In essence, they are looking back at us, the audience, and saying, 'Come on — why aren't you up here with me?' These speeches have undercurrents of impatience and sometimes a hint of frustration or even anger.

As monarch, Queen Elizabeth I had the positional authority by which she could command her troops. But in her Tilbury address she delivers a call to arms, inspiring heartfelt action that supersedes the sense of duty she surmised among her soldiers.

Similarly, the rally cry 'They shall not pass!' delivered by Dolores Ibárruri in her plea for her fellow Spaniards to join in the fight against the fascists elicits a nationalistically motivated call to arms. Both speeches employ the strongest of 'fighting words' — usually not considered the domain of the female speaker.

Imagine the bravery Sojourner Truth would have had to muster when speaking out, as an ex-slave, on the topic of abolition. So incensed was she that one set of human rights should be placed over another that she also persisted with her demand to be counted as a woman. In her clever and demanding address, Truth puts herself square in the firing line, encouraging others to take a stand.

Sometimes a call to action is needed to overcome inertia. If you have ever tried to motivate a group who are disengaged, who don't feel the passion you do, you might be able to understand the fervour of Greta Thunberg's speech at the World Economic Forum. Overcoming inertia or just making people care can be an exasperating business. In this speech, we hear the anger and experience a summary dismissal of every single excuse we can think of — not from a senior policy expert, but from a 16-year-old girl.

We have all felt the temptation to give up — to save our breath, duck the microphone and resist being cast in the role of evangelist. We don't want to be annoying. The lessons here will help you to recognise the situations in which you must resist your own feeling of inertia and be the one to take the lead.

I know I have
the body but of a
weak and feeble
woman; but I have
the heart and
stomach of a king.

Queen Elizabeth I

Queen Elizabeth I

Queen of England

B: 7 September 1533, Greenwich, England, United Kingdom

D: 24 March 1603, Surrey, England, United Kingdom

The heart and stomach of a king

When: 19 August 1588

Where: Mouth of the river Thames, England, United Kingdom

Audience: English troops, assembled in preparation for repelling the expected invasion led by the Spanish Armada

Queen Elizabeth I ascended to the English throne in 1558 at just 25 years old, succeeding her half-sister, Queen Mary. She ruled until her death in 1603.

To say that she came to rule in tumultuous times would be a gross understatement. Elizabeth was the daughter of Henry VIII and Anne Boleyn, his second wife, who had been executed two and a half years after Elizabeth's birth. The now infamous house of Tudor was punctuated with stories of adultery, illegitimacy, treason, assassination, divorce, murder and religious upheaval. These people would make the Lannisters from *Game of Thrones* look like the suburban family next door.

The challenges that the first Elizabeth had to encounter during her reign extended beyond the boundaries of her family. The ongoing conflict between Protestants and Catholics was to take human form as England entered a large-scale and devastating battle with Spain in 1588.

Queen Elizabeth's speech before this battle, included in full here, is a short and powerful piece of oratory. In it, Queen Elizabeth I delivers a stirring battle cry to the English troops, assembled in preparation for repelling the expected invasion led by the Spanish Armada. Coming in at only 312 words and lasting about two minutes, it is a little verbal rocket. This is a battlefield address, presumably delivered to soldiers embodying myriad emotions: fear and excitement, distrust and pride, conviction and doubt. The monarch would have been seeking to unify and galvanise her army with the only remaining tool she had available — her words.

Sometimes called the 'Tilbury Speech' (after the location near the mouth of the River Thames where it is said to have been made), this masterful display continues to deliver a punch more than 430 years later.

<u>WHAT</u> SHE SAID

My loving people.

We have been persuaded by some that are careful of our safety to take heed how we commit ourselves to armed multitudes, for fear of treachery; but I assure you I do not desire to live to distrust my faithful and loving people.

Let tyrants fear, I have always so behaved myself that, under God, I have placed my chiefest strength and safeguard in the loyal hearts and good will of my subjects; and therefore I am come amongst you, as you see, at this time, not for my recreation and disport, but being resolved, in the midst and heat of the battle, to live and die amongst you all; to lay down for my God, and for my kingdom, and my people, my honour and my blood, even in the dust.

I know I have the body but of a weak and feeble woman; but I have the heart and stomach of a king, and of a king of England too, and think foul scorn that Parma or Spain, or any prince of Europe, should dare to invade the borders of my realm; to which rather than any dishonour shall grow by me, I myself will take up arms, I myself will be your general, judge and rewarder of every one of your virtues in the field.

I know already, for your forwardness you have deserved rewards and crowns; and we do assure you in the word of a prince, they shall be duly paid you. In the meantime, my lieutenant-general shall be in my stead, than whom never prince commanded a more noble or worthy subject; not doubting but by your obedience to my general, by your concord in the camp, and your valour in the field, we shall shortly have a famous victory over those enemies of my God, of my kingdom and of my people.

<u>HOW</u> SHE DID THAT

Present character and conviction

Though confronted with threats from all sides, Queen Elizabeth I composes herself before she speaks. An assumptive position, what Aristotle might call ethos or trust in the character of the speaker, is aptly conveyed. The monarch projects controlled power. We hear this in the crescendo, the biblical allusions and the strikingly personal commitment.

This is her platform; her moment to boldly assert her intention to assume the power she clearly takes to be her just birthright. Elizabeth takes aim at any in the crowd who might harbour lingering doubts. Any reservations about her right to command or the justification of the battle are emphatically dispatched.

Elizabeth's tone is one of resolve. It's all or nothing; complete commitment, no matter the cost. Though the salutation covers all her subjects — 'my loving people' — the message is aimed at the troops about to fight. We see absolute clarity of purpose. These men are faced with the imminent proposition of placing their very lives on the line in service of the crown. This speech bestows meaning on that sacrifice. More importantly, she embodies repeated and unmistakable conviction.

The warning is clear and the threat of forceful retaliation is emphasised throughout:

> …I am come amongst you, as you see, at this time, not for my recreation and disport, but being resolved, in the midst and heat of the battle, to live and die amongst you all; to lay down for my God, and for my kingdom, and my people, my honour and my blood, even in the dust.

Total conviction offered by the Queen demands no less than total commitment from each soldier.

Build personal connection

We need to use our imagination when considering the pace and delivery of this message. Over the centuries, artists have tried to capture the moment for us—such as Ferdinand Piloty the Younger's 1861 painting 'Queen Elizabeth I of England, faced with the Spanish Armada 1588, reviews her troops'. Or, we can experience the emotional interpretation of the character by the talented Cate Blanchett (in the movie *Elizabeth: The Golden Age*).

However, the written word is enough to appreciate how these few words would have galvanised an unquestionable bond between monarch and warrior.

She begins with the salutation 'my loving people', and then doubles down, only a few lines later, with 'my faithful and loving people' who are then noted to have 'loyal hearts'. They are said to be deserving of great rewards already and 'shall be duly paid'. (The terms of payment are unclear.)

She shifts between collective pronouns (we, us, ourselves) to the first person, thus asserting her power and personal commitment—'my God, and for my kingdom, and my people, my honour and my blood'. Elizabeth promises to avenge the violation of her kingdom personally—'I myself will take up arms'—as if to say, 'I am with you to the end' (at least in spirit).

Use hyperbole strategically

Well, you'd expect a bit of blood and guts, maybe some glory and triumph—this is, after all, a call to arms. But Elizabeth takes it to the utmost limits by invoking the most heinous enemy imaginable. Just in case her soldiers thought they were about to enter into a battle with some Spaniards about the finer points of contention between the two Christian factions, she sets them straight. She exalts the soldiers and vilifies the enemy with 'foul scorn'—and without any concern for overdoing the drama.

These chosen ones are not just ordinary conscripted fighters; they are 'noble' and 'worthy subjects' and they will be not be fighting the Spanish Armada but 'the enemies of my God'!

Fighting words indeed.

The Tilbury speech stands out in history for its powerful and timeless resonance. These are the words of a monarch delivered in the most pressing circumstances imaginable — and a fine example of words as power.

If de fust woman God ever made was strong enough to turn de world upside down all her one lone, all dese togeder ought to be able to turn it back, and git it right side up again! And now dey is asking to, de men better let 'em.

Sojourner Truth

Sojourner Truth

Abolitionist and human rights advocate

B: 1797, Rifton, NY, United States

D: 26 November 1883, Battle Creek, MI, United States

Ain't I a woman?

When: 1851

Where: Akron, Ohio

Audience: All-white attendees of the Women's Convention

Sojourner Truth was an ex-slave, American abolitionist and activist. In 1851, she delivered an impromptu speech from the steps of the Old Stone Church in front of the all-white attendees of the Women's Convention in Akron, Ohio.

Born to enslaved parents, Truth was sold at the age of about nine or ten, along with a flock of sheep, for 100 dollars. She bore five children and never learned to read or write. Truth grew up without human rights let alone the particular entitlement born of education and, yet, she had a point to make.

No recording exists of this address but her words live on through various re-enactments and public readings. Several artists, including Alison Walker, Cicely Tyson and Kerry Washington, have used their voices to re-activate this remarkable speech first delivered 170 years ago.

Discussion also continues about the accuracy of the version of the speech presented here. The first version to appear in print, presented by Reverend Marius Robinson one month after the convention, seems to have 'smoothed out' some of the language, although Truth is said to have reviewed this version with Robinson. Fellow abolitionist Frances Gage published the version of Truth's speech used here in the *National Anti-Slavery Standard* in 1863. This version has been challenged due to Gage's use of the southern dialect, choice of language, and some clear errors about Truth's life. (Truth lived in New York, for example, and didn't have a southern accent. She had five children, not thirteen, and one son was sold into slavery but Truth went to court and got him back.) All experts agree, however, that Truth's speech moved her audience, and Gage's version is the one that has captured hearts and minds.

Her speech will not be forgotten. It is remarkable for its humour and forthright challenge. For any woman, let alone an ex-slave, to take a stand on women's rights in addition to the fight for the abolition of slavery makes Sojourner Truth a stand-out. Add to that the fact that this particular speech was not planned or rehearsed — but delivered off the cuff. In fact, Truth never learned to read or write. And yet, she used language to its full effect — in part, because of the subtle rhetorical technique.

Sojourner Truth speaks with conviction and confidence. She does not cower or demur. Her strength comes from her faith and dedication to her cause.

Sojourner Truth was sold into slavery. Today, we celebrate the power of her words.

WHAT SHE SAID

Well, chillen, what dar's so much racket dar must be som'ting out o'kilter. I tink dat 'twixt de negroes of de South and de women at de Norf, all a-talking 'bout rights, de white men will be in a fix pretty soon. But what's all this here talking 'bout?

Dat man ober dar say dat woman needs to be helped into carriages, and lifted ober ditches, and to have de best place eberywhar. Nobody eber helps me into carriages, or ober mud-puddles, or gives me any best place.

And ar'n't I a woman? Look at me. Look at my arm! I have plowed and planted and gathered into barns, and no man could head me! And ar'n't I a woman? I could work as much and eat as much as a man (when I could get it) and bear de lash as well. And ar'n't I a woman? I have borne thirteen children, and seen 'em mos' all sold off to slavery, and when I cried out with a mother's grief, none but Jesus heard. And ar'n't I a woman?

Den dey talks 'bout dis ting in de head. What dis dey call it?

[Member of audience whispers, 'Intellect.']

Dat's it, honey. What's dat got to do with women's rights or negroes' rights? If my cup won't hold but a pint, and yourn holds a quart, wouldn't ye be mean not to let me have my little half-measure full?

Den dat little man in black dar, he say woman can't have as much rights as man, 'cause Christ wa'n't a woman. Whar did your Christ come from? Whar did your Christ come from? From God and a woman! Man had not'ing to do with him.

If de fust woman God ever made was strong enough to turn de world upside down all her one lone, all dese togeder ought to be able to turn it back, and git it right side up again! And now dey is asking to, de men better let 'em.

Bleeged to ye for hearin' on me, and now ole Sojourner ha'n't got nothing more to say.

99

<u>HOW</u> SHE DID THAT

Speak from the heart

How can you be an effective orator without the ability to read and write? The answer is to be fully present and speak from the heart. The more powerful rendition of the iconic 'Ain't I a woman?' speech displays the conversational nature of this address. You get the feeling that Sojourner Truth was connecting to the people in the room. She even brings them into her speech with lines such as, 'Dat man ober dar', making the words about them — the people in the room — not some imaginary audience. It's interesting to consider what you might be able to do without notes or a slide presentation.

The impromptu nature of this speech seems to free Truth from the confines of predictable speech patterns. Her language is free flowing. We have touches of humour and personality; 'Nobody eber helps me into carriages, or ober mud-puddles', showing the speaker to be relaxed in her role. She is comfortable communicating in the vernacular, which then allows the audience to transition from a formal, rather distant being, to an equal counterpart in a conversation.

Speaking from the heart will always build the credibility of the speaker. When you share your own experiences, no matter how briefly, and they are relevant to the subject at hand, you will be elevated in the eyes of your audience. They will think, *This person has a right to be here*, and so will be more likely to listen.

Repeat like a preacher

The use of repetition is a well-known rhetorical device that Sojourner Truth uses to great effect. It is also the tool of the preacher. Similarities can be seen between this speech and the iconic Martin Luther King Jnr 'I have a dream' speech. Not least of all because both were preachers. In that tradition, a musicality comes into the use of language.

King used 'I have a dream ... I have a dream ... I have a dream ...' as the precursor to a series of statements. Similarly, Truth used 'Ain't I a woman? ... Ain't I a woman? ... Ain't I a woman?' as a consequent rhetorical question. Truth was herself a travelling preacher, and we hear vestiges of an evangelist in her words.

Repetition, when used appropriately, is an important technique that can help to amplify your message. In this case, the repeating phrase adds considerably more value and brings resonance to the speech. Repetition is also commonly used at the pulpit to encourage parishioners to reflect, and that is echoed in this speech.

In a sense, preachers are the most practical orators. After all, they need to deliver fresh speeches every week in the form of their sermon. Practised speakers learn to rely on a set of tools and give themselves time to remember what comes next. Repeated phrases and words help the audience remember the speech but they also help the speaker to cue their memory.

Appeal to reason

Sojourner Truth makes two appeals to reason in this speech. Her technique is subtle and the arguments are buffered by humour, which only serves to enhance the impact.

Firstly, we have the very rational, 'If my cup won't hold but a pint, and yourn holds a quart, wouldn't ye be mean not to let me have my little half-measure full?' Who could disagree?

Then the cheeky rebuttal of what must have been a recent criticism, that women do not deserve the same rights as a man because Christ was a man. Truth's skilful retort? 'Whar did your Christ come from? From God and a woman! Man had not'ing to do with him.'

In fact, this entire speech is formed in response to criticism. It is a logical rebuttal. Truth was attacked for holding opinions unbefitting a woman, which somehow meant she must not be a 'real' woman. Her response is warm, eloquent and courageous — creating a speech that came into being because she had something to brace against.

The whole country cringes in indignation at these heartless barbarians that would hurl our democratic Spain back down into an abyss of terror and death. However, THEY SHALL NOT PASS!

Dolores Ibárruri

Dolores Ibárruri

Freedom fighter

B: *9 December 1895, Basque Country, Spain*

D: *12 November 1989, Madrid, Spain*

They shall not pass!

When: *19 July 1936*

Where: *Madrid, Spain*

Audience: *Citizens of Madrid*

Dolores Ibárruri was known as 'la Pasionaria'—the 'Passionflower'. She is remembered as a symbol of resistance to Franco fascism during the Spanish Civil War. Ibárruri was a committed communist—in fact, a Stalinist—until her death in 1989.

Ibárruri wrote communist treatises, led hunger strikes, suffered exile, fought as a republican in the Civil War, delivered multiple speeches, spearheaded counter-fascist uprisings and gave birth to six children. She led a life filled with drama, pain and struggle.

This speech, reproduced in full here, was delivered not before a live audience but before press microphones at the Government Ministry Building in Madrid. It was broadcast on Radio Madrid as part of wider efforts to rally the citizens of Spain against Franco's nationalists, who were preparing to launch a military offensive on the city. One of the Communist deputies in the Republican parliament, Ibárruri was known to be a popular and persuasive figure. Her fiery style of delivery was perfectly suited to the moment.

Ibárruri lived her life with passion. 'They shall not pass!' was the battle cry she issued on 19 July 1936, and it lives on as the legacy of la Pasionaria.

WHAT SHE SAID

"

Workers! Farmers! Anti-fascists! Spanish patriots! Confronted with the fascist military uprising, all must rise to their feet, to defend the Republic, to defend the people's freedoms as well as their achievements towards democracy! Through the statements by the government and the Popular Front [parties], the people understand the graveness of the moment. In Morocco, as well as in the Canary Islands, the workers are battling, united with the forces still loyal to the Republic, against the uprising militants and fascists. Under the battle cry, 'Fascism shall not pass; the hangmen of October shall not pass!' workers and farmers from all Spanish provinces are joining in the struggle against the enemies of the Republic that have arisen in arms.

Communists, Socialists, Anarchists and Republican Democrats, soldiers and forces remaining loyal to the Republic combined have inflicted the first defeats upon the fascist foe, who drag through the mud the very same honourable military tradition that they have boasted to possess so many times. The whole country cringes in indignation at these heartless barbarians that would hurl our democratic Spain back down into an abyss of terror and death. However, THEY SHALL NOT PASS! For all of Spain presents itself for battle. In Madrid, the people are out in the streets in support of the Government and encouraging its decision and fighting spirit so that it shall reach its conclusion in the smashing of the militant and fascist insurrection.

Young men, prepare for combat! Women, heroic women of the people! Recall the heroism of the women of Asturias of 1934 and struggle alongside the men in order to defend the lives and freedom of your sons, overshadowed by the fascist menace! Soldiers, sons of the nation! Stay true to the Republican State and fight side by side with the workers, with the forces of the Popular Front, with your parents, your siblings and comrades! Fight for the Spain of February the 16th, fight for the Republic and help them to victory! Workers of all stripes! The government supplies us with arms that we may save Spain and its people from the horror and shame that a victory for the bloody hangmen of October would mean. Let no one hesitate! All stand ready for action. All workers, all antifascists must now look upon each other as brothers in arms. Peoples of Catalonia, Basque Country, and Galicia! All Spaniards! Defend our democratic Republic and consolidate the victory achieved by our people on the 16th of February.

The Communist Party calls you to arms. We especially call upon you, workers, farmers, intellectuals, to assume your positions in the fight to finally smash the enemies of the Republic and of the popular liberties.

Long live the Popular Front! Long live the union of all anti-fascists!

Long live the Republic of the people!

The Fascists shall not pass!

THEY SHALL NOT PASS!

<u>HOW</u> SHE DID THAT

Conjure an audience

An interesting fact about this iconic speech is that it wasn't delivered directly to an audience. Instead, Dolores Ibárruri was broadcast over the radio, just like Winston Churchill in his famous 'We shall fight on the beaches' speech during the darkest times of World War II. In both cases, the speakers mustered the energy and verve of a live performance, summoning their presence to speak as though their audience were with them.

There is a lesson here for when you are delivering virtual presentations or speaking on platforms that distance you from your live audiences. You need to avoid sounding like you are speaking to yourself.

To animate your presentation, conjure an audience. Imagine a group of people is in the room with you and they are nodding and reacting to your words. You might even take a moment to create a handful of personas — name a supporter, for example, as well as a dissenter and a fence sitter.

Create unity

Dolores Ibárruri's battle cry was made in the name of all those loyal to Spain. Rather than only targeting other communists or even left-leaning compatriots, she scoops up every group she can think of: 'Communists, Socialists, Anarchists and Republican Democrats, soldiers and forces remaining loyal to the Republic'. She reaches beyond her ideological supporters with 'workers and farmers from all Spanish provinces'. Groups are made to feel included as they are specifically named: 'Peoples of Catalonia, Basque Country, and Galicia! All Spaniards!' This is a great technique to promote inclusivity.

When you are looking to generate commitment and action, even if facing active resistance, you will need as many supporters as possible. What can you do to name and capture otherwise disparate groups in your audience? Start by thinking about the different segments that might be represented — how can you break them down into subgroups? Consider gender, age, role, education, country of origin and length of tenure. Look for opportunities to call out a range of different groups. This both recognises people's identity and makes them feel included in the collective.

Make it personal

Dolores Ibárruri made the fight against fascism her life's work. Her commitment to preventing Franco's fascist takeover was all-consuming. We hear it in her words, which are absolute: 'Let no one hesitate!' We hear it in her tone — one of anger — as she implores support to 'smash the enemies of the Republic'. And we hear it in her condemnation of the enemy; they are 'militants' and 'hangmen'.

The tone of this address is imperative, and she leaves no room for equivocation. There is no 'gently does it' or even an attempt to offer a single concession. Yet, she demands nothing more from her listeners than she is willing to offer herself.

While you are unlikely to be making such a call to arms, you usually have an opportunity in most speeches or presentations to issue a call for action; to amp up your language and commitment. If you are angry (or frustrated, dismayed or excited), show us. Review your expression, examples and words to ensure alignment between the tone of your speech, your overall purpose and the way you deliver the message.

Too often we see an unnecessary downgrading of emotion in the context of a business presentation. Speakers tell us they are 'excited' with a deadpan expression, or ask the team to be passionate while failing to even show the slightest voice modulation.

Your audience will need to observe coherence between the words you use and your manner of delivery if you are to be believed, trusted and ultimately followed.

And on climate change, we have to acknowledge that we have failed. All political movements in their present form have done so, and the media has failed to create broad public awareness. But *Homo sapiens* have not yet failed.

Yes, we are failing but there is still time to turn everything around. We can still fix this.

Greta Thunberg

Greta Thunberg

Climate change activist

B: *3 January 2003, Stockholm, Sweden*

Our house is on fire

When: *25 January 2019*

Where: *Davos, Switzerland*

Audience: *3000 attendees of the World Economic Forum*

Greta Thunberg is a young Swedish woman who seized the attention of the world by loudly proclaiming her views on climate change. She speaks out as an advocate for radical climate change policy and refuses to accept any barrier that is thrown up as an excuse for anything but immediate radical change.

The striking characteristic that Thunberg exhibits is outrage. Anger can be polarising, certainly, but it will usually draw attention. The outrage of a child is what we see when Greta Thunberg speaks. She is willing to bring her anger to the stage at notable political and NGO gatherings. The contrast between her diminutive appearance and her vocal presence is stark.

Although emotion is always fuelling her words, she manages to keep it contained. Her focus is always on the goal — ruling what is acceptable and what is just playing at the margins. She refuses to be drawn on the minutiae of why certain policies won't work. The practicalities of implementation are not her concern. The role she adopts is the voice of necessary dissent. When she speaks it is to highlight what must be done, not to suggest a mere positive step in the right direction.

As a bright-eyed 16 year old, Greta Thunberg spoke at the Davos World Economic Forum in January 2019 in front of 3000 attendees from around the world as well as a significant media presence.

<u>WHAT</u> SHE SAID

66

Our house is on fire. I am here to say our house is on fire.

According to the IPCC, we are less than twelve years away from not being able to undo our mistakes. In that time, unprecedented changes in all aspects of society need to have taken place, including a reduction of our CO_2 emissions by at least 50 per cent.

And please note that those numbers do not include the aspect of equity, which is absolutely necessary to make the Paris Agreement work on a global scale; nor does it include tipping points or feedback loops like the extremely powerful methane gas released from the thawing Arctic permafrost.

At places like Davos, people like to tell success stories. But their financial success has come with an unthinkable price tag. And on climate change, we have to acknowledge that we have failed. All political movements in their present form have done so, and the media has failed to create broad public awareness. But *Homo sapiens* have not yet failed.

Yes, we are failing but there is still time to turn everything around. We can still fix this. We still have everything in our own hands. But unless we recognise the overall failures of our current systems we most probably don't stand a chance.

We are facing a disaster of unspoken sufferings for enormous amounts of people. And now is not the time for speaking politely or focusing on what we can or cannot say. Now is the time to speak clearly.

Solving the climate crisis is the greatest and most complex challenge that *Homo sapiens* have ever faced. The main solution, however, is so simple that even a small child can understand it. We have to stop our emissions of greenhouse gases. And either we do that or we don't.

You say nothing in life is black or white, but that is a lie. A very dangerous lie. Either we prevent a 1.5 degree of warming or we don't. Either we avoid setting off that irreversible chain reaction beyond human control or we don't. Either we choose to go on as a civilisation or we don't. That is as black or white as it gets. There are no grey areas when it comes to survival.

We all have a choice. We can create transformational action that will safeguard the future living conditions for humankind. Or we can continue with our business as usual, and fail. That is up to you and me.

Some say that we should not engage in activism. Instead we should leave everything to our politicians and just vote for change instead. But what do we do when there is no political will? What do we do when the politics needed are nowhere in sight? Here in Davos, just like everywhere else, everyone is talking about money. It seems that money and growth are our only main concerns. And since the climate crisis is a crisis that has never once been treated as a crisis, people are simply not aware of the full consequences on our everyday life. People are not aware that there is such a thing as a carbon budget, and just how incredibly small that remaining carbon budget is. And that needs to change today.

No other current challenge can match the importance of establishing a wide public awareness and understanding of our rapidly disappearing carbon budget that should and must become a new global currency and the very heart of future and present economics.

We are now at a time in history where everyone with any insight of the climate crisis that threatens our civilisation and the entire biosphere must speak out in clear language, no matter how uncomfortable and unprofitable that may be. We must change almost everything in our current societies. The bigger your carbon footprint is, the bigger your moral duty. The bigger your platform, the bigger your responsibility.

Adults keep saying, 'We owe it to the young people to give them hope.' But I don't want your hope. I don't want you to be hopeful. I want you to panic. I want you to feel the fear I feel every day. And then I want you to act. I want you to act as you would in a crisis. I want you to act as if the house was on fire. Because it is.

99

<u>HOW</u> SHE DID THAT

Choose a powerful metaphor

Greta Thunberg continues the metaphor of a house on fire — something at once universally understood and universally troubling. This house contains children — your children — who are already burning or in imminent danger. Thunberg shows us how a well-crafted metaphor can punctuate a message.

The metaphor is used in the title of the speech, outlined in her hook and further used to create a sense of imminent danger. Thunberg weaves her 'house on fire' imagery through her otherwise fact-infused presentation. Picking up the metaphor again in her conclusion, she successfully imprints the image in the minds of her audience.

Metaphors are such a powerful tool in communication, used to help elucidate meaning and cement understanding. Beware the overused metaphor — 'silver bullets', 'standing on a precipice' and 'rowing in the same direction' have been used to death. Look out for fresh imagery that will make your ideas stand out.

Shake up expected roles

The tone of Thunberg's address is one of condemnation, similar to a parent scolding a child who has been found out not doing what was expected of them — for being irresponsible. But Greta flips the roles. She is the child and has been forced into the role of the parent.

The casting of the roles is extended. Greta assumes the voice of all children — those who traditionally have no actual power but who have the deepest vested interest as heirs to the planet. She uses the first person plural throughout — it is 'we' and 'us' (the children, all of humankind).

In this game of role reversal, she scolds us for playing games, reducing the politics of ideology to a petty squabble as she decries the lack of political will to do what she asserts is needed.

We have been told. We must hang our collective child/adult heads in shame.

Have a clear purpose

Rarely do we hear such direct language used in the expression of the purpose in a speech. Without equivocation or apology Thunberg demands for emissions to be stopped to prevent further warming of 1.5 degrees.

She goes on to educate the audience, forcing a new perspective on what insufficient action looks like through her eyes. She lines up a series of policies, recasts them as peripheral at best and goes about swatting them out of the way. She demands clear language and encourages the audience to accept that it may be uncomfortable and unprofitable. Her speech is striking because she never wavers from the central purpose of her argument.

Thunberg's clarity of purpose transcends her 2019 Davos speech. In fact, we have all come to expect a certain manner and demeanour of forthright outrage every time she stands to speak. A year after this address, at her 2020 Davos speech, she escalated her demands, closing off any potential escape routes and calling for all organisations and countries to immediately stop all investment in the fossil fuel industries. She underscores the urgency of these actions and aligns her own style, pace and pitch to the message she successfully lands.

This is the outcome Thunberg demands. You might not agree, but you cannot say you don't understand exactly what she is calling for. She also clarifies whom she demands this of (everyone: government and business leaders) and she tells us by when (now!) with a clearly defined measure of success (a 1.5-degree target or lower). For a 16-year-old, she seems surprisingly well versed in the ubiquitous corporate SMART objectives.

Using humour to connect and persuade

In *King Lear*, Shakespeare wrote, 'Jesters do oft prove prophets'— another way of saying, 'Many a truth is spoken in jest'.

It may also be true that some truths are best spoken in jest. Humour is a great leveller and connector. Even when we are going through the most challenging situation imaginable, if someone can make us laugh, we will experience that moment of reprieve.

But is humour really a serious route to persuasion? When you look around, you can see much to support this position—and the fact that people may be entertained should not diminish humour as a valuable influence tactic. Of course, in some circumstances, humour might be the last resort, when all rational and emotional attempts have failed. Nellie McClung, the Canadian suffragette who staged a mock parliament, was never going to win a serious audience with the conservative premier who held all the power at the time. She was locked out and ignored. So she made him the butt of her joke. She pointed out the emperor wore no clothes. The result was hilarious—perhaps because she had such great raw materials to work with.

Comedy can also be cathartic. What irritates you but you just can't talk about? Do political correctness or rules of appropriate behaviour get in your way? Now, I'm not suggesting you completely disregard convention or decency, but some professional forums—meetings, conferences and town hall updates, for example—are just too damn boring. Consider the catharsis Dorothy Parker would have felt as she ripped into the superficiality of Hollywood—as only a New Yorker could. Actually, consider the catharsis we all feel when we hear the perfect Dorothy Parker zinger. As a leader, can you put your finger on that thing that everybody hates but nobody wants to talk about? If you can find it and expose it with a joke, you will give people a very satisfying release—and that could be just what you need to kickstart change.

The fact is you can get away with a lot more when you deliver your message in the form of a joke. Roxane Gay is a serious feminist academic.

She often speaks at events or participates in panel discussions and is tenacious and quite solemn. But then, we are gifted with her delightful TED Talk — 'Confessions of a bad feminist' — in which she shares the funniest admissions of her own guilty pleasures and flaws. This makes her and her message more approachable to those who might be resistant.

Broadening people's experience through humour is exemplified with panache by Ruby Wax in her TED Talk, 'What's so funny about mental illness?' As Wax shows in her talk, quite a lot is funny. In this speech, however, the jokes are not the point. The point is to raise awareness, which Wax succeeds at doing; it's just that comedy is the route she takes because that is her craft. It is wonderful to learn from somebody so skilled in the art.

Humour opens doors. If you are dealing with a group of people who resist you, your ideas, your position or the change you are trying to make, maybe a joke could help you get your foot on the very first step. Think of all the times you have been won over — when you didn't like somebody, perhaps, or thought you didn't — but then they made you laugh. It can work like magic. A well-timed and genuine joke can thaw even the most rigid opponent.

Do you need to be funny to be a good speaker? No, of course not. But you do need to be student of human psychology and learn to recognise when a laugh is the best medicine.

Man was made for something higher and holier than voting.

Nellie McClung

Nellie McClung

Author and suffragist

B: 20 October 1873, Chatsworth, ON, Canada

D: 1 September 1951, Victoria, BC, Canada

Should men vote?

When: 28 January 1914

Where: Manitoba, Canada

Audience: Mock parliament

In 1914, Nellie McClung, the Canadian author and suffragist, delivered a satirical address in a mock parliament performance, turning the tables on the prevailing wisdom of the day.

As an early proponent of the Christian women's temperance movement, you might expect McClung to be a thin-lipped, buttoned-up sort of feminist. But this speech reveals a funnier side to her nature. It is a satirical rendition of Canadian politics and a pastiche of her main opponent, the premier of Manitoba, and other male politicians of the time.

Perhaps McClung found nothing funny about the political realities of the day — when, for example, women were considered property of their fathers or husbands under the law. Surely she was not amused but annoyed at having her aspirations continually dashed in favour of more 'deserving' men. But in this speech, she found the humorous side to the predicament of women in Canada at the beginning of the twentieth century.

McClung was battling more than prejudice; she also had to endure the belittling remarks of the men in power, particularly the premier of Manitoba at the time, Rodmond Roblin. When McClung and others met with Premier Roblin in 1914, he flatly refused their request to give women the vote. Roblin went so far as to say in parliament that 'nice women' would not want the vote. Imagine the infuriating reaction this would have triggered.

This seems to be the final straw. McClung, a Canadian prairie woman, activist and apparently secret entertainer, decided to argue back. The evening following her meeting with Roblin, McClung turned his response in parliament into political theatre, selling tickets for a staged mock parliament production to raise awareness for the cause. The first performance was staged at the Walker Theatre in Winnipeg, Manitoba, and then once more in Winnipeg and later in Brandon, Manitoba.

Though clearly capable of rational debate, she spotted a glimmer of opportunity and burst through the door with a cutting satirical address, extracted here, in which she mocked the parliament, the prevailing power of men and the premier himself with all his pompous prejudice. After all, you cannot debate somebody who refuses to listen or even respect your right to speak.

In 1916, Manitoba became the first Canadian province to extend the vote to women.

WHAT SHE SAID

" Gentlemen of the delegation, it gives me great pleasure to welcome you here today. We like delegations, and although this is the first time you have asked us for the vote, we hope it will not be the last. Come any time and ask for anything you like. We wish to congratulate you, too, on the quiet and ladylike way in which you have come into our presence; and we assure you that if the working men in England had fought for their franchise in such a pleasing and dignified way, the results would have been entirely different. If they had used these peaceful means and no other, they might still be enjoying the distinction and privilege of waiting on members of Parliament.

But I cannot do what you ask me to do, for the facts are all against you. Manhood suffrage has not been a success in the unhappy countries where it has been tried. They either do not vote at all, or else they vote too much, and the best men shrink away from the polls as from a pestilence.

…Manhood suffrage would plunge our fair province into a perfect debauchery of extravagance, a perfect nightmare of expense. Think of the increased size of the voters list — we have trouble enough with it now. Of course, with the customary hot-headedness of reformers, you never thought of that, oh, no, just like a man, you never thought of the expense.

…I tell you frankly, I won't do it, for I have always loved and reverenced men. Yet though I love them, I know their frailties. If once they are let vote, they become addicted to it, and even if the polls are only open once every four years, I tell you, I know men, they are creatures of habit, and they'll hang around the polls all the rest of the time.

…Man was made for something higher and holier than voting. Men were made to support families and homes, which are the bulwark of the nation. What is home without a father? What is home without a bank account? The man who pays the grocer rules the world. In this agricultural province, man's place is the farm. Shall I call men away from the useful plough and the necessary harrow to talk loud on street corners about things which do not concern them? Shall I cheat the farm by turning honest ploughmen into dishonest and scheming politicians? I tell you no, for I was born on the farm and I am not ashamed to say so—the farm, the farm, the dear, old farm — we'll never mortgage the farm.

In the United States of America, when men vote, there is one divorce for every marriage, for politics unsettle men, and that leads to unsettled bills, and broken furniture, and broken vows. When you ask me for the vote, you are asking me to break up peaceful and happy homes and wreck innocent lives, and I tell you again, frankly, I will not do it. I am an old-fashioned woman; I believe in the sanctity of marriage. Politics unsettles men, and enters every department of life, with its blighting influence. It even confuses our vital statistics. They tell me that where men vote, when the election is very close, men have been known to come back and vote years after they were dead. Now, do you think I am going to let the hallowed calm of our cemeteries be invaded by the raucous voice of politics?

…I know I am a factor in the affairs of this province. If it were not for this fatal modesty, which on more than one occasion has almost blighted my career, I would say that I know I have written my name large across the province, so large indeed we had to move the boundaries to get it all in, and my most earnest wish for this bright land of promise is that I may long be spared to guide its destiny among the nations of the earth. I know there is no-one but me who can guide the ship of state. I actually tremble when I think what might happen to these leaderless lambs. But I must not dwell on such an overwhelming calamity, but go forward in the strong hope that I may long be spared to be the proud standard-bearer of the grand old flag of this grand old party, which has gone down many times to disgrace but, thank God, never defeat.

<u>HOW</u> SHE DID THAT

Fight absurdity with absurdity

Should women be allowed the right to vote? This was the question flicked away by Nellie McClung's provincial premier the previous day. Largely, his argument centred around the assumption that allowing women the vote would threaten the fabric of family life. He argued 'nice women don't want the vote' and to allow them to vote 'would be a retrograde movement' that would 'break up the home'.

How should one rebut such a ridiculous argument? How do you keep your frustration in check? In McClung's case, you answer with more ridicule — and a mock parliament address, heavy on the mockery.

Perhaps McClung felt that a logical refutation was too obvious, or that it would not capture the attention of her opponents. In any case, her retort was a satirical performance in which she exposed how silly the premier's arguments sounded when played back, with the genders reversed.

Pick your moment

So much of the potency of a speech springs from the speaker's ability to master the art of timing. The impetus for this parody by Nellie McClung was the patronising dismissal of what she felt was a justified and well-reasoned proposal. Shades of Julia Gillard can be seen here, finally reaching her boiling point and firing off her now famous 'misogyny speech' (refer to chapter 5).

McClung spins an unpleasant, potentially humiliating moment into an opportunity to win over supporters — or at least to make more people like her. Because she makes us laugh, we like her; because we like her, we are more likely to listen to what she has to say. And this is the magic of humour and persuasion — like the thin edge of the wedge, humour can force the door open.

If you have ever felt frustrated after being belittled in some way, no matter how subtle, try to resist the urge to shrink away in silence. McClung shows us that if you can find the nerve to laugh, to use humour to underscore the ridiculousness of your antagonist, you are far more likely to generate support.

Persuade stealthily

Some hidden genius is at work behind this otherwise entertaining piece. Of course, you hear the sarcasm, the humour and the withering impact of such a blatant pastiche. But what you also get is a bright light shone on the deceptive reasoning at play among the powerbrokers of the day.

Though Nellie McClung created and delivered this piece with her tongue firmly lodged in her cheek, you can observe the vestiges of a thorough rebuttal. One by one, McClung dismantles the arguments against female suffrage by exposing the flawed reasoning.

Here are a few examples of her stealthy logical refutation.

A 'slippery slope' is a fallacy created in an argument that assumes a transition, usually downward, from A to B to C. Each movement downwards is presented as inevitable — a necessary outcome — but it is not. McClung uses this construction when she says, 'politics unsettle men, and that leads to unsettled bills, and broken furniture, and broken vows'. The slippery slope McClung sets up here is that allowing men to enter politics will 'logically' lead to divorce.

Another device is the 'red herring' — used as an attempt at distraction. Here, random, unrelated but attention-seeking little facts are launched into an argument. They can be pesky because they capture and distract attention. McClung includes a red herring when she argues, 'men have been known to come back and vote years after they were dead.'

Finally, an 'ad hominem' attack is when you attack the person not the argument. McClung also uses this for satirical effect, jumping between categorising men who want the vote as 'hot-headed' reformers and frail beings, vulnerable to addiction. Look out for this fallacy at work when you hear insults peppered through somebody's remarks.

I first went out to Hollywood — oh, many, many years ago. Soooooo long ago that the movie actresses looked flat-chested.

Dorothy Parker

Dorothy Parker

Writer, critic and satirist

B: 22 August 1893, Long Branch, NJ, United States

D: 7 June 1967, New York City, NY, United States

Hollywood, the land I won't return to

When: 10 May 1953

Where: Circle-In-the-Square, New York City, United States

Audience: 1500 people at a ticketed event

With Dorothy Parker's reputation as a sharp-tongued master of wit, you would expect her rant on Hollywood to contain a few scorching burns. You would be correct.

Her remarks are not unfounded — the writer lived and worked in Hollywood for many years but, for her, it always came up short when compared to her home, New York City.

Parker wrote prolifically during her time in Hollywood. She worked as a freelance screenwriter for several movie studios, sometimes collaborated on projects with her husband, Alan Campbell, and even contributed lyrics to songs created by Ralph Rainger and Bing Crosby. It is fair to say she gave Hollywood a good go, so she knew of what she spoke.

The post-war years could be a challenging time for an outspoken politically aware woman like Dorothy Parker, where 'outspoken' would be an understatement. She lent her voice to various causes, including anti-fascism, and landed herself with a 1000+ page dossier with the

FBI. She was listed as a communist and eventually subpoenaed by Joseph McCarthy (during his infamous investigations and hearings into communism in the United States).

At an organised and ticketed performance at Circle-In-the-Square, New York City, in May 1953, Dorothy Parker delivered this one-off piece that she titled, 'Hollywood, the land I won't return to'. In the extracts provided here, look out for classic Dorothy Parker jests, and a model for how to use humour to pave the way.

<u>WHAT</u> SHE SAID

I should have written my speech out to be a little more coherent, but you see what happened. I had a broken wrist. When I go offsides, I want to tell you about it. I have a little dog, a little poodle named Misty, and was taking her for a walk. Well, she stopped suddenly and I didn't. And so when I was in a great cast, and slings and bandages, and all the appurtenances, a ludy who lives in the same building I do came up to me and said, 'What happened to you?' I said, 'Well, I fell over Misty and broke my wrist.' And you know, people say the damnedest things. You know what she said? She said, 'Ah, poor little Misty.'

I think it is an enormous impudence of me to come here and talk to you today. It got me coming down in the cab — the enormity of what I am doing, getting up here and talking to you people. I thought, *What in heaven's name am I doing, doing this?* Then I had one glorious moment when I thought, *I can take just a minute, and I don't have to speak* — but I was stuck here. That's not nice to say because a long time ago the gentleman who runs the theatre said for me to come down here. Well, I thought it just great. I don't know what gets into you as you say that. I suppose it was that in this very room Geraldine Page was discovered.

So I said to the gentleman, 'Well, yes, but what shall I talk about?' And he said, 'Just talk about things like writing in Hollywood.' And so, if you will let me, I'd like to talk about Hollywood. You see, I can talk about Hollywood only from the position of a writer there — 'cause I was supposed to write for many, many years. I wasn't there the whole time. It really was a year on and off, but it seems to me I was there for centuries. Now, I must tell you that the writer goes to Hollywood and just calls himself a writer like those out there. Oh, no, some people leave, and come back, but they write there. You can call yourself a writer, which is a great name, you know, but in Hollywood you can be a writer. You don't need any talent — the last thing you want is talent. You need two things: you need skill and you need a fine memory so that if you know what they did in that wild picture in 1938 ... you're in! You also need, I can't do it, but you need a manual process, which is polishing apples.

Well, I first...is this boring you?...I first went out to Hollywood — oh, many, many years ago. Soooooo long ago that the movie actresses looked flat-chested. When I went out there, I found they were doing very curious things. I went out there the way everybody goes out there, with sheets of paper folded. You know ... I went out. It was a time so long ago they were having what is called 'theme songs'. They did a picture called *I came after to write a theme song*. They told me there had been a picture called *Woman Disputed* and that the theme song was 'Woman Disputed, I Love You'. But I came out to work on a picture called *Dynamite* and you can't very well say 'Dynamite, I Love You'.

So anyway I thought, I was young and prudent, I might go into the producer and see what the picture was about. The producer was Mr Cecil DeMille. So I got in, well, it was like riding a camel through the eye of a needle. But I finally did get in and I said, 'Just tell me what this picture's about.' Well, it was so long and so involved I couldn't possibly remember it to tell you. I do know one thing, that the hero had been accused and convicted of murder — of course, unjustly. He was in the death cell, you see, but luckily had his guitar with him. So I was asked to write the song he would sing.

I got a little nervous while Mr DeMille was telling me all these things and I went back to my office. First, I had said, 'Mr DeMille, the details of these pictures must be...my goodness, it's just staggering.' He said, 'Ah, yes, zebras in the King of Kings.' So I went back to my office and I got a Bible and I felt what in heaven's name are zebras doing in that picture about the life of Christ? I thought, Maybe he said Hebrews?' I couldn't stand it and you can understand why.

Later when I ran into him I asked, 'What are you doing with zebras?' He said, 'Oh, the zebras. They were pulling the chariots of the Magdalene.' He said, 'Terrible, they kick so easily but their legs broke.' You know, well, that was pretty fancy. I should have known this.

…Now I want to talk, I can talk about it, say, from a writer's standpoint. The actors — it seems to me they have an awfully good time. They keep giving one another prizes and they have all this. The writers I think have a fairly tough time, except I didn't. They go out there as I told you. They don't need any talent. They used to. I don't know … things are different. You used to get an awful lot of money. Ladies and gentlemen, there was one time I was so rich I thought that detective stories were wonderful. I think things are different now. Nonetheless, they think they will go out there and they will get this much money, then they will come back east, south or wherever they live, and write that great play about coal miners. They don't … something happens. Nothing comes out of that place. I think, I'm really fairly sure in saying, nothing does.

…Oh, I forgot to tell you, everybody writes. Everybody writes. I was watching a producer who shall be nameless … it's David Selznick. But, anyway, he would come in bashfully, never got in till 6 o'clock in the afternoon and the poor people had to stay on working. And he would say, 'No, not this.' So you change it and the world was made for you and I.

No, I just think that you can't do it. You can't write out there, unless they send you someplace else and then you've made your name someplace else. I would start this little fashion by saying, 'If I hear one say one good word about Hollywood, I hope you'll all do me the courtesy to get up and go home.' But, you know, I find that I can't. Because a place besides Hollywood, or a place besides anything … there must be some people who are brave, gentle, courageous and intelligent, and they are in Hollywood, but oh my God, they are a minority group.

I don't know, I think the great, great trouble is the terrible fear. And I don't mean that just politically. They were scared before. When you say, 'do another' that means fear, doesn't it? Now there they are and look what comes out of it. Well look what once came out of it ... a man who made that place a name in history. A man who made that place a glory, spread that glory around the world. So they kicked out Charlie Chaplin. I don't know if you have the misfortune to read the Hollywood columnists, but I do. What they say about him is so much bunk. They say that he made a great deal of money in America. Well, he's earned a great deal of money in America. Possibly his pictures made money that was almost proportionate to the pleasure they gave. They say America gave him money ... oh, they didn't give him money. He worked for years and years and years. He employed people loyally and generously. So they say he's been given money and a letter with parsley around it. Oh that's the kind of thing they do ... they throw out the only good person they can.

...I don't know what more to say about Hollywood. I just say it is a Stagnation. It is a Horror. The palm trees have been brought in, the poor dears, they died on their feet. Brilliant flowers smell like old dollar bills. Those enormous vegetables taste as if they had been grown in old trunks. That way of having no seasons ... it's just terrible, you can't have any dates. They haven't Easter. Except at Christmas your agent sends you a blotter. I don't know. It's much worse than that now. When I was there — it was pretty bad then. I can only give to you, this message — anybody who isn't living in Hollywood is having a good life!

<u>HOW</u> SHE DID THAT

Play with stream of consciousness

Stream of consciousness is a narrative technique that allows the reader, or the listener, to glimpse inside the mind of the storyteller. If you've read *Catcher in the Rye*, you would be familiar with this spin on storytelling technique. Rather than long swathes of description, we are swept along with the natural if erratic thought patterns of the protagonist and we are jolted by the punchy, spare dialogue.

Dorothy Parker uses this technique in her roast on Hollywood and it works to keep us with her as she rants (in the full version) for more than three thousand words. Rants can be satisfying, particularly if you share in the sentiment of the speaker — as this New York audience likely did. You might recognise that this device is commonly used by stand-up comics — the classic, 'So I was on my way here this evening ...' — as a set up for their situational joke to follow.

Parker maintains the stream of consciousness approach throughout her speech. It has the effect of making us think she is making up her words as she goes along. It feels conversational, inclusive and a bit exciting. Right from the beginning, she releases the tension by fake telling us that she should have 'written my speech out to be a little more coherent' if it weren't for an unfortunate incident involving her pet poodle. She starts us off with a little dark comedy plus a dash of self-deprecating humour, mixed in with her trademark wit, and we are hooked.

You don't have to be funny or capable of Parker-worthy burns to employ this technique in your own speaking style. When telling a story or recounting an event, can you find an opportunity to insert yourself into the story? This will make your audience feel like they are having the experience with you. They will become invested in the challenges that you faced and they will be on your side when you reveal the solution — or the punchline.

Create images that linger

As a career writer, Dorothy Parker was a master of language. Some of her more subtle techniques could be overlooked, but they are at play in the shadows of her more obvious remarks.

Your job as a speaker is to get your audience to appreciate your point of view. If in appreciating your point of view you would like them to form a similar conclusion to your own, you might like to explore the sensory pathways. Create images that are beautiful or moving if you want them to feel kind-hearted towards you. Or if you want them to join you in a sense of disgust, conjure odious smells or ugly vistas.

Parker provides examples of this technique throughout the speech, but the images that leap out are those she stuffs into her final paragraph. We can see the pathetic transplanted palm trees, smell the old dollar bills and taste the cardboard-like insipid vegetables.

Know your style

At the time of her appearance at the Circle-In-The-Square, Dorothy Parker had been doing her 'Dorothy Parker' act for some time. The famous 'Algonquin Table' of wits from New York in the 1920s was years behind her. By this stage in her career, she had produced multiple works of fiction, written many screenplays and dazzled countless salons. It is fair to say she knew how to work a room. More than that, she had crafted, refined and cultivated her unique voice.

You can tell that Parker is at ease with her style and with her performance because the words just flow. It is more than likely that moments in this piece were unscripted. You can imagine her, in the theatre, locking eyes with somebody in the crowd and delivering her lines. Had you been there, you might have felt she was speaking to you over a bottle of wine. This easy flow is just the outward representation of a lot of practice.

You don't need to — and nor should you — emulate Parker's style when delivering your own presentations. If you are not naturally funny, don't try to suddenly land a zinger. If you do not possess her particular gift for sarcasm, don't go there. Instead, build your awareness of the impression you make, cultivate an image of how you would like to be perceived and aim for the outcome instead — which is an easy, natural presence in front of a room.

I firmly believe in 'man work', which is anything I don't want to do, including all domestic tasks, but also: bug killing, trash removal, lawn care and vehicle maintenance. I want no part of any of that.

Roxane Gay

Roxane Gay

Writer, academic and social commentator

B: 15 October 1974, Omaha, NB, United States

Confessions of a bad feminist

When: 28 May 2015

Where: Monterey, California, United States

Audience: TEDWoman event

A humorous take on a serious matter when skilfully handled can magically draw people in. In most cases, we'd rather be entertained than educated.

The TEDWoman event in 2015 was held in Monterey, California. The session themes and speaker bios indicate anyone attending would have needed to buckle up for some stirring feminist platform-making speeches.

Among the line-up was Roxane Gay, a US writer, college professor, activist and social commentator. Her scheduled appearance fitted in perfectly. She is the author of several books, including *Bad Feminist* — a collection of essays on society and popular culture and Gay's own evolution as a woman and feminist. Some essays highlight her personal resistance to the label of feminism and how she came to shift her mindset. That book and its ensuing attention created the foundation and inspiration for this talk.

The speech extracted here (and with over 2 million views online) is legendary because it makes people laugh. Her jokes are the pressure-release valve we all need. In a genre where topics can often be oh-so-serious, Gay is a serious contender. She is seriously well-informed, educated and articulate. But, on this occasion, she was also seriously funny.

Her humour is self-deprecating and identity-deprecating. Someone so accomplished allowing us to see the lighter side is a relief. Her discursive style doesn't prevent her from landing her entreaty: 'I hope that we can all be a little bit brave, when we most need such bravery'.

Roxane Gay is no less a feminist for any of her badness.

WHAT SHE SAID

I am failing as a woman. I am failing as a feminist.

I have passionate opinions about gender equality, but I worry that to freely accept the label of 'feminist' would not be fair to good feminists. I'm a feminist but I'm a rather bad one. So I call myself a 'bad feminist'. Or at least I wrote an essay and then I wrote a book called *Bad Feminist*. And then in interviews people started calling me 'the bad feminist'. So, what started as a bit of an inside joke with myself and a wilful provocation has become a *thing*.

Let me take a step back. When I was younger, mostly in my teens and twenties, I had strange ideas about feminists as hairy, angry, man-hating, sex-hating women. As if those are bad things. These days I look at how women are treated the world over and anger in particular seems like a perfectly reasonable response. But back then I worried about the tone people used when suggesting I might be a feminist. The feminist label was an accusation. It was an F-word and not a nice one. I was labelled a woman who doesn't play by the rules. Who expects too much. Who thinks far too highly of myself for daring to believe I am equal or superior to a man. You don't want to be that rebel woman — until you realise you very much are that woman and cannot imagine being anyone else.

As I got older, I began to accept that I am indeed a feminist and a proud one. I hold certain truths to be self-evident. Women are equal to men. We deserve equal pay for equal work. We have the right to move through the world as we choose, free from harassment or violence. We have the right to easy affordable access to birth control and reproductive services. We have the right to make choices about our bodies, free from legislative oversight or evangelical doctrine. We have the right to respect.

There's more. When we talk about the needs of women, we have to consider the other identities we inhabit. We are not just women;

we are people with different bodies, gender expressions, faiths, sexualities, class backgrounds, abilities and so much more. We need to take into account these differences and how they affect us as much as we account for what we have in common. Without this kind of inclusion, our feminism is nothing.

I hold these truths to be self-evident but let me be clear, I am a mess. I am full of contradictions. There are many ways in which I am doing feminism wrong.

I have another confession. When I drive to work, I listen to thuggish rap at a very loud volume. Even though the lyrics are degrading to women. These lyrics offend me to my core — the classic Ying Yang Twins song 'Salt Shaker' — it is amazing. 'Make it work with your wet T-shirt. Bitch, you gotta shake it till your camel starts to hurt!' Think about it. Poetry, right? I am utterly mortified by my music choices.

I firmly believe in 'man work', which is anything I don't want to do, including all domestic tasks, but also: bug killing, trash removal, lawn care and vehicle maintenance. I want no part of any of that. Pink is my favourite colour. I enjoy fashion magazines and pretty things. I watch *The Bachelor* and romantic comedies, and I have absurd fantasies about fairy tales coming true.

…Too many women, particularly groundbreaking women and industry leaders, are afraid to be labelled as feminists. They're afraid to stand up and say, 'Yes, I am a feminist', for fear of what that label means, for fear of being unable to live up to unrealistic expectations.

Take, for example, Beyoncé or, as I call her, The Goddess. She has emerged, in recent years, as a visible feminist. At the 2014 MTV Video Music Awards, she performed in front of the word 'feminist' 10-feet high. It was a glorious spectacle to see this pop star openly embracing feminism and letting young women and men know that being a feminist is something to celebrate. As the moment faded, cultural critics began endlessly debating whether or not Beyoncé was, indeed, a feminist. They graded her feminism, instead of simply taking a grown, accomplished woman at her word.

We demand perfection from feminists, because we are still fighting for so much, we want so much, we need so damn much.

We go far beyond reasonable, constructive criticism, to dissecting any given woman's feminism, tearing it apart until there's nothing left. We do not need to do that. Bad feminism — or really, more inclusive feminism — is a starting point.

…We can also boldly claim our feminism — good, bad, or anywhere in between. The last line of my book *Bad Feminist* says, 'I would rather be a bad feminist than no feminist at all'. This is true for so many reasons but, first and foremost, I say this because once upon a time, my voice was stolen from me, and feminism helped me to get my voice back.

…In one hand, I hold the power to accomplish anything. And in my other, I hold the humbling reality that I am just one woman.

I am a bad feminist, I am a good woman. I am trying to become better in how I think, and what I say, and what I do, without abandoning everything that makes me human. I hope that we can all do the same. I hope that we can all be a little bit brave, when we most need such bravery.

<u>HOW</u> SHE DID THAT

Be approachable

The thing about contentious issues is that they tend to divide. Sure, there is a time to fight and a time to preach. But what Roxane Gay has cleverly recognised here is that there can also be a time to joke around. If she were to stridently make her case and pit herself against the imagined opposition, she would likely only repel those predisposed to disagree. Instead, humour is used as the bridge to a new middle ground.

Gay's humour is directed at those who might oppose the feminist movement, along with those who are firm believers and for the enjoyment of all. This talk lands beautifully for people who get it. They can connect with Gay's fundamental commitment to her beliefs as well as her self-evaluation of her tiny acts of misalignment. They know themselves to be flawed — no matter how strong the commitment, we can all be very bad at being good. Others, perhaps less committed, might be surprised that it can be fun to be good.

You can find many other instances of Gay's appearances that have a far more serious, even at times combative, tone. These are also powerful in their own right, but perhaps not quite as effective at reaching the ears of her opponents and supporters alike. Humour will draw the audience to you and hopefully to your message as well.

Be yourself, be different, be endearing

Likeability is subjective. And yet, being moved by a speech usually involves some sort of connection being formed with the speaker. Even though this is a big-ticket event, Roxane Gay presents herself in a casual manner as she tells us of her love of inappropriate rap lyrics and fairy-tale endings.

The alchemy of Gay's appearance, language and expression makes us feel like we have been invited to be part of some inner circle. She is confessing some of her flaws, as you might if surrounded by friends — the people you already know, like and trust. This makes us feel we know, like and trust her.

A likely way to make yourself forgettable is to adhere to the rules of the game. Deliver what is expected, no matter how competently, and you won't really stand out. This event included many speakers, with pedigrees as impressive as Gay's. Many fine speeches were delivered at the event, along with myriad statistics, pleas for action and strident calls. The danger of doing what is expected is that you are quickly forgotten.

Nobody at this event would be likely to forget the belly laugh delivered by the bad feminist.

Remove the barriers to receptivity

Roxane Gay uses the TED stage to extend an invitation to the 'club' of feminists. Her approach involves removing one big potential barrier — the feeling that one may not fit in. She expresses her own hesitancy in accepting the label of 'feminist' — the modern 'F-word'. A label that often casts its members in a negative light. You might ask yourself, 'Is that a badge I really want to wear?' Gay delivers a personal account of one woman's struggle to step into the role. More than that, women such as Gay help to shape what we all perceive to be the image of a feminist.

With all the bad press, maybe you are just playing with the idea of identifying as a feminist. Perhaps a dose of imposter syndrome is holding you back. Perhaps a niggling thought that the clubhouse doesn't look much fun has meant you never learned the secret handshake. Knowing that a leading thinker in the field has also felt this way can be reassuring. Now your last remaining barriers have disappeared.

Speakers don't have to be funny, endearing or unique to be effective, but here is an example of how it can certainly work in your favour.

I'm sorry to be the bearer of bad news, but somebody has to be. Your pets are happier than you are. So kitty cat, meow, happy, happy, happy; human beings, screwed. Completely and utterly — so screwed.

Ruby Wax

Ruby Wax

Comedian and mental health advocate

B: *19 April 1953, Evanston, IL, United States*

What's so funny about mental illness?

When: *27 June 2012*

Where: *Edinburgh, Scotland*

Audience: *TEDGlobal*

What is so funny about mental health? What a premise with which to open a speech. But, of course, this is the perfect place to start if you are known as the funny lady. If your reputation was built on making people laugh, why not use that power to raise awareness for a serious issue. In this case, actor, writer and comedian Ruby Wax used her skills as a comic to make a difficult topic more approachable. (Born in the United States, Wax now lives in the United Kingdom.)

Humour is a great leveller. In our modern 'woke' world, we are afraid to openly discuss so many topics. This usually doesn't help a situation. We need to find ways to be uncomfortable and to confront the difficult parts of our existence that might feel shameful or embarrassing. What comedians can do is release that pressure valve. By getting us to laugh, they 'prime the pump', making it possible to listen more attentively to more serious points.

In this speech at TEDGlobal in Edinburgh, Ruby Wax candidly shares her own experience with mental illness. While this is a somewhat educational TED Talk, it is also very personal. The content would not have been nearly so effective if it did not come with the element of personal experience. She leads us to a deeper understanding by being the first to laugh at herself, making it okay for us to chuckle along. Then we are on the inside — we are there with her and we have a better grasp of her experience.

This talk, and Wax's advocacy of mental health in general, is amped up in the credibility department because she holds a master's degree in Mindfulness & Cognitive Therapy from Oxford, and she was awarded the OBE in 2015 for her services to mental health. Not just a funny lady, she is also a credible source of scientific information, data and empirical evidence.

Ruby Wax is a delight to watch in the 2012 TED Talk extracted here (and with more than 3 million views online). Be entertained, and be enlightened.

<u>WHAT</u> SHE SAID

One in four people suffer from some sort of mental illness. So if it was one, two, three, four, it's you, sir. You. Yeah. With the weird teeth. And you next to him. You know who you are. Actually, that whole row isn't right. That's not good. Hi. Yeah. Real bad. Don't even look at me.

I am one of the one in four. Thank you. I think I inherit it from my mother, who used to crawl around the house on all fours. She had two sponges in her hand, and then she had two tied to her knees. My mother was completely absorbent. (Laughter) And she would crawl around behind me going, 'Who brings footprints into a building?!' So that was kind of a clue that things weren't right. So before I start, I would like to thank the makers of Lamotrigine, Sertraline and Reboxetine, because without those few simple chemicals, I would not be vertical today.

…Because, you know, the one thing, one thing that you get with this disease, this one comes with a package, is you get a real sense of shame, because your friends go, 'Oh, come on, show me the lump, show me the x-rays', and, of course, you've got nothing to show, so you're, like, really disgusted with yourself because you're thinking, *I'm not being carpet-bombed. I don't live in a township.* So you start to hear these abusive voices, but you don't hear one abusive voice, you hear about a thousand — 100000 abusive voices, like if the Devil had Tourette's, that's what it would sound like.

But we all know in here, you know, there is no Devil, there are no voices in your head. You know that when you have those abusive voices, all those little neurons get together, and in that little gap you get a real toxic 'I want to kill myself' kind of chemical, and if you have that over and over again on a loop tape, you might have yourself depression. Oh, and that's not even the tip of the iceberg. If you get a little baby, and you abuse it verbally, its little brain sends out chemicals that are so destructive that the little part of its brain that can tell good from bad just doesn't grow, so you might have yourself a homegrown psychotic. If a soldier sees his friend blown up, his brain goes into such high alarm that he can't actually put the experience into words, so he just feels the horror over and over again.

So here's my question. My question is how come when people have mental damage, it's always an active imagination? How come every other organ in your body can get sick and you get sympathy, except the brain?

I'd like to talk a little bit more about the brain, because I know you like that here at TED, so if you just give me a minute here, okay. Okay, let me just say, there's some good news. There is some good news. First of all, let me say, we've come a long, long way. We started off as a teeny, teeny little one-celled amoeba, tiny, just sticking onto a rock, and now, voila, the brain. Here we go. (Laughter) This little baby has a lot of horsepower. It comes completely conscious. It's got state-of-the-art lobes. We've got the occipital lobe so we can actually see the world. We got the temporal lobe so we can actually hear the world. Here we've got a little bit of long-term memory, so, you know that night you want to forget, when you got really drunk? Bye-bye! Gone. So actually, it's filled with 100 billion neurons just zizzing away, electrically transmitting information, zizzing, zizzing.

…But I got a little bad news for you folks. I got some bad news. This isn't for the one in four. This is for the four in four. We are not equipped for the twenty-first century. Evolution did not prepare us for this. We just don't have the bandwidth, and for people who say, oh, they're having a nice day, they're perfectly fine — they're more insane than the rest of us. Because I'll show you where there might be a few glitches in evolution. Okay, let me just explain this to you. When we were ancient man — millions of years ago — and we suddenly felt threatened by a predator, okay? We would — Thank you. I drew these myself. Thank you.

Anyway, we would fill up with our own adrenaline and our own cortisol, and then we'd kill or be killed, we'd eat or we'd be eaten, and then suddenly we'd de-fuel, and we'd go back to normal. Okay. So the problem is, nowadays, with modern man, when we feel in danger, we still fill up with our own chemical. But because we can't kill traffic wardens or eat estate agents, the fuel just stays in our body over and over, so we're in a constant state of alarm, a constant state.

And here's another thing that happened. About 150 000 years ago, when language came online, we started to put words to this constant emergency, so it wasn't just, 'Oh my God, there's a saber-toothed tiger,' which could be, it was suddenly, 'Oh my God, I didn't send the email. Oh my God, my thighs are too fat. Oh my God, everybody can see I'm stupid. I didn't get invited to the Christmas party!' So you've got this nagging loop tape that goes over and over again that drives you insane, so, you see what the problem is? What once made you safe, now drives you insane. I'm sorry to be the bearer of bad news, but somebody has to be. Your pets are happier than you are. So kitty cat, meow, happy, happy, happy; human beings, screwed. Completely and utterly — so screwed.

But my point is if we don't talk about this stuff, and we don't learn how to deal with our lives, it's not going to be one in four. It's going to be four in four who are really, really going to get ill in the upstairs department. And while we're at it, can we please stop the stigma? Thank you.

99

<u>HOW</u> SHE DID THAT

Connect with individual humans

Ruby Wax has a beguiling style that has everything to do with her ability to connect with people. Not with 'people' in the conceptual sense, but with actual people — individual humans. She will look out into the crowd, lock eyes with someone, slow down a little, and smile and nod. For a second, that person is completely drawn into her world. Everyone else sees this happening and maybe they lean forward a bit, knowing they might be next.

It is really quite enchanting. Sure, she can land a joke, but first we need to want to hear them. I could listen to Wax explain how to create a pivot table and be entertained the whole time.

For Wax, this is a characteristic she has likely honed through her years as a stand-up artist, but it is such a simple technique anyone can adopt. The trick is to think about the audience as a collection of humans who are already your friends. You are not talking to a crowd, you are chatting with your mates.

Before you begin, set your belief that the people in the room already know and like you. Engage individuals through eye contact, smiling and nodding. Whatever you do, don't spend the whole talk looking at your screen or over their heads, and definitely don't picture them naked.

Play and have fun

This talk is just so much fun to watch. Why is it fun? Because Ruby Wax is having fun. She is obviously prepared and knows the points she will cover, but she lets herself go in the moment. She gets a little excited and races ahead of herself a bit, but this is endearing. It all comes together to create the overall impression that this is all for us, not her.

Clearly comfortable on stage and conversant in the subject matter, she eschews the technical diagrams and charts. Instead, we get a plasticine brain and hand-drawn stick puppet things. We are put at ease because she uses these childlike show-and-tell props to invite us into the sandpit with her. And so, what might otherwise be a rather heavy and serious subject becomes a delight.

Some topics do not lend themselves to jokes and stunts, I hear you say. Well, if Ruby Wax can talk about her own traumatic experience with mental illness and make us laugh at the same time, you might want to have a re-think. It seems everything has a humorous side, so long as the right person with the right to make the jokes is on the stage.

Anchor to a central message

Ruby Wax wants us to take two things away from this talk. Firstly, we should all be more aware of mental illness so that we stand a chance to do something about it. Secondly, we need to get rid of the stigma.

She makes her thesis explicit at the conclusion of the talk, but everything else is in service of her purpose. Her 'why' is clear and her 'how' makes the best use of her innate skill — humour. The laughter is her way of building a connection with the audience but, in this example, getting the laugh is not enough. We must also formulate a better, more compassionate appreciation for mental illness — and we do.

Encouraging inclusion

Messages of inclusivity require evidence of action. Telling people that they should encourage diversity isn't enough.

In order to inspire change, you must also show people that you are inclusive through openness, awareness and your willingness to learn. The speeches included in this chapter are gentle nudges in the right direction. By using 'we' and 'us', as these speakers do, you will signal your intent. By sharing information that is neither overly pessimistic nor fancifully optimistic, you will demonstrate your pragmatic approach.

Speeches that encourage inclusion often have a moral or ethical component. The speaker knows it and the audience knows it too, so preachiness is to be avoided. By referencing shared values, you can anchor your thesis to the better part of human nature, encouraging individual and group behaviour that serves the common good.

When New Zealand Prime Minister Jacinda Ardern spoke in remembrance of the people who were murdered in the Christchurch mosque attacks, she both signalled and exemplified national support for the families of the victims. Ardern's moving 'They were New Zealanders. They are us' speech highlights her enviable capacity to demonstrate empathy that in no way weakens her ability to lead.

Faith Bandler, the Australian activist for Indigenous rights, manages to deliver a heartfelt message of hope without a hint of revisionism for the sins of the past. With grace and compassion, she champions the move towards reconciliation.

Indira Gandhi demonstrates the strongest possible personal commitment to inclusion by putting her own life on the line. She was aware, before delivering her final speech in 1984, that her life was on the line. She had received the death threats but decided that delivering her speech in person was a necessary manifestation of the message.

Linda Burney was the first Australian Aboriginal woman to be elected to the House of Representatives in the Australian federal parliament. Her inaugural speech to parliament is a poignant artefact of reconciliation. Throughout her address, she balances her respect for the formalities and traditions of the legislature with a heartfelt commitment to the multicultural electorate she represents and the Wiradjuri people from whom she is descended.

Something to take away from these examples, and many others that you may have heard, is the requirement for coherence. Your objective will be instantly lost if your audience senses a lack of alignment between what you say and what you do. People tend to recoil from hypocrisy, so you should first look for ways to demonstrate, through your actions, how you have adopted the spirit of inclusivity.

On a quiet Friday afternoon, a man stormed into a place of peaceful worship and took away the lives of 50 people. That quiet Friday afternoon has become our darkest of days.

Jacinda Ardern

Jacinda Ardern

Prime Minister of New Zealand

B: 26 July 1980, Hamilton, New Zealand

They were New Zealanders. They are us

When: 28 March 2019

Where: Christchurch, New Zealand

Audience: The people of New Zealand

On 15 March 2019, the small country of New Zealand suffered a dreadful trauma. A terrorist attacked worshippers in a mosque in Christchurch, resulting in the deaths of 50 people.

In the days following the tragic mass shooting, New Zealand Prime Minister Jacinda Ardern addressed her parliament in Wellington, the nation's capital. Much has been said about Ardern's leadership style, especially with regards to her communication ability and demonstrative empathy.

Without doubt, Ardern is a people person. She has an innate ability to form instant human connections — in person, and via her speeches and media addresses. She is not afraid to show vulnerability and to share in the pain others have experienced. Consider her voice in contrast with other global political contemporaries. Her personal power and credibility is amplified by what she does not say or do. She offers no self-aggrandisement, no political point-scoring and no dog-whistling.

The poignant address extracted here is a valuable lesson in how a leader can make a difference through their words, reflecting on public sentiment, projecting strength and providing much-needed reassurance.

WHAT SHE SAID

Mr Speaker, Al salam Alaikum. Peace be upon you. And peace be upon all of us.

…On a quiet Friday afternoon, a man stormed into a place of peaceful worship and took away the lives of 50 people.

That quiet Friday afternoon has become our darkest of days.

But for the families, it was more than that.

It was the day that the simple act of prayer — of practising their Muslim faith and religion — led to the loss of their loved ones' lives.

Those loved ones were brothers, daughters, fathers and children.

They were New Zealanders. They are us.

And because they are us, we, as a nation, we mourn them.

We feel a huge duty of care to them. And Mr Speaker, we have so much we feel the need to say and to do.

One of the roles I never anticipated having, and hoped never to have, is to voice the grief of a nation.

At this time, it has been second only to securing the care of those affected, and the safety of everyone.

And in this role, I wanted to speak directly to the families.

We cannot know your grief, but we can walk with you at every stage. We can.

…Mr Speaker, there is one person at the centre of this act of terror against our Muslim community in New Zealand.

A 28-year-old man — an Australian citizen — has been charged with one count of murder. Other charges will follow.

He will face the full force of the law in New Zealand. The families of the fallen will have justice.

He sought many things from his act of terror, but one was notoriety.

And that is why you will never hear me mention his name.

He is a terrorist. He is a criminal. He is an extremist.

But he will, when I speak, be nameless.

And to others, I implore you: speak the names of those who were lost, rather than the name of the man who took them.

He may have sought notoriety, but we in New Zealand will give him nothing. Not even his name.

99

<u>**HOW**</u> SHE DID THAT

Communicate with compassion

As prime minister of New Zealand, Jacinda Ardern has made an impact on New Zealand and the world — not because of her political position but because of her personal style of leadership. She combines strength and compassion, and has projected both in compelling balance through the range of challenges she has faced during her tenure.

In the hours following the shootings in the mosque, Ardern was on the air, reassuring the nation and the citizens of Christchurch. She was on the ground, showing support, solidarity and leadership as soon as she could get there. Then, four days after the shootings, she delivered this speech in the New Zealand parliament.

She has an appreciable ability to read the emotional needs of the people affected by the attack and respond with care and compassion. Often people in leadership roles find situations of personal tragedy or disappointment difficult. Many of us shy away from our own emotions and fail to provide the human support people need. So often, we retreat from discomfort. Ardern shows us how to imbue words with genuine feeling. Stay in the moment, feel the discomfort and respond with mercy.

Respect with recognition and nuance

'Mr Speaker, Al salam Alaikum. Peace be upon you. And peace be upon all of us.' These opening words convey a simple but powerful message. Jacinda Ardern first speaks in Arabic — a sign of respect to the victims. She then uses English, demonstrating a melding of cultures.

Perhaps the most poignant moment in the speech is created by these words that bind the victims to the nation:

> Those loved ones were brothers, daughters, fathers and children.

> They were New Zealanders. They are us.

> And because they are us, we, as a nation, we mourn them.

Throughout this address, we hear genuine respect and recognition for a variety of individuals and groups. In the full version of the speech (see Sources for details), Ardern recognises the particular pain of her fellow House members from the Canterbury region, alluding to the Christchurch earthquake from 2011 that killed 185 people, and a city still in recovery.

Her subtle pausing, attention to particulars, the use of proper nouns and individual names, and the care she takes in pronunciation — all these combine to convey a sense of care.

Ardern's closing sentence in the full version of her speech echoes her theme of unity. For this closing, she first uses English, then Maori, and then Arabic. In another subtle arrangement, Ardern bestows the honour of both primacy and recency to the victims:

> We are one, they are us. Tatau tatau. Al salam Alaikum. Weh Rahmat Allah. Weh Barakaatuh.

Show strength as a leader

In the full version of her speech, Jacinta Ardern uses the specific names of people who confronted the terrorist in the mosque. In contrast, Ardern is very clear in telling parliament that there is one name she will not speak — that of the shooter. A terrorist seeking notoriety will not be given what he wants. She also implores the audience in the House, plus national and international viewers, to avoid naming him:

He is a terrorist. He is a criminal. He is an extremist.

But he will, when I speak, be nameless.

And to others, I implore you: speak the names of those who were lost, rather than the name of the man who took them.

He may have sought notoriety, but we in New Zealand will give him nothing. Not even his name

In this speech, Ardern shows us how emotional resonance can be used to strengthen connection. This is more than a tactic of leadership, and more than a dexterous display of language; this is the way she leads.

It took some time for me to understand, when there are millions in the world today who are hungry, millions who are homeless, millions who are without work, the wrongfully imprisoned, the deaths in custody, the tortured, the mass murder of women and children, why in the name of creation our differences should matter.

Faith Bandler

Faith Bandler

Civil rights activist and author

B: 27 September 1918, NSW, Austraila

D: 13 February 2015, Sydney, NSW, Australia

Faith, hope and reconciliation

When: August 1999

Where: Wollongong, New South Wales, Australia

Audience: Talkin' up Reconciliation convention

Faith Bandler was born and raised in northern New South Wales, Australia. Her father was a South Sea Islander and her mother was of Scottish and Indian descent — so she was very much Australian. Her lineage was integral to the life she led and the work she did in support of Indigenous rights. Notably, she was active in the campaign for the Yes vote in the 1967 referendum on including Aboriginal Australians in the national census and giving the federal government the power to make special laws relating to Indigenous Australians.

Many admirers of Bandler have remarked on her ability to reach across barriers of race, ethnicity and class divisions. When you listen to recordings of her speaking, you immediately have a sense of why. She is measured, yet unequivocally committed to her cause. She speaks with dignity and confers the traits she exhibits onto the people she represents. She always seems to respect others, even those she publicly challenges.

Bandler once said, 'We had politics for breakfast' when asked about her childhood in an interview, highlighting the origins of her lifelong commitment to activism and progress. Her political story begins a generation before; her father was kidnapped from Vanuatu at the age of about to work in the cane fields in Queensland, Australia. Years later, he was then threatened with deportation. Bandler spoke out about such injustices and other issues, including what was known as the White Australia Policy, the prison-like grip of the Aboriginal Welfare Board and Aboriginal deaths in custody.

It seems the achievement of the Yes vote in the 1967 referendum (by overwhelming majority) was only one of many milestones on Bandler's journey. In 1999 at the Talkin' up Reconciliation convention in Wollongong, New South Wales, Bandler (just shy of her eighty-first birthday) spoke eloquently to delegates about Indigenous rights and the need to accelerate the process of reconciliation. Her speech is reproduced in full here.

<u>WHAT</u> SHE SAID

I first would like to thank the Indigenous people of the Illawarra for inviting me to come today. I was here once before and some of those past memories have been stirred with some of you whom I have had a chance to speak with, so thank you.

Lord Mayor, Evelyn Scott, Linda Burney and all honoured guests, when I put my thoughts together to come and speak to you this morning, I found a module in my thinking. It was getting in the way. There was a little sadness because I felt the reconciliation program had slowed since 1967 and then the considerable support for those who sponsored racism excused some of their terrible utterances in the name of free speech, and then the terrible tragedy revealed to us of the stolen children.

So briefly I will try to portray my thoughts of these days and the days before. Earlier we thought our efforts were set in stone. But the track hasn't been easy and it was not so. It is hard to say what we have heard and seen recently, to hear it without shame and anger, and those are two elements which tend to stand in the way of the planning of good strategies.

Some who are here today have lived, breathed, struggled and climbed those ramparts of the rugged past, and when reaching the summit, have seen the ugliness when looking down — the disagreeable habits of those who close their eyes to the past, the willing ignorance and blindness to other peoples' way of life, those who long for a homogeneous society where all think alike.

But I'm pleased to say that out there, there are decent people. They may have different cultures, different political beliefs, but they know there is a need to heal the wounds of the past, the terrible indignities.

My learning was rather hard and slow. It took some time for me to understand, when there are millions in the world today who are hungry, millions who are homeless, millions who are without work, the wrongfully imprisoned, the deaths in custody, the tortured, the mass murder of women and children, why in the name of creation our differences should matter. Why is it so hard to find our commonalities?

The most commonly voiced opinions of some who are willingly blind is that we focus on the failures and faults and too little praise is given. But if praise must be given, it ought not to be given to the powerful but rather to the powerless, who patiently bear the brunt of many misdeeds and indecencies.

So in the struggle to reconcile you said it's about working together. That will mean lightening the burden of that terrible baggage that has to do with our differences. And in the short term, there's a fair bit to do about it.

Many have worked with determination, at most times against tremendous odds, with the talk-back jockeys lined up against them, and those who are deliberately blinkered and our troubled relationships with them. They are chained in their stubbornness, but we are free, and if we need to go forward without them, then we must.

To the youth present, and the not so young, let me say this: this movement should be one wherein we should ask not what is in it for me, but what is in it for us.

The fair-minded people out there can come along with us. None is without fault, none is without blemish, but they greatly outnumber the objectionable and the crude.

At this conference we might ask ourselves if our efforts are enough to make this country a better place for those who come after us. So you, the younger who are present, and those who are not present, have a hard job to do. You have brought change, true, but to eliminate some of the inbuilt attitudes of this society, the task is yet to be tackled.

This year Australia is celebrating 50 years of citizenship. Before 1949 we were all British subjects. Well, some were: it's not 50 years since Indigenous Australians has the right to citizenship.

We are not to forget the White Australia Policy, introduced at the turn of this century, excluded the peoples from South Africa, the peoples from the Pacific Islands and all Asian countries from Australian citizenship rights. Non-Indigenous Australians had the influence of the White Australia Policy, and those to whom it applied were considered, at times, less than human beings.

Thus the campaign for Aboriginal citizenship rights, carried on from 1957 to 1967, was rather difficult. And it's time for us to remember that rights are not handed on a platter by governments, they have to be won.

This conference in its deliberations will consider land rights. In the efforts to hold and protect their land from the invaders in 1788, there were many who lost their lives. There were fierce battles and conflict and, true, there were lulls, in the move for land rights. But even in the most isolated communities, the people spoke about their land.

For the executive of my council, FCAATSI, land rights seemed to be put on the back burner. It was the most poverty stricken in the whole of Australia, so we had to be careful with what few resources we had. These were the matters that had to do with equal wages for equal work, particularly for the Black stockmen, and other needs like housing, education opportunities, freedom of movement, the false arrests. So these problems had to be dealt with and faced and we had to mobilise the forces to meet those needs.

Until 1962. Alex Vesper came down from the community at Woodenbong in the north of NSW, and he drove us on to form a subcommittee for land rights. I recall Alex addressing the 1962 FCAATSI Conference with the bible in one hand and the dictionary in the other hand, and he told us all to get up and fight for land rights. The result of that was that a subcommittee was formed to deal with land rights and Dulcie Fowler was the secretary.

Ken Brindle, whom I know the Illawarra people will remember with great affection, once complained to me that he couldn't talk to Dulcie, because all she could talk about was land rights. Dulcie initiated a petition addressed to the Federal Parliament for Aboriginal people to reclaim their land.

It's a fitting time to mention briefly the struggle of the people for land rights of Mapoon, Weipa and Aurukun, particularly when bauxite was found on their lands. And we might take strength by remembering their brave actions to combat the mining companies.

Jean Jimmy came to the south from Mapoon, and she told us how her people were forced by the police into boats to leave their land and, as they sailed from Mapoon, they saw their houses and their church on fire. Jean Jimmy and her people had an unforgivable fault in the eyes of the white people. They said the land they lived on and the land their forebears lived on for thousands of years was theirs.

Friends, what is reconciliation about? It is about promoting discussion. It is about the rights of the Indigenous people. It's about those rights being enshrined in legislation. It's about being watchful and remembering, and remembering that governments only might implement, and they might not. It's about the violation of the first people's rights, and it's about valuing the differences of those cultures that make up this country.

In 1975, the Racial Discrimination Act was introduced. All rights must now be recognised, and it's our job to make sure that they are. It is rare that a government will deliver out of the goodness of its heart, but history has shown that a genuine people's movement can move more than governments. It can move mountains.

Dear friends, much pain has been endured in the past, and that pain is no longer designated to hopelessness. It's time to move the process of reconciliation forward with a little more speed. That is the task. If not now, when? If not us, who?

<u>HOW</u> SHE DID THAT

Reach across barriers

Former Australian senator John Faulkner was one of the speakers to reflect on Faith Bandler's life's work at her funeral in 2015. He said, 'Her ability to reach across boundaries of race, class, politics and opinion in the pursuit of her great aims was at the heart of her successes.'

Bandler's 1999 speech is the oratorical manifestation of this dimension of her unique character. In her opening, she first thanks the Indigenous people of the Illawarra (the region where the conference was held), and then recognises the dignitaries and assembled guests. She calls upon the young people, and the not so young, who might also be listening. At times she speaks directly to those who have struggled and suffered, and at times she speaks to those whose minds need to change, calling out their 'willing ignorance and blindness'.

She allows the audience to cast themselves in the roles she creates — using phrases such as 'the fair-minded people out there' to build the metaphorical bridge to a meeting of the minds. Through her agile language, she signals inclusivity and she opens the door to reconciliation.

Speeches that encourage inclusivity must invite both sides to the discussion. We often see activists speak eloquently and passionately about their side of the debate to an audience who already agrees with them. What Bandler can teach us is that we must also engage those we seek to persuade. We must be respectful, direct and genuine if we are to open up the possibility of finding commonalities.

Humanise the statistics

Statistics, facts and historical events matter. Having a fact-free discussion when you are proposing a significant change makes no sense. But if your intent is to convince people to come together, you need to find opportunities to humanise your message. Once you have selected some data — the number of people impacted by a new policy, for example — find the story of the one among the many.

When talking about the subject of land rights, Bandler goes beyond the dates and details of the establishment of the subcommittee. She tells us about Alex Vesper who 'came down from the community at Woodenbong'. And we are introduced to secretary Dulcie Fowler and how 'all she could talk about was land rights'. More than just the regions being affected, we have our attention specifically drawn to the communities of Mapoon, Weipa and Aurukun when bauxite was found on their land. The lens is then focused further and we hear what happened to Jean Jimmy and her family as they were forced off their land.

If you are recounting a time line of events, zoom in on a significant inflection point and bring it to life by introducing the characters that made it all possible. You can share the stories of others or re-enact your own memories and mindset to make it real.

Show the way forward

Faith Bandler's call for inclusion illuminates the better part of humanity and shows us what the future might look like. At no point does she diminish or minimise the injustices that were perpetrated against Indigenous Australians. In fact, she reminds us throughout her speech of some of the most tragic and painful periods in our history. But she also hints at a future that could be better and she helps us to understand how we might get there.

The way to progress, according to Bandler, is via reconciliation. The path to reconciliation, in turn, must not ignore all that has happened — 'the violation of the first people's rights'. Instead, it must transcend history to create a new reality. 'Sorry' won't be enough. The forward-looking solution we need is a new attitude: 'it's about valuing the differences of those cultures that make up this country' — all of them.

If you want to encourage the sort of inclusivity heralded by Bandler, you will need to adopt the generosity of spirit she shows us when recounting the past and the hope she tentatively proposes for what might be.

I am here today; I may not be here tomorrow. But the responsibility to look after national interest is on the shoulder of every citizen of India.

... I shall continue to serve until my last breath and when I die, I can say, that every drop of my blood will invigorate India and strengthen it.

Indira Gandhi

Indira Gandhi

Former Prime Minister of India

B: *19 November 1917, Prayagraj, India*

D: *31 October 1984, New Delhi, India*

Last speech of Indira Gandhi at Bhubaneswar

When: *1984*

Where: *Bhubaneswar, Orissa, India*

Audience: *The nation of India*

Indira Gandhi was assassinated by her own bodyguards the day after delivering the speech featured here in 1984. Her words now haunt our memories and the pages of history.

Gandhi served as Prime Minister of India from January 1966 to March 1977 and again from January 1980 until her death in October 1984. She was the daughter of Jawaharlal Nehru, the first and much revered Prime Minister of India, and so far the only female to have served in this position. All politicians, regardless of their pedigree or personal accomplishments, will face challenges to their leadership. Gandhi was raised with an appreciation for this reality.

When she made this speech in Bhubaneswar, in the region of Orissa in the east of India, she was aware she may soon die, because attempts had already been made on her life. She makes specific mention of this in her speech. Imminent threats notwithstanding, Indira Gandhi took the opportunity to address the nation. Her words echo through the years because we now know what was to befall her. The history lends extra significance to what is, in its own right, a powerful address.

A seasoned politician, raised by a serving prime minister, Indira Gandhi would have developed a learned and lived appreciation for political rhetoric. She clearly has a feeling for structure, impact and language. She is able to match her words to her intent and demonstrates mindfulness of the audience and their likely level of receptiveness to change. She shows she appreciates what the audience is thinking and feeling.

The speech extracted here delivers a message of unity and progress — common themes throughout Gandhi's tenure as the prime minister.

<u>WHAT</u> SHE SAID

India, in our long history, has never attacked any country. There have been many invasions against us. People from outside came here and many of them settled here. They proved to be good Indians. Later, they participated with us in the freedom fight. When India was invaded after we achieved our freedom, all of them expressed their solidarity with the people of India. They stood like one wall and faced the challenges. The prime need of the hour is to revive once again the same spirit of solidarity in the hearts and minds of the people. It is not a case of strengthening the hands of Indira Gandhi alone. It means that the hands of millions of people, who live in India, should be strengthened.

The hands of men and women, old and young, scheduled castes and scheduled tribes, people belonging to backward classes indeed, of everybody who's living in India, should be strengthened. They should have the courage and they should have the strength, which will take this country along the road of development. All of us should work hard. It is not only a question of manual labour. It also concerns the mind. Let new ideas be brought in from different sources, so that in this scientific age India could progress.

Whenever I happen to meet scientists I have only one message for them: 'Do something which is of use to the whole of the country.' But if along with this a scientific temper is not cultivated, if we remain prisoners of superstitions, if we continue to quarrel among ourselves, if we tolerate communalism and do not fight against it, if we let casteism or regionalism develop and grow or if we start quarrelling in the name of language, how will we be able to preserve the unity of India? If unity is not preserved, how will we protect our independence? Do not think that if we have won freedom once, we will be able to preserve it for all time to come.

Eternal vigilance is the price of freedom. We have to think about it and do something about it every day. We have to preserve that freedom for our poorer masses, particularly for the people who are backward and are living in backward areas. We should make freedom a reality for them.

...The citizens of India must think of India first. We may belong to any religion or caste or creed, but nationalism is supreme, the love for our country must get priority over everything. But today some people think that they should support or back any agitation which may help in getting votes to them during the elections. But the people in Orissa and the people living in different states, indeed the people of the whole country, must realise that such agitations will pose a greater danger to our country.

...My father used to say that freedom cannot be divided. In the same manner, progress is also indivisible, development is also indivisible. Many countries of the world have become prosperous through scientific development and they are also collecting wealth very rapidly and using it for raising their standard. They are very powerful and even then they want to influence other nations.

...I am here today; I may not be here tomorrow. But the responsibility to look after national interest is on the shoulder of every citizen of India. I have often mentioned this earlier. Nobody knows how many attempts have been made to shoot me; lathis have been used to beat me. In Bhubaneswar itself, a brickbat hit me. They have attacked me in every possible manner. I do not care whether I live or die. I have lived a long life and I am proud that I spend the whole of my life in the service of my people. I am only proud of this and nothing else. I shall continue to serve until my last breath and when I die, I can say that every drop of my blood will invigorate India and strengthen it.

...It means that there is some inherent strength in us; that is why we are surviving. That strength is there inside everybody. But you have to let it develop. If you do not allow it to develop, if you are frustrated, then the inner strength will not take its shape and it will work negatively. There are weaknesses and we have to fight those weaknesses. But if we do not have the courage, if we do not have the necessary morale, then we shall not be able to get over those shortcomings and weaknesses. Without doing this, good work cannot be done. So, it is in your hands, in the hands of the people of Orissa and in the hands of the people of this country what they want to do.

…You have heard me very patiently. I shall repeat that you must give top priority to the unity and integrity of the country. Everything else is secondary. We have to face today's challenges in such a manner that we emerge stronger and our strength continues to grow. If we gain something for the short term and if it weakens us tomorrow or day after, then it is not a thing worth pursuing.

Jai Hind.

99

<u>HOW</u> SHE DID THAT

Use inclusive language

When pointing out shortcomings or areas for further development, Indira Gandhi is careful in her use of the third and first person plural. She warns about a lack of progress for all Indians if they cling to outdated practices, believe in superstitions or continue to fight among themselves. Progress will depend on individual willingness to move past old divisions towards unity. Whenever a criticism is levelled, it is made a collective problem. It is 'we' who must progress. Gandhi makes sure to highlight the opportunities that will be gained if such shortcomings can be overcome.

If you have a message of inclusion, pointing out what is wrong with the current situation is helpful. When criticising the status quo, the use of inclusive language will make your message more palatable. The alternative is to use the second person — *you* are not good enough, *you* are doing it wrong. Such confrontation will likely be met with resistance. Most people will first become defensive if they feel they are being attacked. Even when rational counterarguments are put forward, we tend to cling to old battle lines.

Gandhi, following in her father's path, was committed to the advancement of her country. Of course, this meant she would need to encourage people to let go of some outmoded practices that were limiting progress. Her lesson, aptly demonstrated in the speech, is to approach any form of criticism with language that indicates you are one of the team.

Demonstrate personal commitment

It is impossible to imagine any leader demonstrating a greater level of personal commitment than what is offered by Indira Gandhi in this, her final speech. She overtly puts her life on the line and is willing to die for the benefit of her cause — the future of India.

In most situations, we want to see evidence of commitment from our leaders. Progress requires change and change is often painful. The magical thing about speeches is that they can be an opportunity for a leader to demonstrate their personal commitment.

In your speeches and presentations, move away from lecturing others about what they should do differently. Instead, find instances where you have experienced loss, perhaps made a sacrifice at a time when you were doubtful of the outcome, but can now see the benefits. This might be the perfect time for a well-crafted story. Be sure to select something relevant and appropriate and be genuine in your re-telling.

Elevate the message

As the words flow, Indira Gandhi shifts towards more elevated concepts and language. Clearly, she is working towards a dramatic conclusion and looking to provoke an emotional, patriotic reaction in the audience. She speaks of freedom, self-reliance, internal strength and patriotic pride. If this was the tone of the entire address it might feel too lofty, and disconnected from the experiences of the people listening. This is a classical rhetorical technique called 'peroration' — where the principal points of a speech are repeated in the concluding comments with greater earnestness and force — used to elevate and inspire.

Too many speeches or presentations leave the audience wondering what the takeaway should be. This is an opportunity to gather up all the points you have laid out throughout your address and bring them together in a way that is at once a reminder to the audience and a call to action. Some of the most memorable speeches in history include this technique. Tell us what you hope we have heard and show us the importance.

If there is a god of demography, it is one of his greatest ironies that the seat named after the architect of the White Australia policy has become one of the most multicultural in the country!

Linda Burney

Linda Burney

Australian politician and educator

B: *25 April 1957, Whitton, NSW, Australia*

Inaugural speech

When: *1 September 2016*

Where: *Canberra, Australia*

Audience: *Australian federal House of Representatives*

Linda Burney is a Wiradjuri woman and the first Indigenous female Member of the Australian federal House of Representatives. On 1 September 2016, she delivered her inaugural speech to parliament — and to a gallery filled with supporters, many of whom were Indigenous Australians. Her words were heartfelt and her message was balanced. She managed, in this first federal parliamentary appearance, to add her voice to the ongoing process of reconciliation.

This speech is marked by several poignant moments through which Burney conveys her personal commitment to her Aboriginal heritage as well as her responsibility to the chamber and her electorate of Barton. Rather than segmenting her message into sections and labelling each with the aspects of her identity, she weaves stories of her ancestors through the speech, picking up threads of history along with the various cultures in her constituency and individuals who have played an important role in her life. She does all of this while demonstrating a respect for the conventions of the federal parliamentary apparatus.

The resulting speech, extracted here, is a tapestry — perhaps representing the complexity of Burney's identity in the modern Western world. As Burney herself says, 'The Aboriginal part of my story is important. It is the core of who I am, but I will not be stereotyped and I will not be pigeonholed.'

This is a speech that overtly and covertly encourages inclusivity. Burney, though sometimes trepidacious in her delivery, manages to always exhibit grace and poise. She successfully balances gravity and conviction with respect and occasional moments of levity.

<u>WHAT</u> SHE SAID

❝ It was in this chamber I experienced one of the most remarkable moments of my life. I was in that gallery just up there. It feels like it was just yesterday. But I will tell you that story of truth-telling and generosity in a moment.

Ballumb Ambul Ngunawhal Ngambri yindamarra. Ngadu bang marang Ngadhu Ngu-nha winhanga nha nulabang nguwandang. Ngadhu biyap yuganha. Birrang a ngawaal. Ngadhu, yand yaman gid yal. Yindyamarra. Mandaang. Ngarind-ja.

I have just said, in the language of Wiradjuri, my people: 'I pay respect to the ancient Ngunawhal and Ngambri. I say this: good day. I am giving my first speech and I am deeply moved. I have journeyed to another place — a powerful place. I am one person. I wish in this House to honour, to be respectful, to be gentle and to be polite. I am thankful, happy. I could weep.' However, I say to my elders and to you, Mr Speaker, that that last bit may not always apply in question time!

I mention respectfully the traditional owners of the seat of Barton — three clans of the Eora, the Bidjigal, the Gweagal and the Badigal, custodians of the land from the Cooks River to the shores of Brighton-Le-Sands and out to the Georges River. It is strong country. And to the traditional owners of all the lands from which members of this chamber and the other place* come: these lands are, always were and always will be Aboriginal land — sovereignty never ceded.

So, what was that remarkable moment? Many of you were here. It was the first sitting of the new Labor government, on 13 February 2008. Kevin Rudd was the new prime minister, Jenny Macklin the minister for Indigenous affairs, and Brendan Nelson the opposition leader.

---

* By Australian (and UK) parliamentary tradition, Members of the House of Representatives refer to the Senate as the 'other place'.

Our nation had been holding its breath for a long time, waiting for three words: 'We are sorry'. There was the stubborn refusal of the previous prime minister to apologise for policies that had ripped many thousands of Aboriginal children from their family, culture and country — the devastating effects still felt today. But around the perimeter of this chamber sat some of those children, now old people, still wearing the scars of forced removal on their faces. They were joined by all surviving prime ministers bar one.

Finally, as the words rang out across this chamber, across this land and around the world, 'For this we are sorry', the country cried and began to breathe again.

As the speeches concluded, two women stood and handed the Prime Minister, Leader of the Opposition and Minister an empty coolamon — and I beg the indulgence of the House in carrying a coolamon in here today. It was the most gracious and generous thing I had ever seen. It was profound, a gesture that made us all better people. Friends, a coolamon is what we carried our babies in, which is what made it such an amazing, generous thing to do.

I carry this empty coolamon into this place today as a reminder of that moment, of the power we exercise in this building today, and that it must be for the good of all. It must be gracious. But it has not always been so. But it can be. That day the truth was told in this place, and the power of generosity was writ large. So, Mr Speaker, the significance of coming down from that gallery up there to the floor of this chamber is not lost on me.

Members, in this term of parliament all I want is to be able to stand in this place knowing that the document on which it was founded finally tells the truth. Recognition of the First People in our nation's constitution is the next step on the path we are walking towards a country that can look itself in the eye knowing that we have come of age. Fundamentally, reconciliation is about three things: it is about reciprocity; it is about restitution; and it is about truth-telling. One of the bravest statements I ever heard was in the opening ceremony of the 1997 Reconciliation Convention in Melbourne.

The 10-point plan in the winding back of the native title debate was raging, and the chair of the council at that time is now Senator Patrick Dodson. I was on the executive committee — I am not sure if Patrick liked it or did not — but I think I did okay and I think he did like it. He was an amazing chair. But Senator Dodson said at the opening of that convention, in the presence of the world media, 'There can never be reconciliation without social justice.'

Nor is the significance of a first speech lost on me. It is defining; it sets out what has made you, what you believe in and what you stand for. It talks about the seat and the people whose hopes, hurts, aspirations and loves you carry into this place. It talks of the deep affection you have for those people. Because of the significance, I carry into this chamber this cloak. This cloak was made by my Wiradjuri sister, Lynette Riley, who will sing us into this place now.

[Ms Riley then sang in the Wiradjuri language.]

Thank you, Lynette.

This cloak tells my story. It charts my life. On it is my clan totem, the goanna, and my personal totem, the white cockatoo — a messenger bird and very noisy.

... I would ask all of those listening this afternoon to imagine what it was like for a 13-year-old Aboriginal girl in a school classroom, being taught that her ancestors were the closest thing to Stone Age man on Earth and struggling with your identity.

Being in this chamber today feels a long way from that time.

... In many ways these experiences have been the catalyst for my subsequent life as an advocate for education and social justice. The Aboriginal part of my story is important. It is the core of who I am, but I will not be stereotyped and I will not be pigeonholed. ... In Barton, from the beach in Brighton-Le-Sands you can stand and look towards Botany Bay where the First Fleet in 1788 first entered these shores. Settlement or invasion is a matter of perspective — of whether you were on the shore or on the boats in the middle of the bay. I spoke earlier of truth-telling. Perhaps another great act of honesty and healing would be a permanent remembering of those frontier wars, just down the road at our national war memorial.

The chamber I have come from in New South Wales proudly hangs the Aboriginal and Torres Strait Islander flags. Symbolism is important. I know that symmetry is important in this place, but perhaps we could think that once we get constitutional recognition we could add another two flags to this chamber, coloured red, gold and black, and white, green and blue — the colours and the flags of the two first peoples of this nation.

I will say that I intend to bring the fighting Wiradjuri spirit into this place. This mob behind me knows what that is about. I will bring that spirit into this place for the people of Barton, for the first peoples and for those great Labor values of social justice and equality for all people.

I enter this place as a representative of the people of Barton, a community I have been proud to live in for almost 20 years. If there is a god of demography, it is one of his greatest ironies that the seat named after the architect of the White Australia policy has become one of the most multicultural in the country! Over half of the people in Barton were born overseas. Almost 10 per cent were born in China. We have a well-established post–World War II Greek and European community, a thriving Arabic-speaking community, a rapidly growing Nepalese community, a Macedonian community, an Indian community — you name it. We have people from every corner of the globe. Barton is a kaleidoscope of languages, ethnicities and cultures. I am not sure what Sir Edmund would think of the ethnic wonderland being represented in this place today by, of all people, me — and a Koori woman to boot!

<u>HOW</u> SHE DID THAT

Leverage the power of symbols

Imagine yourself walking into the House of Representatives in Canberra as if you had never seen it before. With fresh eyes, note the symbolism all around you. The layout of the chamber, the elevated position of the speaker, the Australian Coat of Arms (featuring the cross of St George), the Mace, the legal tomes, and the list goes on. All have certain symbolism and connotations. In this context, Linda Burney delivers her inaugural speech as the first Indigenous woman to hold a seat in the federal House of Representatives. While operating in accordance with the traditions of the chamber, she introduces her own symbols.

The contrast between the artefacts of the first Australians Burney brings with her, notably the cloak and the coolamon, and the imposing imagery of colonial power in every corner of the room in which she speaks is powerful. Burney manages to create a productive tension that encourages interest rather than rejection. Because she links the objects to stories, we are able to appreciate the depth of meaning, and this further enhances her message of inclusivity.

Later in her speech, Burney explicitly acknowledges the importance of symbolism when she mentions the flags present in the state parliament she has recently stepped down from. She reminds the assembly that the Aboriginal and Torres Strait Islander flags have a rightful place among the festival of symbolism that abounds in the iconic federal building.

When communicating a message of inclusivity, you must consider any aspect of your presentation, from your visual support, to your appearance, to the diversity or lack thereof in the room; and from the conventions of the event to the unwritten rules of demeanour. What do you see and hear that could potentially divide your audience? What can you do to introduce balance while avoiding potentially vacuous lip service?

Strategically choose your starting point

Linda Burney was hyper aware of the historic significance of her speech — in particular, what it meant in the ongoing campaign for Indigenous rights and reconciliation. She sought to orient the occasion in history. She did not begin by mentioning the arrival of the First Fleet or even Australia's federation; instead she picked out a day in the not too distant past, when Kevin Rudd's 'sorry' speech was delivered — the much anticipated, much delayed symbolic yet significant apology to Australian Aboriginal people delivered by the then Prime Minster back in 2008.

Burney tells us that she was an observer, up in the gallery the day that speech was delivered, and she explains its significance for herself and others.

This is an astute move because it allows her to anchor her argument to a moment of positivity. Although later in the speech we hear of some of the tragic injustices First Nations people have suffered, which must not be forgotten, we have been primed to adopt an attitude of reconciliation.

When you are in control of the microphone, you have the opportunity to frame your message in whatever context best serves your objective. Don't assume you must provide background information in a flat expository way. You can highlight the twists and turns to activate the responses in the audience you are looking for. You might want to provide background in a reverse chronological order, for example, to highlight how far you have come. You might want to leave the past largely out of your talk, and instead focus on what the future might hold.

Lighten up

In the full version of this speech (see Sources), Linda Burney tackles some pretty hefty topics. She tells several stories that help reinforce her message and convey meaning and emotion. But throughout her speech, she also releases the pressure by adding in small moments of levity. These occasional laughs seem well appreciated by her audience and they are endearing.

This is a good example of how personality can be peppered throughout an otherwise serious speech, in a serious context, with serious rules. You should not completely upend the rules of convention, but you can look for tiny moments to inject levity, as Burney does when explaining the image of the cockatoo on her cloak — a personal totem that is also rather noisy. Another example is when she pledges to be gentle and polite, but that 'may not always apply in question time!'

If you can seize small moments to endear yourself to your audience, through humour, self-deprecation, a well-placed hint of sarcasm or a moment of intimacy, you will build a subtle connection with your audience. Remember that people will be far more open to your point of view if they like you.

Harnessing the power of stories

Stories are what we reach for when we want to understand and be understood, when we want to take a concept and bring it to life.

Author Robert Stone said that 'Storytelling is not a luxury to humanity; it's almost as necessary as bread. We cannot imagine ourselves without it because the self is a story.' We use stories to imprint our identity on someone's memory. We don't really need to learn the craft of storytelling, because we already know it. Perhaps we need to relearn the way we used to communicate when we were children. Sometimes we need to strip away the qualifiers, the definitions, the thesis statements and empiricism in favour of a narrative.

At times you want your audience to divine their own meaning, and do not want or need to be explicit, literal or even factual in your communication.

The most powerful stories tend to be those that are autobiographical. We all own our own stories and when told in the first person, they can be moving and powerful. A personal story could actually comprise your whole speech or it could be used to highlight one of its component parts, or as a means of building connections in your introduction.

In the speech included here, Holocaust survivor Eva Kor recounts the horrific treatment she and her twin sister experienced at Auschwitz. Her reality would never be as compelling as it is in her own words. Kor's speech is an example of how ugliness and evil can be reformed into a message of compassion, helping to create a better future.

Josephine Baker is a figure in history who stands out for many as someone who marched, quite determinedly, to the beat of her own drum. In the 1963 March on Washington, Baker took to the stage just before Martin Luther King Jnr, as part of the same demonstration, delivered his iconic 'I have a dream' address. In Baker's case, we learn that her personal story was far more nuanced, more human and more instructive than many would have known. In this speech, she lends her voice and her experience to the struggle for equality.

Russian journalist and writer Svetlana Alexievich demonstrates a mastery of language in her Nobel Lecture that accompanied her prize for literature. In her hands, we see the craft of storytelling come alive. She gives us a deeper understanding of what it means to be human by illuminating our nature in prose.

Finally, consider the iconic poem written and read by Maya Angelou on the occasion of Bill Clinton's inauguration as President of the United States. 'On the pulse of morning' is a stand-out piece of oratory that continues to inspire years after its original delivery. The poem contains the story of a nation and opens the door for us to reimagine the next chapter.

Used in the right context, stories have the power to persuade, motivate and inspire. If you can unearth your own stories to help you to say what you really mean, you know your voice will be authentic and unique — two hallmarks of a great communicator.

Let there be no more wars, no more experiments without informed consent, no more gas chambers, no more bombs, no more hatred, no more killing, no more Auschwitzes.

Eva Kor

Eva Kor

Holocaust survivor, advocate and speaker

B: *31 January 1934, Romania*

D: *4 July 2019, Kraków, Poland*

Surviving the Angel of Death

When: *7 June 2001*

Where: *Berlin, Germany*

Audience: *Biomedical Sciences and Human Experimentation at Kaiser Wilhelm Institutes*

Eva Mozes Kor was a Romanian-born holocaust survivor. Along with her twin sister, she suffered under the horrific human experimentation conducted by the Nazi's, specifically Josef Mengele (known as the 'Angel of Death' by his victims). Her survival is her story, and her story became her life's work.

On 7 June 2001, Eva Kor spoke at the 'Biomedical Sciences and Human Experimentation at Kaiser Wilhelm Institutes — The Auschwitz Connection' symposium in Berlin. She was speaking to the very institute that, as she highlights 'was in charge of our experiments' during the war. This speech is one example among many where Kor brings her story to life, expresses her mission and stills her audience with the power of her chilling, authentic personal story.

Even after her death, the impact of Kor's presentations and advocacy work, including all her moving speeches, lives on through the organisation she founded, CANDLES (Children of Auschwitz Nazi Deadly Lab Experiments Survivors). Her words still influence the field of bio medical research.

In Berlin 2001, a diminutive figure slowly makes her way to the microphone. First, she gets herself comfortable, and then calmly begins. As is the case with many who are vertically challenged, whomever has introduced her needs to adjust the microphone down. She takes her time. Her voice, when it comes, is soft, accented and unhurried. Despite all of this, Kor exudes a tranquil strength.

'Surviving the Angel of Death' is the title of her book and the theme of the speech extracted here, and many of her speeches.

WHAT SHE SAID

...Fifty-seven years ago I was a human guinea pig in Auschwitz. Much progress has been made in order for us to be here at the KWI [Kaiser Wilhelm Institutes]/MPS, the institute that was in charge of our experiments. I thank you for holding this symposium. I hope we can all learn from the past and begin to heal our pain.

Twenty years ago, I began thinking about the other Mengele Twins and started actively searching for them. From the time I began to the time that we made our historic trip to Auschwitz and held the Mock Trial in Jerusalem in 1985, I have mailed out nearly 12 000 letters looking for my fellow survivors. With the help of my late twin sister, Miriam Mozes Zeiger, in 1984 we succeeded in locating 122 individuals/survivors of the Twins' experiments.

I care deeply for the Mengele Twins. Even though I am the founder and the President of CANDLES, I am not a spokesperson for all the twins. I am speaking today only for myself. I know that some of my fellow survivors do not share my ideas. But, we are all here to be honest, learn the truth and learn from this most tragic chapter of human history.

...It was the dawn of an early spring day in 1944 when I arrived in Auschwitz. Our cattle car train came to a sudden stop. I could hear lots of German voices yelling orders outside. We were packed like sardines in the cattle car, and, above the press of bodies, I could see nothing but a small patch of grey sky through the barbed wires on the window.

Our family consisted of my father, age forty-four; my mother, age thirty-eight; my oldest sister, Edit, age fourteen; my middle sister, Aliz, age twelve; and Miriam and I, who were only ten years old.

As soon as we stepped down onto the cement platform, my mother grabbed my twin sister and me by the hand, hoping somehow to protect us. Everything was moving very fast. As I looked around I suddenly realised that my father and two older sisters were gone — I never saw any of them ever again.

As Miriam and I were clutching my mother's hand, an SS hurried by shouting, 'Zwillinge! Zwillinge! Twins — Twins?' He stopped to look at my twin sister and me because we were dressed alike and looked very much alike.

'Are they twins?' he asked.

'Is it good?' asked my mother.

'Yes,' nodded the SS.

'Yes, they are twins,' said my mother.

Without any warning or explanation, he grabbed Miriam and me away from Mother. Our screaming and pleading fell on deaf ears. I remember looking back and seeing my mother's arms stretched out in despair as she was pulled in the opposite direction by an SS soldier. I never got to say goodbye to her and I never got to do so because that was the last time we saw her. All that took thirty minutes. Miriam and I no longer had a family. We were all alone. We did not know what would happen to us. All that was done to us because we were born Jewish. We did not understand why this was a crime.

...Before trying to sleep again, Miriam and I went to the latrine at the end of the barrack. There on that filthy floor were the scattered corpses of three children. Their bodies were naked and shrivelled and their wide-open eyes were looking at me. Then and there, I realised that could happen to Miriam and me unless I did something to prevent it. So I made a silent pledge: 'I will do whatever is within my power to make sure that Miriam and I shall not end up on that filthy latrine floor.'

From that moment on, I concentrated all my efforts, all my talents and all my being on one thing: survival.

In our barrack, we, the children, huddled in our filthy beds crawling with lice and rats. We were starved for food, starved for human kindness and starved for the love of the mothers we once had. We had no rights, but we had a fierce determination to live one more day — to survive one more experiment. No-one explained anything to us nor did anyone try to minimise the risks to our lives. On the contrary, we knew we were there to be subjects of experiments and were totally at the mercy of the Nazi doctors. Our lives depended entirely on the doctors' whims.

Nothing on the face of the Earth can prepare a person for a place like Auschwitz. At age ten, I became part of a special group of children who were used as human guinea pigs by Dr Josef Mengele. Some 1500 sets of multiples were used by Mengele in his deadly experiments. It is estimated that fewer than 200 individuals survived.

...I became very ill after an injection in Mengele's lab. I tried to hide the fact that I was ill because the rumour was that anyone taken to the hospital never came back. The next visit to the lab, they measured my fever and I was taken to the hospital.

The next day a team of Dr Mengele and four other doctors looked at my fever chart and then declared, 'Too bad, she is so young. She has only two weeks to live.'

I was all alone. The doctors I had did not want to heal me. They wanted me dead. Miriam was not with me. I missed her so very much. She was the only kind and loving person I could cuddle up with when I was hungry, cold and scared.

I refused to accept their verdict. I refused to die!

...Three times a week we walked to the main Auschwitz camp for experiments. These lasted six to eight hours. We had to sit naked in a room. Every part of our body was measured, poked and compared to charts and photographed. Every movement was noted. I felt like an animal in a cage.

Three times a week we went to the blood lab. There we were injected with germs and chemicals and they took a lot of blood from us.

...On a white snowy day, January 27th, 1945, four days before my eleventh birthday, Auschwitz was liberated by the Soviets and we were free. We were alive. We had survived. We had triumphed over unbelievable evil.

I have told you my story because there are some important lessons to learn from it: I, Eva Mozes Kor, a survivor of Mengele's medical experiments, have learned that human rights in medical experimentation is an issue that needs to be addressed. Those of you who are physicians and scientists are to be congratulated. You have chosen a wonderful and difficult profession; wonderful because you can save human lives and alleviate human suffering but difficult because you are walking a very narrow line. You have been trained to use good judgement, to be calm, cool and collected, but you cannot forget that you are dealing with human beings. So, make a moral commitment that you will never, ever violate anyone's human rights or take away anyone's human dignity. I appeal to you to treat your subjects and patients with the same respect you would want if you were in their places. Remember that if you are doing your research solely for the sake of science and not for the benefit of mankind, you have crossed that very narrow line and you are heading in the direction of the Nazi doctors and the Dr Mengeles of the world. Medical science can benefit mankind but medical science can also be abused in the name of research.

…I would also like to quote from my Declaration of Amnesty: 'I hope, in some small way, to send the world a message of forgiveness; a message of peace, a message of hope, a message of healing.'

Let there be no more wars, no more experiments without informed consent, no more gas chambers, no more bombs, no more hatred, no more killing, no more Auschwitzes.

🙶

<u>HOW</u> SHE DID THAT

Judge when a personal story is best

Having sound arguments and factual evidence are often required when one is seeking to persuade. But enhancing your rational position by creating emotional resonance will always improve your effectiveness, so long as a sympathetic tone is appropriate. In this case, Eva Kor demonstrates her instinctive knowledge of the importance of personal connection and storytelling to shift people's attitudes.

No doubt, the harrowing details of Kor's experience of being removed from her home and travelling to Auschwitz with her family had been recounted many times. She would have told and re-told audiences stories of her separation from her family and of the torture she suffered in the name of medical research. As a narrator in her own tale, each time she revisited the trauma of experiencing her own pain and that of her twin sister. And yet, she was able to manifest the whole ordeal again and again, each time expressing the right depth of emotion.

Kor's influence goes beyond her skills as a first-person narrator — and these are impressive indeed. She is willing to re-experience her own pain in service of a bigger purpose. Kor's organisation CANDLES shares with others focused on the fact of the holocaust the precept that we must never forget. To forget the evils inflicted in the Nazi camps would be to open up the opportunity for it to happen again. In a way, Kor used her own painful story as insurance against this possibility.

Use imagery that transports the audience

Good storytelling comes to life in the images that are created in the listener's mind. Kor manages to transport the audience to her bunk at Auschwitz — we can hear the rats and share the fear she must have felt as a ten-year-old girl.

Her story is punctuated with details that bring the tale to life. We travel back with her to the 'dawn of an early spring day', we look up with her and see the 'grey sky' and 'barbed wire'. We too are jolted by the SS officer yelling, 'Zwillinge! Zwillinge!', and feel the confusion, heartache and fear.

We feel more than sympathy. We are transported to the most deplorable period of human history and confronted with the reality of evil inflicted upon a child. The audience is unlikely to forget having shared, albeit tangentially, in Kor's story.

Be unapologetically yourself

When Eva Kor speaks, she does not apologise. Though age, stature and language might seem like impediments to persuasive communication, they will not get in her way.

So often, people make apologies — with their words, their body language or their expression — before they even begin to speak. This does nothing but create unnecessary doubt in the minds of your audience. This is not inherently a female trait when speaking, but somehow it seems to manifest more often than it should among women. How you look, how you move and how you sound are who you are and should be used to enhance your presence.

Take a lesson from Kor and don't apologise for who you are. Stand firm in the knowledge that you have a story only you can tell.

I am not a young woman now, friends. My life is behind me. There is not too much fire burning inside me. And before it goes out, I want you to use what is left to light that fire in you.

Josephine Baker

Josephine Baker

Entertainer and activist

B: *3 June 1906, St Louis, MS, United States*

D: *12 April 1975, Paris, France*

March on Washington

When: *28 August 1963*

Where: *Washington DC*

Audience: *250 000 people before a peaceful protest on the capital*

At the historic March on Washington in 1963, Josephine Baker spoke prior to the start of official proceedings, and before Dr Martin Luther King Jnr delivered his iconic 'I have a dream' speech. Civil rights advocate Daisy Bates was the only woman included as part of the official line-up of speakers, but Baker's presence at the event coupled with her international fame earned her a little bit of time at the podium. She used her time to share her personal experience and encourage progress.

If you've heard of Josephine Baker, perhaps you have an image in mind of her as the flamboyant dancer on stage in the cabarets of Paris in the 1920s. The American-born French entertainer seemed to embody a life of freedom. Perhaps you have heard one or more of her one-liners that continue to pop up in popular culture. She was glamorous and a little bit cheeky — like when she said, 'I wasn't really naked. I simply didn't have any clothes on.'

For Baker to live the life she wanted, unencumbered by racial inequality, gender bias and religious oppression, she had to leave the United States.

In Paris, she became an icon of the roaring twenties and she loved her adopted home. Much more than an entertainer, Baker became active in the French resistance during World War II.

Although she had to absent herself from the country of her birth in order to live, she never let go of her commitment to progress. She spent the latter part of her life campaigning for the civil rights movement.

On 28 August 1963 she addressed a crowd larger than she'd ever faced. About 250 000 marched on the US Capitol in a peaceful protest for jobs and freedom. In the speech reproduced in full here, Josephine Baker added her voice, and her story, to the movement.

<u>WHAT</u> SHE SAID

" Friends and family, you know I have lived a long time and I have come a long way. And you must know now that what I did, I did originally for myself. Then later, as these things began happening to me, I wondered if they were happening to you, and then I knew they must be. And I knew that you had no way to defend yourselves, as I had.

And as I continued to do the things I did, and to say the things I said, they began to beat me. Not beat me, mind you, with a club — but, you know, I have seen that done too — but they beat me with their pens, with their writings. And friends, that is much worse.

When I was a child and they burned me out of my home, I was frightened and I ran away. Eventually I ran far away. It was to a place called France. Many of you have been there, and many have not. But I must tell you, ladies and gentlemen, in that country I never feared. It was like a fairyland place.

And I need not tell you that wonderful things happened to me there. Now I know that all you children don't know who Josephine Baker is, but you ask Grandma and Grandpa and they will tell you. You know what they will say. 'Why, she was a devil.' And you know something … why, they are right. I was too. I was a devil in other countries, and I was a little devil in America too.

But I must tell you, when I was young in Paris, strange things happened to me. And these things had never happened to me before. When I left St Louis a long time ago, the conductor directed me to the last car. And you all know what that means.

But when I ran away, yes, when I ran away to another country, I didn't have to do that. I could go into any restaurant I wanted to, and I could drink water anyplace I wanted to, and I didn't have to go to a coloured toilet either, and I have to tell you it was nice, and I got used to it, and I liked it, and I wasn't afraid anymore that someone would shout at me and say, 'Nigger, go to the end of the line.' But, you know, I rarely ever used that word. You also know that it has been shouted at me many times.

So over there, far away, I was happy, and because I was happy I had some success, and you know that too.

Then after a long time, I came to America to be in a great show for Mr Ziegfeld, and you know Josephine was happy. You know that. Because I wanted to tell everyone in my country about myself. I wanted to let everyone know that I made good, and you know too that that is only natural.

But on that great big beautiful ship, I had a bad experience. A very important star was to sit with me for dinner, and at the last moment I discovered she didn't want to eat with a coloured woman. I can tell you it was some blow.

And I won't bother to mention her name, because it is not important and, anyway, now she is dead.

And when I got to New York way back then, I had other blows — when they would not let me check into the good hotels because I was coloured, or eat in certain restaurants. And then I went to Atlanta, and it was a horror to me. And I said to myself, 'My God, I am Josephine, and if they do this to me, what do they do to the other people in America?'

You know, friends, that I do not lie to you when I tell you I have walked into the palaces of kings and queens and into the houses of presidents. And much more. But I could not walk into a hotel in America and get a cup of coffee, and that made me mad. And when I get mad, you know that I open my big mouth. And then look out, 'cause when Josephine opens her mouth, they hear it all over the world.

So I did open my mouth, and you know I did scream, and when I demanded what I was supposed to have and what I was entitled to, they still would not give it to me.

So then they thought they could smear me, and the best way to do that was to call me a communist. And you know, too, what that meant. Those were dreaded words in those days, and I want to tell you also that I was hounded by the government agencies in America, and there was never one ounce of proof that I was a communist. But they were mad. They were mad because I told the truth. And the truth was that all I wanted was a cup of coffee. But I wanted that cup of coffee where I wanted to drink it, and I had the money to pay for it, so why shouldn't I have it where I wanted it?

Friends and brothers and sisters, that is how it went. And when I screamed loud enough, they started to open that door just a little bit, and we all started to be able to squeeze through it. Not just the coloured people, but the others as well, the other minorities too, the Orientals, and the Mexicans, and the Indians, both those here in the United States and those from India.

Now I am not going to stand in front of all of you today and take credit for what is happening now. I cannot do that. But I want to take credit for telling you how to do the same thing, and when you scream, friends, I know you will be heard. And you will be heard now.

But you young people must do one thing, and I know you have heard this story a thousand times from your mothers and fathers, like I did from my mama. I didn't take her advice. But I accomplished the same in another fashion. You must get an education. You must go to school, and you must learn to protect yourself. And you must learn to protect yourself with the pen, and not the gun. Then you can answer them, and I can tell you — and I don't want to sound corny — but friends, the pen really is mightier than the sword.

I am not a young woman now, friends. My life is behind me. There is not too much fire burning inside me. And before it goes out, I want you to use what is left to light that fire in you. So that you can carry on, and so that you can do those things that I have done. Then, when my fires have burned out, and I go where we all go someday, I can be happy.

You know I have always taken the rocky path. I never took the easy one, but as I get older, and as I knew I had the power and the strength, I took that rocky path, and I tried to smooth it out a little. I wanted to make it easier for you. I want you to have a chance at what I had. But I do not want you to have to run away to get it. And mothers and fathers, if it is too late for you, think of your children. Make it safe here so they do not have to run away, for I want for you and your children what I had.

Ladies and gentlemen, my friends and family, I have just been handed a little note, as you probably say. It is an invitation to visit the President of the United States in his home, the White House.

I am greatly honoured. But I must tell you that a coloured woman — or, as you say it here in America, a Black woman — is not going there. It is a woman. It is Josephine Baker.

This is a great honour for me. Someday I want you children out there to have that great honour too. And we know that that time is not someday. We know that that time is now.

I thank you, and may God bless you. And may He continue to bless you long after I am gone.

99

<u>HOW</u> SHE DID THAT

Encourage positivity

Josephine Baker's speech has plenty of down notes but, on balance, one is left with a feeling of positivity. Perhaps her career as a performer meant that Baker had a personal drive to make people feel good. Maybe she looked out at that the massive crowd converging on the US Capitol and she herself felt a sense of renewed hope. Maybe her age, which she mentions in the speech, coupled with her journey from Paris to Washington gave rise to some reflection on what had been achieved in the course of her lifetime. Whatever the reason, Josephine Baker encourages a feeling of positivity, helping people believe that their efforts are not in vain.

Some of Baker's personal story comes through in this speech. We certainly have a sense of the injustices she and her family experienced in a racially divided America. But we also know that there must be much, much more to her story. She resists the temptation to use her time to plumb the depths of injustice or to wallow in the moments of pain. Nor does she continually liken the movement to a 'battle'. If people are to remain motivated, it can't always be about the fight.

When you find yourself advocating for a change, try to look for the moments of light. Are there small victories that can be celebrated? Where do you see the source of positivity for the people you are engaging with? Be careful not to make everything seem like an inevitable ongoing struggle. That can feel circular and exhausting.

At the culmination of a lifetime of struggle, Josephine Baker chose to focus on the things she had achieved and the barriers she had leapt over or walked around. Without a hint of rose-coloured delusion, she passes her spirit of triumph on to the crowd, essentially telling them, 'You can't go wrong; the world is behind you'.

Extrapolate on the theme

Speakers can at times get so caught up in their own message and performance that they forget they are part of a broader agenda. When you find yourself speaking at a conference or event that has a line-up of various speakers, you will maximise your chances of standing out if you first work out where you fit in.

One of the lessons that Josephine Baker imparts with her speech is to begin with a thorough grasp on the theme of the event, and then extrapolate on this theme. She makes the march—which was focused on jobs and freedom—come to life with her own story and her own reflections.

The head of the march, labour unionist and civil rights activist A. Philip Randolph, said the following:

> We are not a pressure group, we are not an organisation or a group of organisations, we are not a mob. We are the advance guard of a massive moral revolution for jobs and freedom.

In Josephine Baker's speech, we can almost hear this framing statement in the subtext. Her perspective is all her own, however, without reference to any official body, movement, political party or company. This is just her story, her life, but so much of what she has to say makes us acutely aware that she was out there in advance of the advance guard. So, her speech, though often left out of the pages of history, does much to inspire and magnify the intent of this historic event.

Be repeatable

You might wonder why the legend of Josephine Baker has lived on all these years. From her infamous performance in a banana skirt, to her comical expressions and her pithy quotes, she continues to occupy a place in our collective hearts.

Baker was many things in her life, but her ability to make a mark and to be memorable transcends all her various roles and activities. The same is true for her public speeches. She tells stories that are repeatable. You can imagine people in the crowd, chatting with each other in the days, weeks or months that followed the march. 'Did you know Josephine Baker is going to the White House to meet President Kennedy?' they might have said, or 'I wonder who that white woman was who refused to sit at Josephine Baker's table' or 'Can you imagine who some of the kings and queens were that Josephine Baker has met?'

When sharing personal details or stories, try to consider how interesting they may be to others. Can you introduce a note of intrigue? Do you have the inside scoop that people would love to hear? Think about the speeches you have seen and the ones you remember the most. Often it is the small facts or anecdotes that you found interesting enough to share. If you can be repeatable, you will be memorable.

I lived in a country where dying was taught to us from childhood. We were taught death. We were told that human beings exist in order to give everything they have, to burn out, to sacrifice themselves.

Svetlana Alexievich

Svetlana Alexievich

Writer

B: *31 May 1948, Ivano-Frankivsk, Ukraine*

On the battle lost

When: *7 December 2015*

Where: *Stockholm, Sweden*

Audience: *Nobel Lecture, Swedish Academy*

Svetlana Alexievich delivered her Nobel Lecture on 7 December 2015, at the Swedish Academy, Stockholm. She had been awarded the Nobel Prize for Literature for her 'polyphonic writings, a monument to suffering and courage in our time'. As a masterful storyteller, she channels many voices, illuminating the human condition.

Alexievich is a Belarusian journalist and novelist who writes in Russian. She is also an outspoken critic of the regimes of her homeland and the Soviet and post-Soviet systems, and a staunch anti-totalitarian, anti-Stalinist advocate for the victims she finds in every corner. She has written fiction and non-fiction featuring stories that highlight the victims of oppression — giving voice to all who endured the Soviet regime. Her writing brings the stories of human suffering out of the shadows.

In the lecture extracted here, Alexievich exemplifies much of what drives her writing. You will find, peppered throughout her speech, fine examples of masterful literary devices, delivered with startling personal conviction. She is adamant in her political stance but not strident. She leaps from the specific to the general then back again in a head-spinning display of the practised novelist.

<u>WHAT</u> SHE SAID

66

I do not stand alone at this podium ... There are voices around me, hundreds of voices. They have always been with me, since childhood. I grew up in the countryside. As children, we loved to play outdoors, but come evening, the voices of tired village women who gathered on benches near their cottages drew us like magnets. None of them had husbands, fathers or brothers. I don't remember men in our village after World War II. During the war, one out of four Belarusians perished, either fighting at the front or with the partisans. After the war, we children lived in a world of women. What I remember most is that women talked about love, not death. They would tell stories about saying goodbye to the men they loved the day before they went to war, they would talk about waiting for them, and how they were still waiting. Years had passed, but they continued to wait: 'I don't care if he lost his arms and legs, I'll carry him.' No arms ... no legs ... I think I've known what love is since childhood.

Here are a few sad melodies from the choir that I hear.

...Flaubert called himself a human pen; I would say that I am a human ear. When I walk down the street and catch words, phrases and exclamations, I always think — how many novels disappear without a trace! Disappear into darkness. We haven't been able to capture the conversational side of human life for literature. We don't appreciate it; we aren't surprised or delighted by it. But it fascinates me, and has made me its captive. I love how humans talk. I love the lone human voice. It is my greatest love and passion.

The road to this podium has been long — almost forty years, going from person to person, from voice to voice. I can't say that I have always been up to following this path. Many times I have been shocked and frightened by human beings. I have experienced delight and revulsion. I have sometimes wanted to forget what I heard, to return to a time when I lived in ignorance. More than once, however, I have seen the sublime in people, and wanted to cry.

I lived in a country where dying was taught to us from childhood. We were taught death. We were told that human beings exist in order to give everything they have, to burn out, to sacrifice themselves. We were taught to love people with weapons. Had I grown up in a different country, I couldn't have travelled this path. Evil is cruel, you have to be inoculated against it. We grew up among executioners and victims. Even if our parents lived in fear and didn't tell us everything — and more often than not they told us nothing — the very air of our life was poisoned. Evil kept a watchful eye on us.

I have written five books, but I feel that they are all one book. A book about the history of a utopia.

Varlam Shalamov once wrote: 'I was a participant in the colossal battle, a battle that was lost, for the genuine renewal of humanity'. I reconstruct the history of that battle, its victories and its defeats. The history of how people wanted to build the Heavenly Kingdom on earth. Paradise! The City of the Sun! In the end, all that remained was a sea of blood, millions of ruined human lives. There was a time, however, when no political idea of the twentieth century was comparable to communism (or the October Revolution as its symbol); a time when nothing attracted Western intellectuals and people all around the world more powerfully or emotionally. Raymond Aron called the Russian Revolution the 'opium of intellectuals'. But the idea of communism is at least two thousand years old. We can find it in Plato's teachings about an ideal, correct state; in Aristophanes' dreams about a time when 'everything will belong to everyone'. In Thomas More and Tommaso Campanella, later in Saint-Simon, Fourier and Robert Owen. There is something in the Russian spirit that compels it to try to turn these dreams into reality.

...Twenty years ago, we bid farewell to the 'Red Empire' of the Soviets with curses and tears. We can now look at that past more calmly, as an historical experiment. This is important, because arguments about socialism have not died down. A new generation has grown up with a different picture of the world, but many young people are reading Marx and Lenin again. In Russian towns there are new museums dedicated to Stalin, and new monuments have been erected to him.

The 'Red Empire' is gone, but the 'Red Man,' *Homo sovieticus*, remains. He endures.

My father died recently. He believed in communism to the end. He kept his party membership card. I can't bring myself to use the word *sovok*, that derogatory epithet for the Soviet mentality, because then I would have to apply it my father and others close to me, my friends. They all come from the same place — socialism. There are many idealists among them. Romantics. Today they are sometimes called slavery romantics. Slaves of utopia. I believe that all of them could have lived different lives, but they lived Soviet lives. Why? I searched for the answer to that question for a long time — I travelled all over the vast country once called the USSR, and recorded thousands of tapes. It was socialism, and it was simply our life. I have collected the history of 'domestic', 'indoor' socialism, bit by bit. The history of how it played out in the human soul. I am drawn to that small space called a human being — a single individual. In reality, that is where everything happens...

<u>HOW</u> SHE DID THAT

Use metaphors

As an accomplished novelist and journalist, Svetlana Alexievich's mastery of language should come as no surprise. Her use of metaphor is particularly powerful in this Nobel Prize acceptance speech.

When referencing her past, a world lived among women because so many of the men had died in World War II, she speaks of 'the sad melodies from the choir' that she hears. Later she describes herself as a 'human ear', catching 'words, phrases and exclamations'. Alexievich uses these metaphors to give us some insight as to the role of conversation, language and expression in how she makes sense of the world.

A metaphor is when one thing is used to represent another, even though there may not be a connection to the literal meaning. Metaphors are endemic in human communication. We often reach for a metaphor (or its cousin, the simile) to create shared understanding or to bring a statement to life. When crafting a communication, you might be inspired to use a metaphor that will have the dual purpose of clarifying your meaning and enhancing your language.

A word of warning: the metaphor, when overplayed, can turn into a cliché. The cliché, in turn, can become meaningless jargon — a kind of verbal gas that should be avoided in your presentations. Rid your speech of 'silver bullets', 'four prongs' and 'low-hanging fruit'! Try not to 'boil the ocean' or 'move the needle'. And never, ever 'open the kimono'. That is something Alexievich, with all her storytelling skill, would never do.

Be shocking and personal

The experiences that Svetlana Alexievich exposes in her writing would be shocking to most. In the full version of this Nobel acceptance speech (see Sources), she continues to expose the horrific. Her willingness to get out of the way and let us see the bare reality of her life and the lives of her characters is what makes the lecture so memorable. You won't forget the impact of the revelation from the 'second voice' in her choir of voices, the woman whose baby died because she exposed herself to radiation while pregnant. Nor the confronting words from the 'third voice': 'The first time I killed a German, I was 10 years old'. Or when she shares her own conflicted feelings about her father's dying commitment to the communist ideal.

Much is said of this quality called 'authenticity' in our modern communication and leadership parlance. It sometimes seems like a tortured justification for oversharing or a platform for a false display of empathy. But here is an example of what authenticity really means. Alexievich shares the personal to illuminate bigger concerns — truths of human experience, dangers of ideology or the persistent suffering of war. She makes larger matters real by connecting them to the intensely individual. She isn't sharing her pain or that of others for the sake of it. It is a literary and oratorical sacrifice with purpose.

Punctuate with specifics

Stories come to life when punctuated with specific, personal details. These tiny vignettes evoke human emotion. We are moved by stories not only through their grand literary arcs, but also by the small, poignant, sometimes mundane details. This intimate lens somehow humanises the plotline.

In the full version of her speech, Svetlana Alexievich makes us see 'ashes and smashed bricks' or newlyweds holding hands. In her own words, she reminds us, 'I'm interested in little people. The little, great people, is how I would put it, because suffering expands people.'

Storytelling is such a useful tool of communication and when wielded in the right context, with the right audience, it can add great depth to your speech. To bring your stories to life, practise adding layers of detail. Go back through your experience — what did you see, hear, touch or smell? Can you evoke a greater connection with your story by inviting the audience into your world?

Alexievich is a master of language. Not just a 'human ear', but much more like Flaubert's human pen. She definitely succeeds in creating, as she muses in this lecture, true meaning with words.

Here, on the pulse of
this fine day

You may have
the courage

To look up and out, and
upon me, the

Rock, the River, the Tree,
your country.

Maya Angelou

Maya Angelou

Poet and author

B: *4 April 1928, St Louis, MS, United States*

D: *28 May 2014, Winston-Salem, NC, United States*

On the pulse of morning

When: *20 January 1993*

Where: *Washington DC, United States*

Audience: *The nation of the United States*

Not technically a speech but a poem, 'On the pulse of morning' was spoken aloud before a live audience of thousands, and a global audience of millions. Maya Angelou, the American author and poet, delivered this poem in Washington DC at the inauguration of US President Bill Clinton in January 1993.

Maya Angelou knew that her piece had to reflect the significance of the occasion. She had to take a reading of the social and political context, along with the highest stated intention of the Clinton campaign, and then use her artistic skill to craft and perform a poem that would evoke the intended spirit. This was a challenge equal to the mastery of Maya Angelou.

Upon reflection, one can look back on this day and observe what is essentially the same message delivered in two different forms, by two different but outstanding speakers. The themes of hope and unity were also central in Clinton's inaugural address. But here we have a poetic treatment of the themes, written and spoken by a known and beloved literary icon. In one context, we understand the message on an intellectual level. In the other, we feel it.

As a poet, author and activist, Maya Angelou regularly spoke out on the issues that mattered most to her. Looking back on this historic day and the poem reproduced in full here, we can celebrate the words she so masterfully assembled and so confidently delivered.

<u>WHAT</u> SHE SAID

A Rock, A River, A Tree
Hosts to species long since departed,
Marked the mastodon, The dinosaur, who left dried tokens
Of their sojourn here
On our planet floor,
Any broad alarm of their hastening doom
Is lost in the gloom of dust and ages.

But today, the Rock cries out to us, clearly, forcefully,
Come, you may stand upon my
Back and face your distant destiny,
But seek no haven in my shadow.
I will give you no hiding place down here.

You, created only a little lower than
The angels, have crouched too long in
The bruising darkness,
Have lain too long
Face down in ignorance.
Your mouths spilling words

Armed for slaughter.
The Rock cries out to us today, you may stand upon me,
But do not hide your face.

Across the wall of the world,
A River sings a beautiful song. It says,
Come, rest here by my side.

Each of you, a bordered country,
Delicate and strangely made. Proud,
Yet thrusting perpetually under siege.
Your armed struggles for profit
Have left collars of waste upon
My shore, currents of debris upon my breast.

Yet, today I call you to my riverside,
If you will study war no more. Come,
clad in peace and I will sing the songs
The Creator gave to me when I
And the Tree and the Rock were one.
Before cynicism was a bloody sear across your
brow and when you yet knew you still
knew nothing.
The River sang and sings on.

There is a true yearning to respond to
The singing River and the wise Rock.
So say the Asian, the Hispanic, the Jew,
The African, the Native American, the Sioux,
The Catholic, the Muslim, the French, the Greek,
The Irish, the Rabbi, the Priest, the Sheikh,
The Gay, the Straight, the Preacher,
The privileged, the homeless, the Teacher.
They all hear
The speaking of the Tree.

They hear the first and last of every Tree
Speak to humankind today.
Come to me, here beside the River.
Plant yourself beside the River.

Each of you, descendant of some passed on
Traveller, has been paid for.
You, who gave me my first name, you,
Pawnee, Apache, Seneca, you,
Cherokee Nation, who rested with me, then
forced on bloody feet,
Left me to the employment of
Other seekers — desperate for gain,
starving for gold.
You, the Turk, the Arab, the Swede, the German, the Eskimo, the Scot,
You, the Ashanti, the Yoruba, the Kru, bought,

Sold, stolen, arriving on a nightmare
Praying for a dream.
Here, root yourselves beside me.
I am that Tree planted by the River,
Which will not be moved.
I, the Rock, I the River, I the Tree
I am yours — your passages have been paid.
Lift up your faces, you have a piercing need
For this bright morning dawning for you.
History, despite its wrenching pain,
Cannot be unlived, but if faced
With courage, need not be lived again.

Lift up your eyes upon
This day breaking for you.
Give birth again
To the dream.

Women, children, men,
Take it into the palms of your hands,
Mould it into the shape of your most
Private need. Sculpt it into
The image of your most public self.
Lift up your hearts
Each new hour holds new chances
For new beginnings.
Do not be wedded forever
To fear, yoked eternally
To brutishness.

The horizon leans forward,
Offering you space to place new steps of change.
Here, on the pulse of this fine day
You may have the courage
To look up and out, and upon me, the
Rock, the River, the Tree, your country.
No less to Midas than the mendicant.
No less to you now than the mastodon then.

Here on the pulse of this new day
You may have the grace to look up and out
And into your sister's eyes, and into
your brother's face, your country
And say simply
Very simply
With hope — Good morning.

<u>HOW</u> SHE DID THAT

Just say YES

Imagine you are asked to speak in front of a crowd, a really big crowd — what is your instinctive response? Do you jump at the chance, or quickly cast around for an excuse to get out of it? Do you have a visceral reaction? Most of us would feel some form of fear. This fear is a barrier to greatness.

One of the most wonderful lessons from Maya Angelou's incredible address at Clinton's inauguration is the way it came about. Before knowing what she would say and certainly before considering if she was worthy of speaking at such an event, Angelou simply said YES.

Maintain congruence

Oprah Winfrey had a special relationship with Maya Angelou — one of friendship, admiration and mentorship. She had this to say about the treasured author:

> What is most impressive to me about Maya Angelou is not what she has done or written or spoken. It is how she has done it all. She moves through the world with unshakeable calm confidence and a fiery fierce grace and abounding love ... she is a master.

And that is it exactly. A congruence existed between who Maya Angelou was — the public image she projected over decades — and how she performed on this momentous day. This is a difficult trait to master and probably requires years of personal reflection and conscious development; nonetheless, we can all be inspired by her example.

How can you learn to elevate your presence with Angelou as your benchmark? The first thing is to have and be aware of your personal principles. What is it you stand for as a professional, as a volunteer, as a consultant or as a leader? Whether you are having a one-on-one conversation, chairing a meeting, delivering a speech or having a casual chat, people will come to know what you stand for. Through consistency of message and congruence of behaviour, you will build long-term trust.

Use the beauty of language

Maya Angelou was a writer and poet at the peak of her career when she wrote and performed 'On the pulse of morning', so we expect some literary flair. Angelou delivers on these expectations with aplomb. In just over five minutes, we receive perfectly constructed metaphors, symbolism, repetition and alliteration. The techniques, of course, fade into the background. What remains with the audience is a feeling of hope and a message of inclusion.

You might be unlikely to craft and recite a poem to communicate your message, but that does not mean you cannot learn from this piece — no matter how 'lacking in creativity' you think you are. The ability to use language to evoke emotion is something we could all work harder on in many areas of our lives. Creating a message of hope and conjuring inclusiveness are concepts that translate in many settings. Maya Angelou uses the metaphor of nature for her poem. How could you use the power of language to bring your talk to life?

Sources

Chapter 1

Michelle Obama: Speech in support of Hillary Clinton's presidential campaign at the 2016 Democratic National Convention in Philadelphia. Originally supplied to news outlets by the White House, you can find a transcript of this speech at: www.nytimes.com/2020/08/17/us/politics/Michelle-Obama-speech-transcript-video.html.

Nora Ephron: Commencement speech for the graduating class of 1996 at Wellesley College; www.wellesley.edu/events/commencement/archives/1996commencement.

Florence Nightingale: 1881 letter to trainee nurses at St Thomas' Hospital in London. This letter is housed at the Florence Nightingale Museum in the United Kingdom, but you can find a scan of the speech at https://ehive.com/collections/201880/objects/1392780/letter-from-florence-nightingale-to-the-nurses-at-st-thomas-hospital-6-may-1881.

Virginia Woolf: Speech to the female students from Newnham College and Girton Colleges at the University of Cambridge, England. A transcription of this speech can be found at: www.speech.almeida .co.uk/virginia-woolf. *Note:* This site also provides a link to actor Fiona Shaw performing the speech.

Chapter 2

Brené Brown: TED Talk at the 2010 TEDxHouston; www.ted.com/talks/brene_brown_the_power_of_vulnerability/transcript?language=en#t-1193206.

Hannah Arendt: 1964 televised interview with German journalist Günter Gaus; www.rbb-online.de/zurperson/interview_archiv/arendt_hannah .html. The version that appears in this book is a 1994 translation by Joan Stambaugh.

Marie Curie: Nobel Lecture, delivered in 1911 upon acceptance of second Nobel Prize, in Stockholm, Sweden; www.nobelprize.org/prizes/ chemistry/1911/marie-curie/lecture.

Margaret Atwood: Delivered as part of the five-part lecture series for the CBC Radio Massey Lecture Series; www.cbc.ca/radio/ideas/ the-2008-cbc-massey-lectures-payback-debt-and-the-shadow-side- of-wealth-1.2946880. *Note:* This lecture was recorded in front of a live audience in St Johns Newfoundland, Canada. Text might be slightly different from what appears in the later published book, *Payback: Debt and the Shadow Side of Wealth.*

Chapter 3

Eleanor Roosevelt: Address to the United Nations General Assembly in Paris in 1948; *The Department of State Bulletin*, Volume 19 (19 December 1948), 751., https://archive.org/details/sim_department- of-state-bulletin_1948-12-19_19_494/page/n1/mode/2up. The full audio of this speech can be found at www.americanrhetoric.com/speeches/ eleanorrooseveltdeclarationhumanrights.htm.

Nancy Astor: Inaugural speech to the British House of Commons in 1920; https://www.parliament.uk/globalassets/documents/upload/lady-astor- maiden-speech-in-the-house-of-commons2.pdf.

Malala Yousafzai: Address to the United Nations General Assembly in New York as part of Youth Takeover Day; malala.org/newsroom/archive/ malala-un-speech.

Naomi Klein: Speech delivered at the 2014 Bioneers Annual Conference; bioneers.org/naomi-klein-this-changes-everything-bioneers.

Chapter 4

Mary Wollstonecraft: Extract from *A Vindication of the Rights of Woman*, 1792; oll.libertyfund.org/quote/mary-wollstonecraft-s-i-have-a-dream-speech-from-1792; full text: https://www.google.com.au/books/edition/A_Vindication_of_the_Rights_of_Woman/qhcFAAAAQAAJ?hl=en&gbpv=0.

Emmeline Pankhurst: Speech on women's suffrage made in New York City in October 2013; Marcus, J. (ed), 1987, *Women's Source Library, Volume VIII: Suffrage and the Pankhursts*, Routledge, pp. 153–165. An online version of this is available at: speakingwhilefemale.co/womans-vote-pankhurst5.

Betty Friedan: Farewell address to the 1970 convention of the National Organization for Women; Friedan, B., 1978, *It Changed My Life: Writings on the Women's Movement*, Random House, pp. 180–183. An online version of this is available at: speakingwhilefemale.co/womens-lives-friedan.

Audre Lorde: Speech delivered at the Lesbian and Literature panel of the 1977 Modern Language Association conference; genius.com/Audre-lorde-the-transformation-annotated#song-info. *Note:* This was later published in many of Audre's books, including *The Cancer Journals* and *Sister Outsider*; also reproduced in Shneer, D. and Aviv, C., 2006, *American Queer, Now and Then*, Routledge.

Chapter 5

Julia Gillard: Speech made in 2012 in the Australian House of Representatives in response to comments made by then Leader of the Opposition; https://parlinfo.aph.gov.au/parlInfo/search/display/display.w3p;query=Id:%22chamber/hansardr/5a0ebb6b-c6c8-4a92-ac13-219423c2048d/0039%22. Also featured: www.smh.com.au/politics/federal/transcript-of-julia-gillards-speech-20121010-27c36.html.

Sylvia Rivera: Speech made at the gay pride Christopher Street Liberation Day in 1973; A recording of this speech is available from LoveTapesCollective at https://vimeo.com/234353103.

Margaret Thatcher: 1980 speech delivered to the Conservative Party Conference in Brighton, UK; www.margaretthatcher.org/document/104431.

Hillary Clinton: Address to the 1995 United Nations Fourth World Conference for Women in Beijing, China; www.un.org/esa/gopher-data/conf/fwcw/conf/gov/950905175653.txt.

Chapter 6

Ruth Bader Ginsburg: Arguing as *amicus curiae* in favour of Frontiero in the US Supreme Court case of Frontiero *v.* Richardson. A version of this can be read at: www.oyez.org/cases/1972/71-1694.

Barbara Jordan: Address to the House Judiciary Committee arguing for the impeachment of President Nixon. A version of this can be read at: millercenter.org/the-presidency/impeachment/my-faith-constitution-whole-it-complete-it-total.

Margaret Sanger: Speech in favour of women's reproductive rights at the Park Theatre, New York City, in 1921. Collected as part of the NYU Margaret Sanger Papers Project, a version of this speech can be found at: www.americanrhetoric.com/speeches/margaretsangermoralityofbirthcontrol.htm.

Angela Merkel: 2009 address to a joint session of the US Congress in Washington; www.c-span.org/video/?289781-1/german-chancellor-address-joint-meeting-congress.

Chapter 7

Queen Elizabeth I: Tilbury address to British troops before the expected invasion led by the Spanish Armada; www.bl.uk/learning/timeline/item102878.html.

Sojourner Truth: 1851 speech made at the Old Stone Church in front of attendees of the Women's Convention in Ohio; sojournertruthmemorial .org/sojourner-truth/her-words

Delores Ibárruri: 1936 speech from the Government Ministry Building in Madrid, broadcast on Radio Madrid to rally the citizens against Franco's nationalists. A version of this can be read at: speakola.com/ political/dolores-ibarruris-no-pasaran-spanish-civil-war-1936.

Greta Thunberg: Address at the 2019 Davos World Economic Forum. A version of this can be read at: www.theguardian.com/environment/ 2019/jan/25/our-house-is-on-fire-greta-thunberg16-urges-leaders-to-act-on-climate.

Chapter 8

Nellie McClung: Part of performance staged in 1914 at the Walker Theatre in Winnipeg, Manitoba. A version of this can be read at: greatcanadianspeeches.ca/2017/04/20/nellie-mcclung.

Dorothy Parker: 1953 speech at Circle-In-the-Square, New York City; dorothyparker.com/2017/03/in-lost-1953-speech-dorothy-parker-rips-hollywood.html.

Roxane Gay: TED Talk at the 2015 TEDWoman in Monterey, California; www.ted.com/talks/roxane_gay_confessions_of_a_bad_feminist/ transcript?language=en.

Ruby Wax: TED Talk at the 2012 TEDGlobal in Edinburgh, Scotland; www.ted.com/talks/ruby_wax_what_s_so_funny_about_mental_illness/ transcript?language=en#t-147960.

Chapter 9

Jacinda Ardern: Address to New Zealand Parliament following the 2019 Christchurch terrorist attack; www.beehive.govt.nz/release/ pm-house-statement-christchurch-mosques-terror-attack.

Faith Bandler: Speech at the 1999 Talkin' up Reconciliation convention in Wollongong, Australia. Versions of this can be read at: www .theguardian.com/australia-news/2016/jan/26/notable-speeches- by-indigenous-australians-we-refuse-to-be-pushed-into-the- background and https://speakola.com/ideas/faith-bandler-faith- hope-reconciliation-1999.

Indira Gandhi: Last speech, made in 1984 in Bhubaneswar, eastern India; www.nationalheraldindia.com/people/indira-gandhi-if-we- tolerate-communalism-how-will-be-preserve-indias-unity.

Linda Burney: Inaugural speech to the Australian House of Representatives in 2016; parlinfo.aph.gov.au/parlInfo/search/display/ display.w3p;query=Id:%22chamber/hansardr/f706773d-28cd-4fb7- b62a-9ed884a645d8/0196%22.

Chapter 10

Eva Kor: Speech at the 'Biomedical Sciences and Human Experimentation at Kaiser Wilhelm Institutes — The Auschwitz Connection' symposium in Berlin; candlesholocaustmuseum.org/ learn/evas-2001-speech-on-healing.html; www.mpg.de/10424339/ Speeches_Symposium_2001_Biomedical-Sciences___-Human_ Experimentation.pdf

Josephine Baker: Speech made before the start of official proceedings at the March on Washington civil rights demonstration in the United States in 1963; www.blackpast.org/african-american-history/speeches-african- american-history/1963-josephine-baker-speech-march-washington/.

Svetlana Alexievich: Nobel Lecture, delivered in 2015 upon acceptance of Nobel Prize for Literature, in Stockholm, Sweden; www.nobelprize .org/prizes/literature/2015/alexievich/25408-nobel-lecture-2015/.

Maya Angelou: Poem delivered at the 1993 inauguration of US President Bill Clinton in Washington DC; www.youtube.com/ watch?v=59xGmHzxtZ4. Appears in *On the pulse of morning* by Maya Angelou.

Index

Abbey, Edward (*Desert Solitaire*) 122
Abbott, Tony 169
Aboriginal citizenship rights 327
absurdity, fighting with absurdity 281
achievements, acknowledging 96
ad hominem attacks, deflecting 68
against the grain, going 155
aiming high 115
Ain't I a woman? (speech, 1851), Sojourner Truth 167, 240, 251–256
Alexievich, Svetlana, *On the battle lost* (Nobel Lecture, 2015) 353, 375–381
American Birth Control League 226
American Dream 234
amicus curiae (friend of the court) 204
Analytical Review, Mary Wollstonecraft wrote articles for 132
anaphora, using 198
'Ancient Balances', 1st lecture in series by Margaret Atwood 80–83

Angelou, Maya, *On the pulse of morning* (poem, 1993) 353, 383–390
anger, controlling and weaponising 174
approachable, being 300
Arden, Jacinta, *They were New Zealanders. They are us* (address, 2019) 312, 315–320
Arendt, Hannah, *The banality of evil* (TV interview, 1964) 48–49, 61–68
arguing logically 197–198
Argument in Frontiero v. Richardson (address, 1973), Ruth Bader Ginsburg 200, 203–212
Aron, Raymond, on the Russian Revolution 376
Articles of Impeachment during Watergate (TV speech, 1974), Barbara Jordan 200–201, 215–223
Astor, Nancy, *Maiden speech to UK House of Commons* (1920) 88, 101–107
Asturias, women of (1934) 260
attacks on women 18
attention, capturing 166

Atwood, Margaret
— *Payback: Debt and the shadow side of wealth* (lecture, 2008) 49, 79–86
audience
— conjuring an 262
— empowering an 115
— inviting to do the work 43
— using imagery that transports the 362–363
— warming up an 236
audiences, engaging with questions 163–164
Auschwitz, twins in 357–361
authenticity 380
awe, bringing to process of discovery 56–57

Bad Feminist (book), Roxane Gay 295
Bader Ginsburg, Ruth, *Argument in Frontiero v. Richardson* (address, 1973) 200, 203–212
Baker, Josephine, *March on Washington speech* (1963) 352, 365–373
Bandler, Faith, *Faith, hope and reconciliation* (speech, 1999) 312, 323–331
barriers, reaching across 329
barriers to receptivity, removing 301
Barton, parliamentary seat of 346
basic rights, deprivation of 112
battle, knowing joy of 142
Be the heroine of your life, Nora Ephron (speech, 1996) 3, 15–23

beauty of language, using the 390
Becoming (book), Michelle Obama 6
Becquerel, Henri 73
being enough 55
Berra, Yogi, quotation from speech by 19
best person to speak, confirming you are the 211
Beyoncé 298–299
Bidjigal clan 343
birth control, principle of 227
blame and politics today 54
brain, activity of the 306–307
Branson, Richard, launches Virgin Earth challenge 121
brave, being 105
bravery, embodying 116
Bright, John (reformist MP, 1867) 141–142
Brindle, Ken 328
Brown, Brené, *The power of vulnerability* (TED talk, 2010) 48, 51–58
Burke, Edmund, *A Vindication of Natural Society* (1756) 132, 135
Burney, Linda, *Inaugural speech to Parliament* (2016) 313, 341–349

Call to women's strike for equality (speech, 1970), Betty Friedan 129, 136, 149–155
CANDLES (Children of Auschwitz Nazi Deadly Lab Experiments Survivors) 356, 357, 362
Carson, Rachel (*Silent Spring*) 122

Catcher in the Rye, J. D.
Salinger 291
central idea, establishing
synergy with 57
central message,
anchoring to a 309
change, beginnings of 88–89
chaos, bringing order to 180
Chaplin, Charlie 290
character, presenting 246
Churchill, Winston,
verbal exchange with
Nancy Astor 107
Cialdini, Robert 228
citizenship rights of Aborigines 329
clarity, using contrast for 31
clear purpose, having a 271
Clinton, Bill
— effect of Michelle Obama's
speech on 12
— inauguration as President 383
Clinton, Hillary
— Michelle Obama's
support for 8–9
— *Women's rights are human
rights* (speech, 1995) 191–198
cloak brought by Linda
Burney 345, 347
common ideas, exploring new
perspectives on 84
communism 377
compassion,
communicating with 318
complexity, accepting 67
Confessions of a bad feminist
(TED Talk, 2015), Roxane Gay
274–275, 293–301
congruence, maintaining
389–390

connect, taking time to 58
connection and shame 52–53
consent, withholding of by the
people 143
'consistency and commitment'
tactic of persuasion 228
content, signposting
transitions in 76–77
contrast
— gaining clarity by using 31
— using to highlight the
point 44–45
contribution of others,
recognising 189
conviction, presenting 246
coolamon brought by Linda
Burney 344, 347
counterargument, creating the 146
counterarguments,
stepping over 97
courage 53
credit
— claiming 76
— giving 75
Curie, Dr Marie, *Radium
and the new concepts in
chemistry* (Nobel Lecture,
1911) 49, 71–77
Curie, Pierre 73–74

Davos, Greta Thunberg at
(2020) 271
debates, elevating 124
debt, concept of 80–83
deductive arguments 222
delivery, embodying the 11–12
DeMille, Cecil 288–289
different, being 300–301

difficult questions, being prepared to face 66–67

disaster capitalism 119

discovery, bringing awe and wonder to 56–57

Dodson, Senator Patrick 345

drama, adding a touch of 212

drunkenness among women (pre-1914) 104

Earth, attitudes towards 122

Eden, Anthony 185

education
— equally for boys and girls 132
— as only solution 113

Eichmann, Adolf, trial of 61

Eichmann in Jerusalem: A Report on the Banality of Evil, Hannah Arendt 61–62

Elizabeth I, Queen, *The heart and stomach of a king* (speech, 1588) 240, 243–248

eloquence 102

emotional appeal, balanced wth logos and ethos 192

emotional connections, forming 114

emotional resonance, persuasion by 201

endearing, being 300–301

energy, shifting 181

enough, being 55

Eora clan 343

Ephron, Nora, *Be the heroine of your life* (speech, 1996) 3, 15–23

ethical argument, not using an 210

ethics, appealing to 98

ethos (character of the speaker) 192

evocative language, using 144

expected roles, shaking up 270–271

extra, giving a little bit 175

Faith, hope and reconciliation (speech, 1999), Faith Bandler 312, 323–331

fear, using 159–162

fear of disconnection, as shame 52–53

feelings, numbing 54

female experience, inequity of 36

The Feminine Mystique (1963), Betty Friedan 149

finishing strongly 164

First People, recognition of 344

flags, as symbols 346, 347

Flaubert, Gustave, as human pen 376, 381

forbidden topics 82

Fowler, Dulcie 327, 330

Friedan, Betty, *Call to women's strike for equality* (speech, 1970) 129, 136, 149–155

Fry, Christopher, *The lady's not for burning* (1948) 183

fun, having 308–309

Gage, Francis, his version of Truth's speech (1863) 252

Gandhi, Indira, *Last speech of Indira Gandhi at Bhubaneswar* (1984) 312, 333–339

Gaus, Günter, TV interviewer of Hannah Arendt 62–65

Gay, Roxane, *Confessions of a bad feminist* (TED Talk, 2015) 274–275, 293–301
gear changes for serious messages 22–23
gender parity 211
Gillard, Julia, *Misogyny speech* (2012) 166, 169–175
going against the grain 155
Good Girls Revolt (book), Nora Ephron 15
good woman, being a 27
gravitas, cultivating 221
Grimke, Sara (1837) 209
groundwork, laying the 137
Gweagal clan 343

having everything 19
heart, speaking from the 180–181, 255
The heart and stomach of a king (speech, 1588), Queen Elizabeth I 240, 243–248
hecklers, handling 188
Heseltine, Michael 185
high virtue, encouraging 32–33
higher purpose, appealing to a 98
Hollywood, the land I won't return to (stage performance, 1953), Dorothy Parker 274, 285–293
homes, ownership of 185
Homo sovieticus (the Red Man) 378
hook, beginning with a 126
human dignity, raising 98
humanising statistics 330
humans, connecting with individual 308

humour
— and persuasion 274
— using 105–106
hyperbole, strategic use of 247–248

Ibárruri, Dolores, *They shall not pass!* (speech, 1936) 240, 259–263
imagery that transports the audience, using 362–363
images that linger, creating 292
impeachment of President Richard Nixon 217–220
Inaugural speech to Parliament (2016), Linda Burney 313, 341–349
inclusive, being 229
inclusive language, using 338
inclusivity, messages of 312–313
indigenous worldview, effect of 124
individual humans, connecting with 308
inductive arguments 22
inequity of female experience 36
inflation, defeat of 186
influence, concept of 33
inner strength 336

Jimmy, Jean 328, 330
Johnson, Joseph (sponsor of Mary Wollstonecraft) 131–132
Jordan, Barbara, *Articles of Impeachment during Watergate* (TV speech, 1974) 200–201, 215–223

kairos 166, 174
Kennedy, John F. in Berlin
    (1963) 234
kings, as inferior to common
    men 133–134
Klein, Naomi, *This changes
    everything* (speech, 2014)
    89, 119–126
knowledge, morality of 227
Kor, Eva, *Surviving the Angel
    of Death* (speech, 2001)
    352, 355–363

'la Pasionaria' (Dolores
    Ibárruri) 259
'Lady with the Lamp' 25
The lady's not for burning,
    Christopher Fry (1948) 183
The lady's not for turning (speech,
    1980), Margaret Thatcher
    167, 183–189
land rights 329
language, using the beauty of 390
*Last speech of Indira Gandhi at
    Bhubaneswar* (1984), Indira
    Gandhi 312, 333–339
leader, showing strength
    as a 320
leadership, emphasising
    nature of 32
learning
    — emphasising nature of 32
    — as prerequisite for teaching 28
lightening up 348–349
'like a woman' 28
limbic response, provoking a 144
logic, arguing with 197–198
logos (rational argument) 192

Lorde, Audre, *Your silences will
    not protect you* (speech, 1977)
    129, 157–164

McClung, Nellie, *Should men vote?*
    (stage performance, 1914)
    274, 277–283
McDuck, Scrooge 82
Macklin, Jenny 343–344
*Maiden speech to UK House of
    Commons* (1920), Nancy Astor
    (1920) 88, 101–107
Malala *see* Yousafzai, Malala
March on Washington speech
    (1963), Josephine Baker
    352, 365–373
marriage, for women 18
mechanics of persuasion,
    exposing 45
memorable, being 115
Mengele, Josef 355, 359
Merkel, Angela, *Speech to US
    Congress* (2009) 201,
    231–237
message, elevating the 339
metaphor
    — choosing a powerful 270
    — using 188–189, 379
Misogyny speech (2012), Julia
    Gillard 166, 169–175
misunderstanding, limiting
    opportunities for 31
moment, picking your
    281–282
The morality of birth control
    (speech, 1921), Barbara
    Sanger 201, 225–229
morality of knowledge 227

name dropping, judicious
use of 237
naming opponents 228–229
National Anti-Slavery Standard,
version of Truth's speech
(1863) 252
nationalism 336
Nehru, Jawaharlal 333
Nelson, Brendan 343–344
Nightingale, Florence, *What
makes a good nurse* (letter,
1881) 3, 25–33
Nixon, President Richard,
impeachment of 217–220
nuance
— accepting 67
— showing respect with 318–319
nursing 27–30

Obama, Michelle, *When they
go low, we go high* (speech,
2016) 3, 5–12
obedience 27–28
Occasio (Roman god) 174–175
*On the adoption of the Universal
Declaration of Human Rights*,
Eleanor Roosevelt (speech,
1948) 88, 91–98
On the battle lost (Nobel Lecture,
2015), Svetlana Alexievich
353, 375–381
On the pulse of morning (poem,
1993), Maya Angelou
353, 383–390
One girl among many (speech,
2013), Malala Yousafzai
88–89, 109–116
oneself, being 41

opponents, naming and
rebutting 228–229
opportunistic, being 154
opportunity, inequalities
of 36
oppression, women's
44–45
order to chaos, bringing 180
others, recognising
contribution of 189
Our house is on fire (speech,
2019), Greta Thunberg
240–241, 265–271

Paine, Thomas 132
Pankhurst, Emmeline, *Why we
are militant* (speech, 1913)
128, 139–146
Parker, Dorothy, *Hollywood,
the land I won't return to*
(stage performance, 1953)
274, 285–293
passion, speaking with 223
past triumphs, echoing 228
pathos
— achieving 114
— Bill Clinton as
practitioner of 12
*Payback: Debt and the shadow
side of wealth* (lecture, 2008),
Margaret Atwood 49, 79–86
pennies 83
people, connecting with 308
peroration 339
personal
— being 380
— connecting to the universal 10
— making it 263

personal commitment,
demonstrating 338–339
personal connection
— building 247
— identifying a 236–237
personal conviction, showing 197
personal principles, your 389–390
personal stories
— doing the work with 21
— judging when this is best 362
persuading stealthily 282
persuasion, exposing
mechanics of 45
Peterson, Jordan 229
picking your moment 281–282
Planned Parenthood Federation
of America 226
playing 308–309
poetic language, playing with 163
politics today, and blame 54
'polluter pays' model 123
positive resilience, showing 96–97
positivity, encouraging 371
power of three, emphasising
with the 145
The power of vulnerability
(TED talk, 2010), Brené
Brown 48, 51–58
powerful metaphor, choosing a 270
pragmatic goals, setting 210–211
praise, using 236
preacher, repeating like a 255–256
prepared speeches 85–86
presentations, planning 48
principle of contrast 44
pro-water movement 123
purpose, having a clear 270
purpose (of Declaration), raising to
spiritual level 98

question, daring to 135
questions, engaging the audience
with 163–164
quietness 30

race, bears no relation to ability 206
Racial Discrimination Act
(1975) 328
radioactivity 73–74
Radium and the new concepts
in chemistry (Nobel
Lecture, 1911), Dr Marie
Curie 49, 71–77
rage of women, cause of 152
Rama Rau, Santha, at Nora
Ephron's graduation 17
Randolph, A. Philip (head of
March on Washington) 372
ranting 291
rational arguments,
presenting 200, 222
rational creatures, women as 137
Rational Dissenters (later
Unitarians) 132
Reagan, Ronald in Berlin
(1987) 234
reason
— appealing to 256–257
— submitting to 133
rebutting opponents 228–229
receptivity, removing barriers to 301
reciprocity 344
recognition, showing respect
with 318–319
reconciliation
— concept of 328, 331
— content of 344–345
'red herring' device 282

Reform Act (1867), passing of 142
Reform Bill (1832), passing of 141
repeatable, being 372–373
repeating like a preacher
    255–256
repetition, using 198
resilience, showing positive
    96–97
restitution 344
revolution, effect of term in
    England 141
rhetorical flourishes, applying 11
Richards, Ann (at Barbara Jordan's
    funeral) 216
rights, deprivation of basic 112
Riley, Lynette (cloak maker) 345
Rivera, Sylvia, *Y'all better quiet
    down* (speech, 1973)
    166, 177–181
Roblin, Rodmond (premier of
    Manitoba, 1914) 278
Roosevelt, Eleanor, *On the
    adoption of the Universal
    Declaration of Human Rights*
    (speech, 1948) 88, 91–98
Rudd, Kevin, 'Sorry' speech
    343–344, 348
Russian spirit 377
Rutherford, Ernest 73

Sanger, Margaret, *The morality of
    birth control* (speech, 1921)
    201, 225–229
self, looking beyond 136
self-awareness 221
serious messages, gear
    changes for 22–23
Seton, Ernest Thompson 89

settlement or invasion 345–346
sex
  — bears no relation to ability
    206
  — effect when considered
    dirty 152
  — as suspect criterion 205, 206
sex discrimination 205–209
sexism 169–172
Shakespeare, Judith 39–41
Shakespeare's sister (speech, 1928),
    Virginia Woolf 3, 35–45
Shalamov, Varlam, on
    communism 377
Shoah 233
shocking, being 380
Should men vote? (stage
    performance, 1914), Nellie
    McClung 274, 277–283
silence is no protection 160–161
'slippery slope' fallacy 282
socialism 378
'Sorry' speech (Kevin
    Rudd) 344, 348
Soviet amendments to *Universal
    Declaration of Human
    Rights* 93, 96–97
Spanish Armada 244
*Speaking the Truth with Eloquent
    Thunder*, Barbara Jordan ed.
    Max Sherman 221
specifics, punctuating
    with 380–381
Speech to US Congress (2009),
    Angela Merkel 201, 231–237
speeches, planning 48
spider's web, fiction being like a 39
starting point, strategically
    choosing your 348

starting as you mean to continue 107

statistics, humanising 330

Stewart, Martha, Nora Ephron's reference to 17

Stone, Robert, on storytelling 352

stories, letting do the work 21

storyteller, Brené Brown as 52

stream of consciousness, playing with 291

strength, showing as a leader 320

strike, women on 153

structure, creating a 22

style, knowing your 292–293

suiting you, present in a way that is 85–86

Surviving the Angel of Death (speech, 2001), Eva Kor 352, 355–363

suspect classification, gender as 210

symbolism of flags 346

symbols, leveraging the power of 347

synergy, establishing with central idea 57

taking a stand, knowing when to 174–175

tenacity 102

terrorists, psyche of 116

Thatcher, Margaret, *The lady's not for turning* (speech, 1980) 167, 183–189

theme, extrapolating on the 372

theme selection 22

They shall not pass! (speech, 1936), Dolores Ibárruri 240, 259–263

They were New Zealanders. They are us (address, 2019), Jacinta Ardern 312, 315–320

This changes everything (speech, 2014), Naomi Klein 89, 119–126

Thoreau, Henry David (*Walden*) 122

thoroughness 28, 32

Thunberg, Greta
— at Davos (2020) 271
— *Our house is on fire* (speech, 2019) 240–241, 265–271

'Tilbury Speech', Queen Elizabeth I 245

time, giving subject what it deserves 85

tone and content, cleaving 67

transitions in content, signposting 76–77

tricolon (rule of three), using 11, 145, 223

Truth, Sojourner, *Ain't I a woman?* (speech, 1851) 167, 240, 251–256

truth telling 344

Tudor, house of 243

twins in Auschwitz 357–361

two-sex revolution 151

Unitarians (were Rational Dissenters) 132

unity, creating 262–263

universal, connecting personal to 10

value signalling, using 236

Vesper, Alex 327, 330

video clips, using 126

A Vindication of Natural Society, Edmund Burke (1756) 135

A Vindication of the Rights of Woman (1792), Mary Wollstonecraft 128

Virgin Earth challenge (Richard Branson) 121

virtue, encouraging high 32–33

voices outside your field, invoking 125

Vonnegut, Kurt, forward vision of 122, 125

vulnerability, embracing 54

Wallace, Mike, TV interview with Barbara Sanger (1957) 226

warming up an audience 236

Wax, Ruby, *What's so funny about mental illness?* (TED Talk, 2012) 275, 303–309

way forward, showing the 330–331

'We, the people' 217

What makes a good nurse (letter, 1881), Florence Nightingale 3, 25–30

What remains? The language remains (TV interview, 1964), Hannah Arendt 48–49, 61–68

What's so funny about mental illness? (TED Talk, 2012), Ruby Wax 275, 303–309

When they go low, we go high (speech, 2016), Michelle Obama 3, 5–12

White Australia Policy 329

Whitelaw, Willie 185

Why we are militant (speech, 1913), Emmeline Pankhurst 128, 139–146

wife-beating 39

Wirandjuri language and people 343

Wollstonecraft, Mary
— *A Vindication of the Rights of Woman* (1792) 128, 131
— *I have a dream* (presentation, 1792) 131–137

women
— drunkenness among (pre-1914) 104
— as rational creatures 137
— on strike 153

women and children, suffering of 112

women and fiction, Virginia Woolf's thoughts on 37

women's movement, supporting 128

women's nature 27

women's oppression 44–45

women's rights 297

Women's rights are human rights (speech, 1995), Hillary Clinton 191–198

Women's Social and Political Union (WSPU) 139

wonder, bringing to process of discovery 56–57

Woolf, Virginia, *Shakespeare's sister* (speech, 1928) 3, 35–45

words, letting flow 154–155

work
— inviting audience to do the 43
— letting stories do the 21

world view, showing your 237

Y'all better quiet down (speech, 1973), Sylvia Rivera 166, 177–181

YES, just saying 389

you, presenting in a way that suits 85–86

Your silences will not protect you (speech, 1977), Audre Lorde 129, 157–164

yourself
— being 175, 300–301
— being unapologetically 363

Yousafzai, Malala, *One girl among many* (speech, 2013) 88–89, 109–116

Printed and bound by CPI Group (UK) Ltd, Croydon, CR0 4YY
18/02/2022

03112945-0001